Praise for *Agile Analytics*

"This book does a great job of explaining why and how you would implement Agile Analytics in the real world. Ken has many lessons learned from actually implementing and refining this approach. Business Intelligence is definitely an area that can benefit from this type of discipline."

—Dale Zinkgraf, Sr. Business Intelligence Architect

"One remarkable aspect of *Agile Analytics* is the breadth of coverage—from product and backlog management to Agile project management techniques, from self-organizing teams to evolutionary design practices, from automated testing to build management and continuous integration. Even if you are not on an analytics project, Ken's treatment of this broad range of topics related to products with a substantial data-oriented flavor will be useful for and beyond the analytics community."

—Jim Highsmith, Executive Consultant, ThoughtWorks, Inc., and author of *Agile Project Management*

"Agile methods have transformed software development, and now it's time to transform the analytics space. *Agile Analytics* provides the knowledge needed to make the transformation to Agile methods in delivering your next analytics projects."

—Pramod Sadalage, coauthor of *Refactoring Databases: Evolutionary Database Design*

"This book captures the fundamental strategies for successful business intelligence/analytics projects for the coming decade. Ken Collier has raised the bar for analytics practitioners—are you up to the challenge?"

—Scott Ambler, Chief Methodologist for Agile and Lean, IBM Rational Founder, Agile Data Method

"A sweeping presentation of the fundamentals that will empower teams to deliver high-quality, high-value, working business intelligence systems far more quickly and cost effectively than traditional software development methods."

—Ralph Hughes, author of *Agile Data Warehousing*

This page intentionally left blank

AGILE ANALYTICS

AGILE ANALYTICS

A VALUE-DRIVEN APPROACH TO BUSINESS INTELLIGENCE AND DATA WAREHOUSING

KEN COLLIER

✦✦ Addison-Wesley

Upper Saddle River, NJ • Boston • Indianapolis • San Francisco
New York • Toronto • Montreal • London • Munich • Paris • Madrid
Capetown • Sydney • Tokyo • Singapore • Mexico City

Many of the designations used by manufacturers and sellers to distinguish their products are claimed as trademarks. Where those designations appear in this book, and the publisher was aware of a trademark claim, the designations have been printed with initial capital letters or in all capitals.

The author and publisher have taken care in the preparation of this book, but make no expressed or implied warranty of any kind and assume no responsibility for errors or omissions. No liability is assumed for incidental or consequential damages in connection with or arising out of the use of the information or programs contained herein.

The publisher offers excellent discounts on this book when ordered in quantity for bulk purchases or special sales, which may include electronic versions and/or custom covers and content particular to your business, training goals, marketing focus, and branding interests. For more information, please contact:

U.S. Corporate and Government Sales
(800) 382-3419
corpsales@pearsontechgroup.com

For sales outside the United States please contact:

International Sales
international@pearson.com

Visit us on the Web: informit.com/aw

Library of Congress Cataloging-in-Publication Data

Collier, Ken, 1960–
  Agile analytics : a value-driven approach to business intelligence and data warehousing / Ken Collier.
       p.   cm.
  Includes bibliographical references and index.
  ISBN 978-0-321-50481-4 (pbk. : alk. paper)
1. Business intelligence—Data processing. 2. Business intelligence—Computer programs. 3. Data warehousing. 4. Agile software development. 5. Management information systems. I. Title.
  HD38.7.C645 2012
  658.4'72—dc23
                                   2011019825

ISBN-13: 978-0-321-50481-4
ISBN-10:   0-321-50481-X
Text printed in the United States on recycled paper at RR Donnelley in Crawfordsville, Indiana.
First printing, July 2011

This book is dedicated to my wife and best friend, Beth, who never once asked, "How come it's taking you so long to finish that darn book?"

This page intentionally left blank

CONTENTS

This page intentionally left blank

FOREWORD
BY JIM HIGHSMITH

I was introduced to Ken Collier through a mutual friend about seven years ago. We started meeting for coffee (a two-person Agile group in Flagstaff, Arizona) every week or so to talk about software development, a sprinkling of Agile here and there, skiing, mountain biking, and Ken's analytics projects. Early on, as Ken talked about a project that was faltering and I talked about Agile, he decided to try out Agile on his next project. As he quipped, "It couldn't be worse!"

Over the years I've heard every reason imaginable why "Agile won't work in my company because we are different." Ken never had that attitude and from the beginning kept trying to figure out not *if* Agile would work on business intelligence and data warehousing projects, but *how* it would work. Ken saw each impediment as an opportunity to figure out an Agile way to overcome it. From developing user stories that traversed the entire analytics software stack, to figuring out how to do continuous integration in that same diverse stack, Ken has always *been* Agile, just as he was learning to *do* Agile. Today, Ken champions the cause of *being* Agile and not just *doing* Agile.

Over subsequent analytics projects, one that ran for over three years, delivering releases every quarter, Ken took the fundamental Agile management and development practices and came up with innovative ways to apply them. Business intelligence and data warehousing developers have been reluctant to embrace Agile (although that is changing) in part because it wasn't clear how to apply Agile to these large, data-centric projects. However, analytics projects suffered from the same problems as more typical IT projects—they took too long, cost too much, and didn't satisfy their customers. In our current turbulent business era these kinds of results are no longer acceptable.

One remarkable aspect of *Agile Analytics* is the breadth of coverage—from product and backlog management, to Agile project management techniques, to self-organizing teams, to evolutionary design practices, to automated testing, to build management and continuous integration. Even if you are not on an analytics project, Ken's treatment of this broad range of topics related to products with a substantial data-oriented flavor will be useful for and beyond the analytics community.

In each subject area he has taken the basic Agile practices and customized them to analytics projects. For example, many BI and data warehouse teams are far behind their software development counterparts in configuration management. With execution code in Java, Ruby, and other languages, stored procedures, SQL, and tool-specific code in specialized tools, analytics teams often have poor "code" management practices. Ken spends several chapters on reviewing techniques that software developers have been using and showing how those techniques can be adapted to an analytics environment. Ken often asks analytics teams, "If your servers went down hard today, how long would it take you to rebuild?" The responses he typically receives vary from a few weeks to never! The automation of the build, integration, and test process is foreign to many analytics teams, so Ken spends a chapter each on version control and build automation, showing how to build a fast-paced continuous integration environment.

The book also devotes a chapter to explaining how to customize test-driven development (TDD) to an analytics environment. Comprehensive, automated testing—from unit to acceptance—is a critical piece of Agile development and a requirement for complete continuous integration.

The breadth of Ken's topic coverage extends to architecture. While he advocates architecture evolution (and evolutionary design is covered in Chapter 6, "Evolving Excellent Design"), he describes architectural patterns that are adaptive. In Chapter 6 he introduces an adaptable analytics architecture, one that he used on a large project in which change over time was a key part of the challenge. This architecture advocates a "data pull" in contrast to the traditional "data push" approach, much like Kanban systems.

What I like about Ken's book can be summarized by three points: (1) It applies Agile principles and practices to analytics projects; (2) it addresses technical and management practices (doing Agile) and core Agile principles (being Agile); and (3) it covers an astonishingly wide range of topics—from architecture to build management—yet it's not at all superficial. This is quite an accomplishment. Anyone participating in data-centric or business analytics projects will benefit from this superb book.

—*Jim Highsmith*
Executive Consultant
Thoughtworks, Inc.

FOREWORD
BY WAYNE ECKERSON

Several years ago, I spearheaded the development of Web sites for The Data Warehousing Institute's local chapters. I had established the program two years earlier and worked closely with many of the officers to grow the chapters and host events.

As the "business driver" of the project, I knew exactly what functionality the chapter Web sites needed. I had researched registration and collaboration systems and mapped their capabilities to my feature matrix. I was ready to wheel and deal and get a new system up and running in three months.

Unfortunately, the project went "corporate." The president assigned someone to manage the project, an IT person to collect requirements, and a marketing person to coordinate integration with our existing Web site. We established a regular time to meet and discuss solutions. In short order, the project died.

My first sense of impending doom came when I read the requirements document compiled by the IT developer after I had e-mailed her my requirements and had a short conversation. When I read the document—and I'm technically astute—I no longer recognized my project. I knew that anyone working from the document (i.e., vendor or developer) would never get close to achieving the vision for the Web sites that I felt we needed.

This experience made me realize how frustrated business people get with IT's traditional approach to software development. Because I witnessed how IT translates business requirements into IT-speak, I now had a greater understanding of why so many business intelligence (BI) projects fail.

Agile to the rescue. When I first read about Agile development techniques, I rejoiced. Someone with a tad of business (and common) sense had finally infiltrated the IT community. Everything about the methodology made perfect sense. Most important, it shifts the power in a development project from the IT team to business users for whom the solution is being built!

However, the Agile development methodology was conceived to facilitate software projects for classic transaction-processing applications.

Unfortunately, it didn't anticipate architecture- and data-laden development projects germane to business intelligence.

Fortunately, BI practitioners like Ken Collier have pioneered new territory by applying Agile methods to BI and have lived to tell about their experiences. Ken's book is a fount of practical knowledge gleaned from real project work that shows the dos and don'ts of applying Agile methods to BI.

Although the book contains a wealth of process knowledge, it's not a how-to manual; it's really more of a rich narrative that gives would-be Agile BI practitioners the look, feel, smell, and taste of what it's like to apply Agile methods in a real-world BI environment. After you finish reading the book, you will feel as if you have worked side by side with Ken on a project and learned from the master.

—*Wayne Eckerson*
 Founder and President
 BI Leadership Forum
 Formerly Director of Research and Services, TDWI

PREFACE

WHEN DW/BI PROJECTS GO BAD

Most data warehouse developers have experienced projects that were less than successful. You may even have experienced the pain of a failed or failing project. Several years ago I worked for a midsize company that was seeking to replace its existing homegrown reporting application with a properly architected data warehouse. My role on the project was chief architect and technical lead. This project ended very badly and our solution was ultimately abandoned. At the outset the project appeared poised for success and user satisfaction. However, in spite of the best efforts of developers, project managers, and stakeholders, the project ran over budget and over schedule, and the users were less than thrilled with the outcome. Since this project largely motivated my adaptation of Agile principles and practices to data warehouse and business intelligence (DW/BI) development, I offer this brief retrospective to help provide a rationale for the Agile DW/BI principles and practices presented throughout this book. It may have some similarities to projects that you've worked on.

About the Project

This section summarizes the essential characteristics of the project, including the following:

- **Existing application.** The company's existing reporting application was internally referred to as a "data warehouse," which significantly skewed users' understanding of what a data warehouse application offers. In reality the data model was a replication of parts of one of the legacy operational databases. This replicated database did not include any data scrubbing and was wrapped in a significant amount of custom Java code to produce the reports required. Users had, at various times, requested new custom reports, and the application had become overburdened with highly specialized and seldom used reporting features. All of the reports could be classified as canned reports. The system was not optimized for analytical activities, and advanced analytical capabilities were not provided.

- **Project motivation.** Because the existing "data warehouse" was not architected according to data warehousing best practices, it had reached the practical limits of maintainability and scalability needed to continue meeting user requirements. Additionally, a new billing system was coming online, and it was evident that the existing system could not easily be adapted to accommodate the new data. Therefore, there was strong executive support for a properly designed data warehouse.
- **External drivers.** The data warehousing project was initially envisioned by a sales team from one of the leading worldwide vendors of data warehousing and business intelligence software. In providing guidance and presales support, this sales team helped the project sponsors understand the value of eliciting the help of experienced business intelligence consultants with knowledge of industry best practices. However, as happens with many sales efforts, initial estimates of project scope, cost, and schedule were overly ambitious.
- **Development team.** The development team consisted exclusively of external data warehousing contractors. Because the company's existing IT staff had other high-priority responsibilities, there were no developers with deep knowledge of the business or existing operational systems. However, the development team had open access to both business and technical experts within the company as well as technology experts from the software vendor. While initial discovery efforts were challenging, there was strong participation from all stakeholders.
- **Customer.** The primary "customer" for the new data warehouse was the company's finance department, and the project was sponsored by the chief financial officer. They had a relatively focused business goal of gaining more reliable access to revenue and profitability information. They also had a substantial volume of existing reports used in business analysis on a routine basis, offering a reasonable basis for requirements analysis.
- **Project management.** Project management (PM) responsibilities were handled by corporate IT using traditional Project Management Institute/Project Management Body of Knowledge (PMBOK) practices. The IT group was simultaneously involved in two other large development projects, both of which had direct or indirect impact on the data warehouse scope.
- **Hosted environment.** Because of limited resources and infrastructure, the company's IT leadership had recently decided to partner with an application service provider (ASP) to provide hosting services for newly developed production systems. The data warehouse

was expected to reside at the hosting facility, located on the west coast of the United States, while the company's headquarters were on the east coast. While not insurmountable, this geographic separation did have implications for the movement of large volumes of data since operational systems remained on the east coast, residing on the corporate IT infrastructure.

Project Outcome

The original project plan called for an initial data warehouse launch within three months but had an overly ambitious scope for this release cycle. Project completion was a full eight months after project start, five months late! User acceptance testing did not go well. Users were already annoyed with project delays, and when they finally saw the promised features, there was a large gap between what they expected and what was delivered. As is common with late projects, people were added to the development team during the effort to try to get back on track. As Fred Brooks says, "Adding more people to a late project only makes it later" (Brooks 1975). Ultimately, project costs far exceeded the budget, users were unsatisfied, and the project was placed on hold until further planning could be done to justify continued development.

Retrospective

So who was to blame? Everybody! Users felt that the developers had missed the mark and didn't implement all of their requirements. Developers felt that the users' expectations were not properly managed, and the project scope grew out of control. Project sponsors felt that the vendors overpromised and underdelivered. Vendors felt that internal politics and organizational issues were to blame. Finally, many of the organization's IT staff felt threatened by lack of ownership and secretly celebrated the failure.

The project degenerated into a series of meetings to review contracts and project documents to see who should be held responsible, and guess what? Everyone involved was partially to blame. In addition to the normal technical challenges of data warehouse development, the following were identified as root causes of project failure:

- The contract did not sufficiently balance scope, schedule, and resources.
- Requirements were incomplete, vague, and open-ended.
- There were conflicting interpretations of the previously approved requirements and design documents.

- Developers put in long nights and weekends in chaotic attempts to respond to user changes and new demands.
- The technical team was afraid to publicize early warning signs of impending failure and continued trying to honor unrealistic commitments.
- Developers did not fully understand the users' requirements or expectations, and they did not manage requirements changes well.
- Users had significant misconceptions about the purpose of a data warehouse since existing knowledge was based on the previous reporting application (which was not a good model of a warehouse).
- Vendors made ambitious promises that the developers could not deliver on in the time available.
- The project manager did not manage user expectations.
- IT staff withheld important information from developers.
- The ASP partner did not provide the level of connectivity and technical support the developers expected.

Hindsight truly is 20/20, and in the waning days of this project several things became apparent: A higher degree of *interaction* among developers, users, stakeholders, and internal IT experts would have ensured accurate understanding on the part of all participants. Early and frequent *working software*, no matter how simplistic, would have greatly reduced the users' misconceptions and increased the accuracy of their expectations. Greater emphasis on *user collaboration* would have helped to avoid conflicting interpretations of requirements. A project plan that focused on *adapting to changes* rather than meeting a set of "frozen" contractual requirements would have greatly improved user satisfaction with the end product. In the end, and regardless of blame, the root cause of this and many other data warehousing project failures is the disconnect in understanding and expectations between developers and users.

ABOUT THIS BOOK

About the same time I was in the throes of the painful and failing project just described, I met Jim Highsmith, one of the founding fathers of the Agile movement, author of *Adaptive Software Development*, *Agile Software Development Ecosystems*, and *Agile Project Management* and one of the two series editors for the Agile Software Development Series of which this book is a part. Jim listened to my whining about our project difficulties and gave me much food for thought about how Agile methods might be adapted to DW/BI systems development. Unfortunately, by the time I met Jim it was too late to right that sinking ship. However, since then Jim and I have become good friends, exchanging ideas over coffee on a mostly weekly basis. Well, mostly he shares good ideas and I do my best to absorb them. Jim has become my Agile mentor, and I have devoted my professional life since we first met to ensuring that I never, ever work on another failing DW/BI project again. Now that may seem like an audacious goal, but I believe that (a) life is too short to suffer projects that are doomed to fail; (b) Agile development is the single best project risk mitigation approach we have at our disposal; and (c) Agile development is the single best means of innovating high-value, high-quality, working DW/BI systems that we have available. That's what this book is about:

- Mitigating DW/BI project risk
- Innovating high-value DW/BI solutions
- Having fun!

Since my last painful project experience I have had many wonderful opportunities to adapt Agile development methods to the unique characteristics of DW/BI systems development. Working with some very talented Agile DW/BI practitioners, I have successfully adapted, implemented, and refined a comprehensive set of project management and technical practices to create the Agile Analytics development method.

This adaptation is nontrivial as there are some very significant and unique challenges that we face that mainstream software developers do not. DW/BI developers deal with a hybrid mix of integrating commercial software and writing some custom code (ETL scripting, SQL, MDX, and application programming are common). DW/BI development teams often have a broad and disparate set of skills. DW/BI development is based on large data volumes and a complex mixture of operational, legacy, and specialty systems. The DW/BI systems development platform is often a high-end dedicated server or server cluster, making it harder to replicate for sandbox development and testing. For these reasons and more, Agile software development methods do not always easily transfer to DW/BI systems development, and I have met a few DW/BI developers who have given up trying. This book will introduce you to the key technical and project management practices that are essential to Agile DW/BI. Each practice will be thoroughly explained and demonstrated in a working example, and I will show you how you might modify each practice to best fit the uniqueness of your situation.

This book is written for three broad audiences:

- DW/BI practitioners seeking to learn more about Agile techniques and how they are applied to the familiar complexities of DW/BI development. For these readers I provide the details of Agile technical and project management techniques as they relate to business intelligence and data-centric projects.
- Agile practitioners who want to know how to apply familiar Agile practices to the complexities of DW/BI systems development. For these readers I elaborate upon the traits of business intelligence projects and systems that make them distinctly different from software development projects, and I show how to adapt Agile principles and practices to these unique characteristics.
- IT and engineering management who have responsibility for and oversight of program portfolios, including data warehousing, business intelligence, and analytics projects. This audience may possess neither deep technical expertise in business intelligence nor expertise in Agile methods. For these readers I present an introduction to an approach that promises to increase the likelihood of successful projects and delighted customers.

Although this book isn't a primer on the fundamentals of DW/BI systems, I will occasionally digress into coverage of DW/BI fundamentals for the benefit of the second audience. Readers already familiar with business intelligence should feel free to skip over these sections.

By the way, although I'm not an expert in all types of enterprise IT systems, such as enterprise resource planning (ERP) implementations, I have reason to believe that the principles and practices that make up Agile Analytics can be easily adapted to work in those environments as well. If you are an IT executive, you might consider the broader context of Agile development in your organization.

WHY AN AGILE DW/BI BOOK?

In the last couple of years the Agile software development movement has exploded. Agile success stories abound. Empirical evidence continues to increase and strongly supports Agile software development. The Agile community has grown dramatically during the past few years, and many large companies have adopted agility across their IT and engineering departments. And there has been a proliferation of books published about various aspects of Agile software development.

Unfortunately, the popularity of Agile methods has been largely lost on the data and business intelligence communities. For some strange reason the data community and software development community have always tended to grow and evolve independently of one another. Big breakthroughs that occur in one community are often lost on the other. The object-oriented boom of the 1990s is a classic example of this. The software development community has reaped the tremendous benefits of folding object orientation into its DNA, yet object-oriented database development remains peripheral to the mainstream for the data community.

Whenever I talk to groups of DW/BI practitioners and database developers, the common reaction is that Agile methods aren't applicable to data-centric systems development. Their arguments are wide and varied, and they are almost always based on myths, fallacies, and misunderstandings, such as "It is too costly to evolve and change a data model. You must complete the physical data model before you can begin developing reports and other user features."

The reality is that there is nothing special about data-centric systems that makes Agile principles irrelevant or inappropriate. The challenge is that Agile practices must be adapted, and a different tool set must be adopted for data-centric systems development. Although many of the current books on Agile concepts and techniques are directly relevant to the data community, most of them do not speak directly to the data-minded reader. Unfortunately, many current Agile books are too narrowly focused on new, green-field software development using all the latest platforms, frameworks, and programming languages. It can be difficult for readers to extrapolate the ideas presented in these books to database development, data warehouse development, ERP implementation, legacy systems development, and so forth.

Agile author and database expert Scott Ambler has written books on Agile database development and database refactoring (a distinctly Agile practice) to engage the database community in the Agile dialogue. Similarly, I've written this book to engage the DW/BI community in the Agile movement because Agile is simply a better way to work on large, complex DW/BI systems. In 2008 Ralph Hughes's book *Agile Data Warehousing* hit the shelves (Hughes 2008). Ralph does a great job of adapting Scrum and eXtreme Programming (XP) techniques to the nuances of data warehousing, and many of those concepts are also present in this book. Additionally, this book aims to dive into many of the technical practices that are needed to develop in an Agile manner.

WHAT DO I MEAN BY AGILE ANALYTICS?

A word about terminology: I've chosen the title *Agile Analytics* more because it's catchy and manageable than because it precisely captures my focus. Face it, *Agile Data Warehousing, Business Intelligence, and Analytics* would be a mouthful. By and large the data warehousing community has come to use the term *data warehousing* to refer to back-end management and preparation of data for analysis and *business intelligence* to refer to the user-facing front-end applications that present data from the warehouse for analysis. The term *analytics* is frequently used to suggest more advanced business intelligence methods involving quantitative analysis of data (e.g., predictive modeling, statistical analysis, etc.). Moreover, the industry term *business intelligence* is sometimes an ambiguous and broadly encompassing term that includes anything to do with data-driven business processes (business performance management, customer relationship management, etc.) or decision support (scorecards, dashboards, etc.).

My use of the moniker Agile Analytics should not imply that Agile methods are applicable only to a certain class of user-facing BI application development. Agile methods are applicable and adaptable to data warehouse development as well as business intelligence and analytical application development. For many people Agile BI development tends to be easier to imagine, since it is often assumed that the data warehouse has been built and populated. Certainly a preexisting data warehouse simplifies the effort required to build BI applications. However, you should not take this to mean that the data warehouse must be completed prior to building BI applications. In fact, Agile Analytics is a user-value–driven approach in which high-valued BI capabilities drive the evolutionary development of the data warehouse components needed to support those capabilities. In this way we avoid overbuilding the warehouse to support more than its intended purpose.

In this book I focus primarily on the core of most flavors of DW/BI systems, the data warehouse. My use of the term *business intelligence* or *BI* throughout this book should be assumed to include analytic as well as reporting and querying applications. When I use the term *DW/BI system*, you should infer that I mean the core data warehouse along with any presentation applications that are served by the warehouse such as a finance dashboard, a forecasting portal, or some other BI application. However, the DW/BI acronym is somewhat clunky, and I may occasionally use BI alone. In most of these cases you should assume that I mean to include relevant DW components as well. I'll also address some of the advanced BI concepts like data mining and data visualization. I'll leave it to the reader to extrapolate the practices to more specific BI projects such as CRM implementations. The principles still apply.

WHO SHOULD READ THIS BOOK?

An Agile DW/BI team is made up of more than just developers. It includes the customer (user) community, who provide requirements; the business stakeholder community, who are monitoring the impact of the BI system on business improvements; and the technical community, who develop, deploy, and support the DW/BI system. These communities are connected by a project manager, a business analyst (or product owner), and an executive sponsor. Each of these communities plays a crucial role in project success, and each of these communities requires a well-defined set of Agile practices to be effective in its role. This book is intended for both business and technical readers who are involved in one or more of the communities described.

Not everything in the book is meant for everyone on the list, but there is something here for everyone. I have worked with many organizations that seek Agile training, mentoring, and coaching. Occasionally I have to dispel the myth that agility applies only to developers and techies.

At one company with which I was invited to work, the executive who sponsored the training said something like, "If our engineers could just start doing Agile development, we could finish projects faster and our customers would be happier." This statement represents some unfortunate misconceptions that can be a buzzkill for Agile teams.

First, successful agility requires a change in the mind-set of all team members. Customer community members must understand that their time is required to explore and exercise newly completed features, and to provide continuous input and feedback on the same. Management community members must adapt their expectations as project risk and uncertainty unfolds, and as the team adapts to inevitable change. The technical community must learn a whole new way of working that involves lots of discipline and rigor. And the project interface community must be committed to daily project involvement and a shift in their role and contribution to project success.

Second, Agile doesn't always mean faster project completion. Even the best project teams still have a finite capacity to complete a scope of work. Agility is not a magic wand that makes teams work faster. Agile practices do steer teams to focus on the high-value and riskiest features early. Therefore, it is possible that an Agile DW/BI system can be launched into production earlier, as soon as the most critical features are complete and accepted. However, I would caution against expecting significantly faster project cycles, especially in the beginning. On the other hand, you should expect a significant increase in quality and customer delight over traditional DW/BI development approaches.

The bottom line is that successful adoption of Agile DW/BI requires awareness, understanding, and commitment from the members of all of the aforementioned project communities. For this reason I have tried to design this book to provide something relevant for everyone.

How This Book Is Organized

This book is divided into two parts. Part I, "Agile Analytics: Management Methods," is focused on Agile project management techniques and delivery team coordination. It includes the following chapters:

- Chapter 1, "Introducing Agile Analytics," provides an overview and baseline for this DW/BI approach.
- Chapter 2, "Agile Project Management," introduces an effective collection of practices for chartering, planning, executing, and monitoring an Agile Analytics project.
- Chapter 3, "Community, Customers, and Collaboration," introduces a set of guidelines and practices for establishing a highly collaborative project community.
- Chapter 4, "User Stories for BI Systems," introduces the story-driven alternative to traditional requirements analysis and shows how use cases and user stories drive the continuous delivery of value.
- Chapter 5, "Self-Organizing Teams Boost Performance," introduces an Agile style of team management and leadership as an effective alternative to more traditional command-and-control styles.

This first part is written for everyone involved in an Agile Analytics project, from executive sponsors, to project managers, to business analysts and product owners, to technical leads and delivery team members. These chapters establish a collection of core practices that shape the way an Agile project community works together toward a successful conclusion.

Part II of the book, "Agile Analytics: Technical Methods," is focused on the technical methods that are necessary to enable continuous delivery of business value at production-quality levels. This part includes the following chapters:

- Chapter 6, "Evolving Excellent Design," shows how the evolutionary design process works and how to ensure that it results in higher-quality data models and system components with minimal technical debt.
- Chapter 7, "Test-Driven Data Warehouse Development," introduces a collection of practices and tools for automated testing, and for taking a test-first approach to building data warehouse and business intelligence components.
- Chapter 8, "Version Control for Data Warehousing," introduces a set of techniques and tools for keeping the entire DW/BI system under version control and configuration management.
- Chapter 9, "Project Automation," shows how to combine test automation and version control practices to establish an automated continuous integration environment that maintains confidence in the quality of the evolving system.
- Chapter 10, "Final Words," takes a look at some of the remaining factors and considerations that are critical to the successful adoption of an Agile Analytics approach.

I think of this part as a collection of modern development practices that should be used on every DW/BI project, be it Agile or traditional (e.g., "waterfall"). However, these technical practices are essential when an Agile Analytics approach is taken. These methods establish the minimally sufficient set of technical practices needed to succeed in the continuous, incremental, and evolutionary delivery of a high-value DW/BI system.

Of course, these technical chapters should be read by technical team leads and delivery team members. However, I also recommend that nontechnical project team members read the introductory sections of each of these chapters. Doing so will help nontechnical members establish a shared understanding of the purpose of these practices and appreciate the value of the technical team's efforts to apply them.

How Should You Read This Book?

I like to think of Agile Analytics techniques as supporting one of the following focal points:

- **Agile DW/BI management**: the set of practices that are devoted to how you run your project, including precursors to agility, Agile project management methods, the Agile team, developer-user interface, and so on
- **Agile DW/BI technical methods**: the set of practices that are devoted to the development and delivery of a high-value, high-quality, working DW/BI system, including specific technical practices like story-driven development, test-driven development, build automation, code management, refactoring, and so on

The chapters are organized into these major sections. Each chapter is dedicated to a key practice or related set of practices, beginning with an executive-level overview of the salient points of the chapter and progressing into deeper coverage of the topic. Some of the chapter topics are rich enough to deserve to be entire books. In these cases, my aim is to give the reader a solid understanding of the topic, and ideally the motivation needed for a deeper self-study of its mechanics.

If you are reading this to gain a high-level understanding of Agile DW/BI, the initial overview at the beginning of each chapter will suffice. My goal in these overviews is to provide an accurate portrayal of each of the Agile DW/BI practices, but these sections aren't intended to give you all the techniques needed to apply the practice.

If you are a data warehouse manager, project sponsor, or anyone who needs to have a good working understanding of the practices without getting bogged down in the technical details, I recommend reading the middle sections of each chapter, especially the project management chapters. These sections are designed to provide a deep enough understanding of the topic to either use the techniques or understand how they are used on your project.

If you are a member of the day-to-day project team (project managers, technical team members, business analysts, product managers, etc.), I recommend reading the details and examples in each of the project management chapters (Part I, "Agile Analytics: Management Methods"). These are designed to give you a concrete set of techniques to apply in your release planning, iteration planning, and all other project management and user collaboration activities. If you are a member of the technical community, the chapters in Part II, "Agile Analytics: Technical Methods," are intended for you.

A word about DW/BI technologies: I am a technology agnostic. I have done DW/BI development using a variety of technology stacks that are IBM-DB2-centric, Oracle-centric, SAS-centric, and Microsoft-centric, as well as a variety of hybrid technology stacks. While some technologies may lend themselves to Agile DW/BI better than others, I am confident that the guiding principles and practices introduced in this book are technology-independent and can be effective regardless of your tool choices.

As this book goes to press, there are an increasing number of data warehouse and business intelligence tool vendors that are branding their products as Agile. Tools and tool suites from forward-thinking vendors such as WhereScape, Pentaho, Balanced Insight, and others offer some exciting possibilities for enabling agility. While I do not believe that you must have these types of tools to take an Agile approach, they certainly do offer some powerful benefits to Agile delivery teams. The Agile software development community has greatly benefited from tools that help automate difficult development activities, and I look forward to the benefits that our community stands to gain from these vendors. At the same time I would caution you not to believe that you must have such tools before you can start being Agile. Instead, I encourage you to get started with Agile techniques and practices and adopt tools incrementally as you determine that they are of sufficient benefit.

This page intentionally left blank

ACKNOWLEDGMENTS

I would never have gotten the experience and knowledge I needed to write this book without the contributions of several key people. These friends and colleagues have my respect and gratitude for the many valuable interactions I've had with them, and the collaborations that ultimately resulted in the Agile Analytics approach.

Foremost, my good friend Jim Highsmith has been my trusted adviser and mentor since the beginning of my Agile journey. Jim was just starting to write the first edition of *Agile Project Management* when I first met him, and he made book-writing look so easy that I decided to give it a try. As it turns out, it's much harder than he makes it look. My weekly breakfast discussions with Jim were critical in shaping the concepts in this book. He voluntarily served as my developmental editor, reviewing early drafts of sections and chapters and helping me pull things together in a more cohesive and coherent fashion. Jim continues to challenge my assumptions and gives me new ideas and new ways to think about the complexities of development. He also didn't give up on me when book-writing wasn't my highest priority. Thanks, Jim.

Jim introduced me to Luke Hohmann at a time when Luke was looking for somebody with both data warehousing experience and Agile knowledge. Luke is one of the most visionary people I've ever met. I was fortunate enough to be the chief architect for one of Luke's innovative ideas: a complex, hosted, enterprise DW/BI product offering from one of Luke's clients. The complexity of this project and Luke's deep knowledge of Agile techniques challenged me (and our team) to figure out how to apply Agile software methods to the nuances of DW/BI development. The concepts in this book stem from that experience and have been refined and matured on subsequent projects. Luke has become a great friend over the past seven years, and I value his wisdom and vision. Thanks, Luke.

My team on the aforementioned project remains one of the best Agile teams I have yet experienced either as a participant or as an Agile trainer. This team included David Brink, Robert Daugherty, James Slebodnick, Scott Gilbert, Dan O'Leary, Jonathon Golden, and Ricardo Aguirre. Each team member brought a special set of skills and perspectives, and over that first three-plus-year-long project these friends and teammates helped me figure out effective ways to apply Agile techniques to DW/BI development. I've since had other project opportunities to work with many of these friends, further refining Agile Analytics concepts. These team members deserve much of the credit for validating and tweaking Agile Analytics practices in a complex and real-life situation. Thanks, guys.

Jim Highsmith also introduced me to Scott Ambler along the way. Scott has led the charge in applying Agile to data-centric systems development. Fortunately for all of us, Scott is a prolific writer who freely shares his ideas in his many books and on his ambysoft.com Web site. I have benefited greatly from the conversations I've had with him, as well as from his writings on Agile Modeling, Agile Data, Agile Unified Process, and Database Refactoring (together with Pramod Sadalage). In the early days of my focus on Agile in DW/BI, Scott and I regularly lamented our perceptions that the data community wasn't paying attention to the benefits of agility, while the software community wasn't paying attention to the unique challenges of database development and systems integration. Scott gave much of his time reviewing this book. He has given me much to think about and shared ideas with me that I might otherwise have missed. Thanks, Scott.

I don't think I truly understood what it means for somebody to have "the patience of a saint" before working with Addison-Wesley editor Chris Guzikowski and editorial assistant Raina Chrobak. As it turns out, I am a painfully slow author who is not very good at applying Agile principles to book-writing deadlines. Huge thanks go to Raina and Chris, who were amazingly patient as I slipped deadline after deadline. I hope I have future opportunities to redeem myself as an author.

Ralph Hughes's *Agile Data Warehousing* book hit the shelves as I was writing this book. Ralph and I were acquainted at that time and since have become friends and colleagues. I am grateful for his work in this area and for the discussions I've had with him and the experiences he has shared. Although I have tried not to duplicate what Ralph has already published, I am confident that our approaches are consistent with and complementary to one another. I look forward to future collaborations with Ralph as our ideas mature and evolve.

Finally, the ideas presented in this book have benefited tremendously from smart and thoughtful people willing to review its early drafts and give me guidance. In addition to Scott's and Jim's reviews, special thanks go to Jonathon Golden, my go-to guru on project automation, and Israel Gat, expert on Agile leadership and technical debt. My gratitude also goes to DW/BI experts Wayne Eckerson and Dale Zinkgraf and to Agile data expert Pramod Sadalage for their feedback. Their contributions were invaluable.

ABOUT THE AUTHOR

Ken Collier got excited about Agile development in 2003 and was one of the first to start combining Agile methods with data warehousing, business intelligence, and analytics. These disciplines present a unique set of challenges to the incremental/evolutionary style of Agile development. Ken has successfully adapted Agile techniques to data warehousing and business intelligence to create the Agile Analytics style. He continues to refine these ideas as a technical lead and project manager on several Agile DW/BI project teams. Ken also frequently trains data warehousing and business intelligence teams in Agile Analytics, giving him the opportunity to exercise this approach with various technologies, team dynamics, and industry domains. He has been an invited keynote speaker on the subject of Agile DW/BI at several U.S. and international conferences, including multiple TDWI (The Data Warehousing Institute) World Conferences as well as HEDW (Higher Education Data Warehousing) annual conferences.

In nearly three decades of working in advanced computing and technology, Ken has experienced many of the trends that come and go in our field, as well as the ones that truly transform the state of our practices. With an M.S. and Ph.D. in computer science engineering, Ken is formally trained in software engineering, data management, and machine learning. He loves challenging problems in the areas of systems architecture and design, systems/software development lifecycles, project leadership, data warehousing, business intelligence, and advanced analytics. Ken also loves helping organizations adopt and tailor effective approaches and solutions that might not otherwise be apparent. He combines a deep technical foundation with sound business acumen to help bridge the gaps that often exist between technical and business professionals.

Ken is the founder and president of KWC Technologies, Inc., and is a senior consultant with the Cutter Consortium in both the Agile Development and Business Intelligence practice areas. Ken has had the privilege of working as a software engineer for a large semiconductor company. He has spent several years as a tenured professor of computer science engineering. He has directed the data warehousing and business intelligence solutions group for a major consulting firm. And, most recently, he has focused on enabling organizational agility, including Agile software engineering, Agile Analytics, and Agile management and leadership for client companies.

This page intentionally left blank

PART I

AGILE ANALYTICS: MANAGEMENT METHODS

This page intentionally left blank

Chapter 1

INTRODUCING AGILE ANALYTICS

Like Agile software development, Agile Analytics is established on a set of core values and guiding principles. It is not a rigid or prescriptive methodology; rather it is a style of building a data warehouse, data marts, business intelligence applications, and analytics applications that focuses on the early and continuous delivery of business value throughout the development lifecycle. In practice, Agile Analytics consists of a set of highly disciplined practices and techniques, some of which may be tailored to fit the unique data warehouse/business intelligence (DW/BI) project demands found in your organization.

Agile Analytics includes practices for project planning, management, and monitoring; for effective collaboration with your business customers and management stakeholders; and for ensuring technical excellence by the delivery team. This chapter outlines the tenets of Agile Analytics and establishes the foundational principles behind each of the practices and techniques that are introduced in the successive chapters in this book.

Agile is a reserved word when used to describe a development style. It means something very specific. Unfortunately, "agile" occasionally gets misused as a moniker for processes that are ad hoc, slipshod, and lacking in discipline. Agile relies on discipline and rigor; however, it is not a heavyweight or highly ceremonious process despite the attempts of some methodologists to codify it with those trappings. Rather, Agile falls somewhere in the middle between just enough structure and just enough flexibility. It has been said that Agile is simple but not easy, describing the fact that it is built on a simple set of sensible values and principles but requires a high degree of discipline and rigor to properly execute. It is important to accurately understand the minimum set of characteristics that differentiate a true Agile process from those that are too unstructured or too rigid. This chapter is intended to leave you with a clear understanding of those characteristics as well as the underlying values and principles of Agile Analytics. These are derived directly from the tried and proven foundations established by the Agile software community and are adapted to the nuances of data warehousing and business intelligence development.

ALPINE-STYLE SYSTEMS DEVELOPMENT

I'm a bit of an armchair climber and mountaineer. I'm fascinated by the trials and travails of climbing high mountains like Everest, Annapurna, and others that rise to over 8,000 meters above sea level. These expeditions are complicated affairs involving challenging planning and logistics, a high degree of risk and uncertainty, a high probability of death (for every two climbers who reach the top of Annapurna, another one dies trying!), difficult decisions in the face of uncontrollable variables, and incredible rewards when success is achieved. While it may not be as adventuresome, building complex business intelligence systems is a lot like high-altitude climbing. We face lots of risk and uncertainty, complex planning, difficult decisions in the heat of battle, and the likelihood of death! Okay, maybe not that last part, but you get the analogy. Unfortunately the success rate for building DW/BI systems isn't very much better than the success rate for high-altitude mountaineering expeditions.

Climbing teams first began successfully "conquering" these high mountains in the 1950s, '60s, and '70s. In those early days the preferred mountaineering style was known as "siege climbing," which had a lot of similarities to a military excursion. Expeditions were led in an autocratic command-and-control fashion, often by someone with more military leadership experience than climbing experience. Climbing teams were supported by the large numbers of porters required to carry massive amounts of gear and supplies to base camp and higher. Mounting a siege-style expedition takes over a year of planning and can take two months or more to execute during the climbing season. Siege climbing is a yo-yo-like affair in which ropes are fixed higher and higher on the mountain, multiple semipermanent camps are established at various points along the route, and loads of supplies are relayed by porters to those higher camps. Finally, with all this support, a small team of summit climbers launches the final push for the summit on a single day, leaving from the high camp and returning to the same. Brilliant teams have successfully climbed mountains for years in this style, but the expeditions are prohibitively expensive, time-consuming to execute, and fraught with heavyweight procedures and bureaucracy.

Traditional business intelligence systems development is a lot like siege climbing. It can result in high-quality, working systems that deliver the desired capabilities. However, these projects are typically expensive, exhibiting a lot of planning, extensive design prior to development, and long development cycles. Like siege-style expeditions, all of the energy goes into one shot at the summit. If the summit bid fails, it is too time-consuming to return to base camp and regroup for another attempt. In my lifetime (and I'm not that old yet) I've seen multiple traditional DW/BI projects with budgets of $20 million or more, and timelines of 18 to 24 months, founder. When such projects fail, the typical management response is to cancel the project entirely rather than adjust, adapt, and regroup for another "summit attempt."

In the 1970s a new mountaineering method called "alpine-style" emerged, making it feasible for smaller teams to summit these high peaks faster, more cheaply, and with less protocol. Alpine-style mountaineering still requires substantial planning, a sufficient supporting team, and enough gear and supplies to safely reach the summit. However, instead of spending months preparing the route for the final summit push, alpine-style climbers spend about a week moving the bare essentials up to the higher camps. In this style, if conditions are right, summits can be reached in a mere ten days. Teams of two to three climbers share a single tent and sleeping bag, fewer ropes are needed, and the climbers can travel much lighter and faster. When conditions are not right, it is feasible for alpine-style mountaineers to return to base camp and wait for conditions to improve to make another summit bid.

Agile DW/BI development is much like alpine-style climbing. It is essential that we have a sufficient amount of planning, the necessary support to be successful, and an appropriate amount of protocol. Our "summit" is the completion of a high-quality, working business intelligence system that is of high value to its users. As in mountaineering, reaching our summit requires the proper conditions. We need just the right amount of planning—but we must be able to adapt our plan to changing factors and new information. We must prepare for a high degree of risk and uncertainty—but we must be able to nimbly manage and respond as risks unfold. We need support and involvement from a larger community—but we seek team self-organization rather than command-and-control leadership.

Agile Analytics is a development "style" rather than a methodology or even a framework. The line between siege-style and alpine-style mountaineering is not precisely defined, and alpine-style expeditions may include some siege-style practices. Each style is best described in terms of its values and guiding principles. Each alpine-style expedition employs a distinct set of climbing practices that support a common set of values and principles. Similarly, each Agile DW/BI project team must adapt its technical, project management, and customer collaboration practices to best support the Agile values and principles.[1]

---

1. I'm not the first Agile advocate to discuss the analogy between climbing and Agile development. Jim Highsmith made a similar analogy in his 2000 book, *Adaptive Software Development: A Collaborative Approach to Managing Complex Systems* (Highsmith 2000).

Premier mountaineer Ed Viesturs has a formula, or core value, that is his cardinal rule in the big mountains: "Getting to the top is optional. Getting down is mandatory." (Viesturs and Roberts 2006) I love this core value because it is simple and elegant, and it provides a clear basis for all of Ed's decision making when he is on the mountain. In the stress of the climb, or in the midst of an intensely challenging project, we need just such a basis for decision making—our "North Star." In 2000, a group of the most influential application software developers convened in Salt Lake City and formed the Agile Alliance. Through the process of sharing and comparing each of their "styles" of software development, the *Agile Manifesto* emerged as a simple and elegant basis for project guidance and decision making. The Agile Manifesto reads:[2]

Manifesto for Agile Software Development

We are uncovering better ways of developing software by doing it and helping others do it. Through this work we have come to value:

Individuals and interactions *over processes and tools*
Working software *over comprehensive documentation*
Customer collaboration *over contract negotiation*
Responding to change *over following a plan*

That is, while there is value in the items on the right, we value the items on the left more.

With due respect to the Agile Alliance, of which I am a member, I have adapted the Agile Manifesto just a bit in order to make it more appropriate to Agile Analytics:

Manifesto for Agile Analytics Development

We are uncovering better ways of developing data warehousing and business intelligence systems by doing it and helping others do it. Through this work we have come to value:

Individuals and interactions over processes and tools
Working DW/BI systems over comprehensive documentation
End-user and stakeholder collaboration over contract negotiation
Responding to change over following a plan

That is, while there is value in the items on the right, we value the items on the left more.

---

2. www.agilealliance.org

I didn't want to mess with the original manifesto too much, but it is important to acknowledge that DW/BI systems are fundamentally different from application software. In addition to dealing with large volumes of data, our efforts involve systems integration, customization, and programming. Nonetheless, the Agile core values are very relevant to DW/BI systems development. These values emphasize the fact that our primary objective is the creation of high-quality, high-value, working DW/BI systems. Every activity related to any project either (a) directly and materially contributes to this primary objective or (b) does not. Agile Analytics attempts to maximize a-type activities while acknowledging that there are some b-type activities that are still important, such as documenting your enterprise data model.

WHAT IS AGILE ANALYTICS?

Throughout this book I will introduce you to a set of Agile DW/BI principles and practices. These include technical, project management, and user collaboration practices. I will demonstrate how you can apply these on your projects, and how you can tailor them to the nuances of your environment. However, the title of this section is "What Is Agile Analytics?" so I should probably take you a bit further than the mountaineering analogy.

Here's What Agile Analytics Is

So here is a summary of the key characteristics of Agile Analytics. This is simply a high-level glimpse at the key project traits that are the mark of agility, not an exhaustive list of practices. Throughout the remainder of this book I will introduce you to a set of specific practices that will enable you to achieve agility on your DW/BI projects. Moreover, Agile Analytics is a development style, not a prescriptive methodology that tells you precisely what you must do and how you must do it. The dynamics of each project within each organization require practices that can be tailored appropriately to the environment. Remember, the primary objective is a high-quality, high-value, working DW/BI system. These characteristics simply serve that goal:

- **Iterative, incremental, evolutionary.** Foremost, Agile is an iterative, incremental, and evolutionary style of development. We work in short *iterations* that are generally one to three weeks long, and never more than four weeks. We build the system in small *increments* or "chunks" of user-valued functionality. And we *evolve* the working system by adapting to frequent user feedback. Agile development is like driving around in an unfamiliar city; you want to avoid going very far without some validation that you are on the right course.

Short iterations with frequent user reviews help ensure that we are never very far off course in our development.

- **Value-driven development.** The goal of each development iteration is the production of user-valued features. While you and I may appreciate the difficulty of complex data architectures, elegant data models, efficient ETL scripts, and so forth, users generally couldn't care less about these things. What users of DW/BI systems care about is the presentation of and access to information that helps them either solve a business problem or make better business decisions. Every iteration must produce at least one new user-valued feature in spite of the fact that user features are just the tip of the architectural iceberg that is a DW/BI system.
- **Production quality.** Each newly developed feature must be fully tested and debugged during the development iteration. Agile development is not about building hollow prototypes; it is about incrementally evolving to the right solution with the best architectural underpinnings. We do this by integrating ruthless testing early and continuously into the DW/BI development process.[3] Developers must plan for and include rigorous testing in their development process. A user feature is "Done" when it is of production quality, it is successfully integrated into the evolving system, and developers are proud of their work. That same feature is "Done! Done!" when the user accepts it as delivering the right value.
- **Barely sufficient processes.** Traditional styles of DW/BI development are rife with a high degree of ceremony. I've worked on many projects that involved elaborate stage-gate meetings between stages of development such as the transition from requirements analysis to design. These gates are almost always accompanied by a formal document that must be "signed off" as part of the gating process. In spite of this ceremony many DW/BI projects struggle or founder. Agile DW/BI emphasizes a sufficient amount of ceremony to meet the practical needs of the project (and future generations) but nothing more. If a data dictionary is deemed important for use by future developers, then perhaps a digital image of a whiteboard table or a simple spreadsheet table will suffice. Since our primary objective is the production of high-quality, high-value, working systems, we must be able to minimize the amount of ceremony required for other activities.

---

3. Historically database and data warehouse testing has lacked the rigor, discipline, and automation that have benefited software development efforts (www.ambysoft.com/surveys/dataQualitySeptember2006.html).

- **Automation, automation, automation.** The only way to be truly Agile is to automate as many routine processes as possible. Test automation is perhaps the most critical. If you must test your features and system manually, guess how often you're likely to rerun your tests? Test automation enables you to frequently revalidate that everything is still working as expected. Build automation enables you to frequently build a version of your complete working DW/BI system in a demo or preproduction environment. This helps establish continuous confidence that you are never more than a few hours or days away from putting a new version into production. Agile Analytics teams seek to automate any process that is done more than once. The more you can automate, the more you can focus on developing user features.
- **Collaboration.** Too often in traditional projects the development team solely bears the burden of ensuring that timelines are met, complete scope is delivered, budgets are managed, and quality is ensured. Agile business intelligence acknowledges that there is a broader project community that shares responsibility for project success. The project community includes the subcommunities of users, business owners, stakeholders, executive sponsors, technical experts, project managers, and others. Frequent collaboration between the technical and user communities is critical to success. Daily collaboration within the technical community is also critical. In fact, establishing a collaborative team workspace is an essential ingredient of successful Agile projects.
- **Self-organizing, self-managing teams.** Hire the best people, give them the tools and support they need, then stand aside and allow them to be successful. There is a key shift in the Agile project management style compared to traditional project management. The Agile project manager's role is to enable team members to work their magic and to facilitate a high degree of collaboration with users and other members of the project community. The Agile project team decides how much work it can complete during an iteration, then holds itself accountable to honor those commitments. The Agile style is not a substitute for having the right people on the team.

Guiding Principles

The core values contained in the Agile Manifesto motivate a set of guiding principles for DW/BI systems design and development. These principles often become the tiebreaker when difficult trade-off decisions must be made. Similarly, the Agile Alliance has established a set of principles for software development.[4] The following Agile Analytics principles borrow liberally from the Agile Alliance principles:

- Our highest priority is to satisfy the DW/BI user community through early and continuous delivery of working user features.
- We welcome changing requirements, even late in development. Agile processes harness change for the DW/BI users' competitive advantage.
- We deliver working software frequently, providing users with new DW/BI features every few weeks.
- Users, stakeholders, and developers must share project ownership and work together daily throughout the project.
- We value the importance of talented and experienced business intelligence experts. We give them the environment and support they need and trust them to get the job done.
- The most efficient and effective method of conveying information to and within a development team is face-to-face conversation.
- A working business intelligence system is the primary measure of progress.
- We recognize the balance among project scope, schedule, and cost. The data warehousing team must work at a sustainable pace.
- Continuous attention to the best data warehousing practices enhances agility.
- The best architectures, requirements, and designs emerge from self-organizing teams.
- At regular intervals, the team reflects on how to become more effective, then tunes and adjusts its behavior accordingly.

Take a minute to reflect on these principles. How many of them are present in the projects in your organization? Do they make sense for your organization? Give them another look. Are they realistic principles for your organization? I have found these not only to be commonsense principles, but also to be effective and achievable on real projects. Furthermore, adherence to these principles rather than reliance on a prescriptive and ceremonious process model is very liberating.

Myths and Misconceptions

There are some myths and misconceptions that seem to prevail among other DW/BI practitioners and experts that I have talked to about this style

---

4. www.agilemanifesto.org/principles.html

of development. I recently had an exchange on this topic with a seasoned veteran in both software development and data warehousing who is certified at the mastery level in DW/BI and data management and who has managed large software development groups. His misunderstanding of Agile development made it evident that myths and misconceptions abound even among the most senior DW/BI practitioners. Agile Analytics is not:

- **A wholesale replacement of traditional practices.** I am not suggesting that everything we have learned and practiced in the short history of DW/BI systems development is wrong, and that Agile is the new savior that will rescue us from our hell. There are many good DW/BI project success stories, which is why DW/BI continues to be among the top five strategic initiatives for most large companies today. It is important that we keep the practices and methods that work well, improve those that allow room for improvement, and replace those that are problematic. Agile Analytics seeks to modify our general approach to DW/BI systems development without discarding the best practices we've learned on our journey so far.

- **Synonymous with Scrum or eXtreme Programming (XP).** Scrum is perhaps the Agile flavor that has received the most publicity (along with XP) in recent years. However, it is incorrect to say that "Agile was formerly known as eXtreme Programming," as one skeptic told me. In fact, there are many different Agile development flavors that add valuable principles and practices to the broader collective known as Agile development. These include Scrum, Agile Modeling, Agile Data, Crystal, Adaptive, DSDM, Lean Development, Feature Driven Development, Agile Project Management (APM), and others.[5] Each is guided by the core values expressed in the Agile Manifesto. Agile Analytics is an adaptation of principles and practices from a variety of these methods to the complexities of data-intensive, analytics-based systems integration efforts like data warehousing and data mart development.

- **Simply iterating.** Short, frequent development iterations are an essential cornerstone of Agile development. Unfortunately, this key practice is commonly misconstrued as *the* definition of agility. Not long ago I was asked to mentor a development team that had "gone Agile" but wasn't experiencing the expected benefits of agility. Upon closer inspection I discovered that they were planning in four-week "iterations" but didn't expect to have any working features until

---

5. For a great survey of the various Agile flavors I highly recommend reading *Agile Software Development Ecosystems* (Highsmith 2002).

about the sixth month of the project. Effectively they had divided the traditional waterfall model into time blocks they called iterations. They completely missed the point. The aim of iterative development is to demonstrate working features and to obtain frequent feedback from the user community. This means that every iteration must result in demonstrable working software.

- **For systems integration; it's only for programming.** Much of our effort in DW/BI development is focused on the integration of multiple commercial tools, thereby minimizing the volume of raw programming required. DW/BI tool vendors would have us believe that DW/BI development is simply a matter of hooking up the tools to the source systems and pressing the "Go" button. You've probably already discovered that building an effective DW/BI system is not that simple. A DW/BI development team includes a heterogeneous mixture of skills, including extraction, transformation, load (ETL) development; database development; data modeling (both relational and multidimensional); application development; and others. In fact, compared to the more homogeneous skills required for applications development, DW/BI development is quite complex in this regard. This complexity calls for an approach that supports a high degree of customer collaboration, frequent delivery of working software, and frequent feedback—aha, an Agile approach!

- **An excuse for ad hoc behavior.** Some have mistaken the tenets of Agile development for abandonment of rigor, quality, or structure, in other words, "hacking." This misperception could not be farther from the truth. Agility is a focus on the frequent delivery of high-value, production-quality, working software to the user community with the goal of continuously adapting to user feedback. This means that automated testing and quality assurance are critical components of all iterative development activities. We don't build prototypes; we build working features and then mature those features in response to user input. Others mistake the Agile Manifesto as disdain of documentation, which is also incorrect. Agile DW/BI seeks to ensure that a sufficient amount of documentation is produced. The keyword here is *sufficient*. Sufficiency implies that there is a legitimate purpose for the document, and when that purpose is served, there is no need for additional documentation.

In my work with teams that are learning and adopting the Agile DW/BI development style, I often find that they are looking for a prescriptive methodology that makes it very clear which practices to apply and when. This is a natural inclination for new Agile practitioners, and I will provide some recommendations that may seem prescriptive in nature. In fact you may benefit initially by creating your own "recipe" for the application of Agile DW/BI principles and practices. However, I need to reemphasize that Agile Analytics is a style, not a methodology and not a framework. Figuratively, you can absorb agility into your DNA with enough focus, practice, and discipline. You'll know you've reached that point when you begin applying Agile principles to everything you do such as buying a new car, remodeling a bathroom, or writing a book.

DATA WAREHOUSING ARCHITECTURES AND SKILL SETS

To ensure that we are working from a common understanding, here is a very brief summary of data warehouse architectures and requisite skill sets. This is not a substitute for any of the more comprehensive technical books on data warehousing but should be sufficient as a baseline for the remainder of the book.

Data Warehousing Conceptual Architectures

Figure 1.1 depicts an abstracted classical data warehousing architecture and is suitable to convey either a Kimball-style (Kimball and Ross 2002) or an Inmon-style (Inmon 2005) architecture. This is a high-level conceptual architecture containing multiple layers, each of which includes a complex integration of commercial technologies, data modeling and manipulation, and some custom code.

The data warehouse architecture includes one or more *operational source systems* from which data is extracted, transformed, and loaded into the data

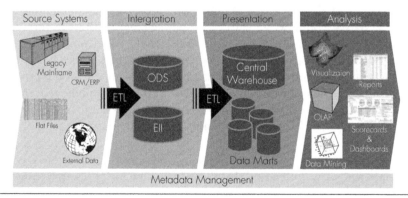

Figure 1.1 Classical data warehouse architecture

warehouse repositories. These systems are optimized for the daily transactional processing required to run the business operations. Most DW/
BI systems source data from multiple operational systems, some of which
are legacy systems that may be several decades old and reside on older
technologies.

Data from these sources is extracted into an *integration tier* in the architecture that acts as a "holding pen" where data can be merged, manipulated,
transformed, cleansed, and validated without placing an undue burden on
the operational systems. This tier may include an operational data store or
an enterprise information integration (EII) repository that acts as a system
of record for all relevant operational data. The integration database is typically based on a relational data model and may have multiple subcompo-
nents, including pre-staging, staging, and an integration repository, each
serving a different purpose relating to the consolidation and preprocessing
of data from disparate source systems. Common technologies for staging
databases are Oracle, IBM DB2, Microsoft SQL Server, and NCR Teradata.
The DW/BI community is beginning to see increasing use of the open-
source database MySQL for this architectural component.

Data is extracted from the staging database, transformed, and loaded into a
presentation tier in the architecture that contains appropriate structures for
optimized multidimensional and analytical queries. This system is designed
to support the data slicing and dicing that define the power of a data warehouse. There are a variety of alternatives for the implementation of the
presentation database, including normalized relational schemas and denor-
malized schemas like star, snowflake, and even "starflake." Moreover, the
presentation tier may include a single enterprise data warehouse or a collection of subject-specific data marts. Some architectures include a hybrid
of both of these. Presentation repositories are typically implemented in the
same technologies as the integration database.

Finally, data is presented to the business users at the *analysis tier* in the
architecture. This conceptual layer in the system represents the variety of
applications and tools that provide users with access to the data, including
report writers, ad hoc querying, online analytical processing (OLAP), data
visualization, data mining, and statistical analysis. BI tool vendors such as
Pentaho, Cognos, MicroStrategy, Business Objects, Microsoft, Oracle, IBM,
and others produce commercial products that enable data from the presentation database to be aggregated and presented within user applications.

This is a generalized architecture, and actual implementations vary in the details. One major variation on the Kimball architecture is the Inmon architecture (Inmon 2005), which inserts a layer of *subject-specific data marts* that contain subsets of the data from the main warehouse. Each data mart supports only the specific end-user applications that are relevant to the business subject area for which that mart was designed. Regardless of your preferences for Kimball- versus Inmon-style architectures, and of the variations found in implementation detail, Figure 1.1 will serve as reference architecture for the discussions in this book. The Agile DW/BI principles and practices that are introduced here are not specific to any particular architecture.

Diverse and Disparate Technical Skills

Inherent in the implementation of this architecture are the following aspects of development, each requiring a unique set of development skills:

- **Data modeling.** Design and implementation of data models are required for both the integration and presentation repositories. Relational data models are distinctly different from dimensional data models, and each has unique properties. Moreover, relational data modelers may not have dimensional modeling expertise and vice versa.
- **ETL development.** ETL refers to the *extraction* of data from source systems into staging, the *transformations* necessary to recast source data for analysis, and the *loading* of transformed data into the presentation repository. ETL includes the selection criteria to extract data from source systems, performing any necessary data transformations or derivations needed, data quality audits, and cleansing.
- **Data cleansing.** Source data is typically not perfect. Furthermore, merging data from multiple sources can inject new data quality issues. Data hygiene is an important aspect of data warehouse that requires specific skills and techniques.
- **OLAP design.** Typically data warehouses support some variety of online analytical processing (HOLAP, MOLAP, or ROLAP). Each OLAP technique is different but requires special design skills to balance the reporting requirements against performance constraints.
- **Application development.** Users commonly require an application interface into the data warehouse that provides an easy-to-use front end combined with comprehensive analytical capabilities, and one that is tailored to the way the users work. This often requires

some degree of custom programming or commercial application customization.

- **Production automation.** Data warehouses are generally designed for periodic automated updates when new and modified data is slurped into the warehouse so that users can view the most recent data available. These automated update processes must have built-in fail-over strategies and must ensure data consistency and correctness.
- **General systems and database administration.** Data warehouse developers must have many of the same skills held by the typical network administrator and database administrator. They must understand the implications of efficiently moving possibly large volumes of data across the network, and the issues of effectively storing changing data.

WHY DO WE NEED AGILE ANALYTICS?

In my years as a DW/BI consultant and practitioner I have learned three consistent truths: Building successful DW/BI systems is hard; DW/BI development projects fail very often; and it is better to fail fast and adapt than to fail late after the budget is spent.

First Truth: Building DW/BI Systems Is Hard

If you have taken part in a data warehousing project, you are aware of the numerous challenges, perils, and pitfalls. Ralph Kimball, Bill Inmon, and other DW/BI pioneers have done an excellent job of developing reusable architectural patterns for data warehouse and DW/BI implementation. Software vendors have done a good job of creating tools and technologies to support the concepts. Nonetheless, DW/BI is just plain hard, and for several reasons:

- **Lack of expertise.** Most organizations have not previously built a DW/BI system or have only limited experience in doing so.
- **Lack of experience.** Most organizations don't build multiple DW/BI systems, and therefore development processes don't get a chance to mature through experience.
- **Ambitious goals.** Organizations often set out to build an enterprise data warehouse, or at least a broad-reaching data mart, which makes the process more complex.
- **Domain knowledge versus subject matter expertise.** DW/BI practitioners often have extensive expertise in business intelligence but not in the organization's business domain, causing gaps in

understanding. Business users typically don't know what they can, or should, expect from a DW/BI system.

- **Unrealistic expectations.** Business users often think of data warehousing as a technology-based plug-and-play application that will quickly provide them with miraculous insights.
- **Educated user phenomenon.** As users gain a better understanding of data warehousing, their needs and wishes change.
- **Shooting the messenger.** DW/BI systems are like shining a bright light in the attic: You may not always like what you find. When the system exposes data quality problems, business users tend to distrust the DW/BI system.
- **Focus on technology.** Organizations often view a DW/BI system as an IT application rather than a joint venture between business stakeholders and IT developers.
- **Specialized skills.** Data warehousing requires an entirely different skill set from that of typical database administrators (DBAs) and developers. Most organizations do not have staff members with adequate expertise in these areas.
- **Multiple skills.** Data warehousing requires a multitude of unique and distinct skills such as multidimensional modeling, data cleansing, ETL development, OLAP design, application development, and so forth.

These unique DW/BI development characteristics compound the already complex process of building software or building database applications.

Second Truth: DW/BI Development Projects Fail Often

Unfortunately, I'm not the only one who has experienced failure on DW/BI projects. A quick Google search on "data warehouse failure polls" results in a small library of case studies, postmortems, and assessment articles. Estimated failure rates of around 50 percent are common and are rarely disputed.

When I speak to groups of business intelligence practitioners, I often begin my talks with an informal survey. First I ask everyone who has been involved in the completion of one or more DW/BI projects to stand. It varies depending on the audience, but usually more than half the group stands up. Then I ask participants to sit down if they have experienced projects that were delivered late, projects that had significant budget overruns, or projects that did not satisfy users' expectations. Typically nobody is left standing by the third question, and I haven't even gotten to questions about acceptable quality or any other issues. It is apparent that most experienced DW/BI practitioners have lived through at least one project failure.

While there is no clear definition of what constitutes "failure," Sid Adelman and Larissa Moss classify the following situations as characteristic of limited acceptance or outright project failure (Moss and Adelman 2000):

- The project is over budget.
- The schedule has slipped.
- Some expected functionality was not implemented.
- Users are unhappy.
- Performance is unacceptable.
- Availability of the warehouse applications is poor.
- There is no ability to expand.
- The data and/or reports are poor.
- The project is not cost-justified.
- Management does not recognize the benefits of the project.

In other words, simply completing the technical implementation of a data warehouse doesn't constitute success. Take another look at this list. Nearly every situation is "customer"-focused; that is, primarily end users determine whether a project is successful.

There are literally hundreds of similar evaluations of project failures, and they exhibit a great deal of overlap in terms of root causes: incorrect requirements, weak processes, inability to adapt to changes, project scope mismanagement, unrealistic schedules, inflated expectations, and so forth.

Third Truth: It Is Best to Fail Fast and Adapt

Unfortunately, the traditional development model does little to uncover these deficiencies early in the project. As Jeff DeLuca, one of the creators of Feature Driven Development (FDD), says, "We should try to break the back of the project as early as possible to avoid the high cost of change later downstream." In a traditional approach, it is possible for developers to plow ahead in the blind confidence that they are building the right product, only to discover at the end of the project that they were sadly mistaken. This is true even when one uses all the best practices, processes, and methodologies.

What is needed is an approach that promotes early discovery of project peril. Such an approach must place the responsibility of success equally on the users, stakeholders, and developers and should reward a team's ability to adapt to new directions and substantial requirements changes.

As we observed earlier, most classes of project failure are user-satisfaction-oriented. If we can continuously adapt the DW/BI system and align with user expectations, users will be satisfied with the outcome. In all of my past involvement in traditional DW/BI implementations I have consistently seen the following phenomena at the end of the project:

- **Users have become more educated about BI.** As the project progresses, so does users' understanding of BI. So, what they told you at the beginning of the project may have been based on a misunderstanding or incorrect expectations.
- **User requirements have changed or become more refined.** That's true of *all* software and implementation projects. It's just a fact of life. What they told you at the beginning is much less relevant than what they tell you at the end.
- **Users' memories of early requirements reviews are fuzzy.** It often happens that contractually speaking, a requirement is met by the production system, but users are less than thrilled, having reactions like "What I really meant was . . ." or "That may be what I said, but it's not what I want."
- **Users have high expectations when anticipating a new and useful tool.** Left to their own imaginations, users often elevate their expectations of the BI system well beyond what is realistic or reasonable. This only leaves them disappointed when they see the actual product.
- **Developers build based on the initial snapshot of user requirements.** In waterfall-style development the initial requirements are reviewed and approved, then act as the scoping contract. Meeting the terms of the contract is not nearly as satisfying as meeting the users' expectations.

All these factors lead to a natural gap between what is built and what is needed. An approach that frequently releases new BI features to users, hears user feedback, and adapts to change is the single best way to fail fast and correct the course of development.

Is Agile Really Better?

There is increasing evidence that Agile approaches lead to higher project success rates. Scott Ambler, a leader in Agile database development and Agile Modeling, has conducted numerous surveys on Agile development in an effort to quantify the impact and effectiveness of these methods. Beginning in 2007, Ambler conducted three surveys specifically relating to IT project success rates.[6] The 2007 survey explored success rates of different IT project types and methods. Only 63 percent of traditional projects and data warehousing projects were successful, while Agile projects experienced a 72 percent rate of success. The 2008 survey focused on four success criteria: quality, ROI, functionality, and schedule. In all four areas Agile methods significantly outperformed traditional, sequential development approaches. The 2010 survey continued to show that Agile methods in IT produce better results.

I should note here that traditional definitions of success involve metrics such as on time, on budget, and to specification. While these metrics may satisfy management efforts to control budgets, they do not always correlate to customer satisfaction. In fact, scope, schedule, and cost are poor measures of progress and success. Martin Fowler argues, "Project success is more about whether the software delivers value that's greater than the cost of the resources put into it." He points out that XP 2002 conference speaker Jim Johnson, chairman of the Standish Group, observed that a large proportion of features are frequently unused in software products. He quoted two studies: a DuPont study, which found that only 25 percent of a system's features were really needed, and a Standish study, which found that 45 percent of features were never used and only 20 percent of features were used often or always (Fowler 2002). These findings are further supported by a Department of Defense study, which found that only 2 percent of the code in $35.7 billion worth of software was used as delivered, and 75 percent was either never used or was canceled prior to delivery (Leishman and Cook 2002).

Agile development is principally aimed at the delivery of high-priority value to the customer community. Measures of progress and success must focus more on value delivery than on traditional metrics of on schedule, on budget, and to spec. Jim Highsmith points out, "Traditional managers expect projects to be on-track early and off-track later; Agile managers expect projects to be off-track early and on-track later." This statement reflects the notion that incrementally evolving a system by frequently seeking and adapting to customer feedback will result in building the right solution, but it may not be the solution that was originally planned.

The Difficulties of Agile Analytics

Applying Agile methods to DW/BI is not without challenges. Many of the project management and technical practices I introduce in this book are

---

6. The detailed results are available at www.ambysoft.com/surveys/.

adapted from those of our software development colleagues who have been maturing these practices for the past decade or longer. Unfortunately, the specific practices and tools used to custom-build software in languages like Java, C++, or C# do not always transfer easily to systems integration using proprietary technologies like Informatica, Oracle, Cognos, and others. Among the problems that make Agile difficult to apply to DW/BI development are the following:

- **Tool support.** There aren't many tools that support technical practices such as test-driven database or ETL development, database refactoring, data warehouse build automation, and others that are introduced in this book. The tools that do exist are less mature than the ones used for software development. However, this current state of tool support continues to get better, through both open-source as well as commercial tools.
- **Data volume.** It takes creative thinking to use lightweight development practices to build high-volume data warehouses and BI systems. We need to use small, representative data samples to quickly build and test our work, while continuously proving that our designs will work with production data volumes. This is more of an *impediment* to our way of approaching the problem rather than a *barrier* that is inherent in the problem domain. Impediments are those challenges that can be eliminated or worked around; barriers are insurmountable.
- **"Heavy lifting."** While Agile Analytics is a feature-driven (think business intelligence features) approach, the most time-consuming aspect of building DW/BI systems is in the back-end data warehouse or data marts. Early in the project it may seem as if it takes a lot of "heavy lifting" on the back end just to expose a relatively basic BI feature on the front end. Like the data volume challenge, it takes creative thinking to build the smallest/simplest back-end data solution needed to produce business value on the front end.
- **Continuous deployment.** The ability to deploy new features into production frequently is a goal of Agile development. This goal is hampered by DW/BI systems that are already in production with large data volumes. Sometimes updating a production data warehouse with a simple data model revision can require significant time and careful execution. Frequent deployment may look very different in DW/BI from the way it looks in software development.

The nuances of your project environment may introduce other such difficulties. In general, those who successfully embrace Agile's core values and guiding principles learn how to effectively adapt their processes to mitigate these difficulties. For each of these challenges I find it useful to ask the question "Will the project be better off if we can overcome this difficulty despite how hard it may be to overcome?" As long as the answer to that question is yes, it is worth grappling with the challenges in order to make Agile Analytics work. With time and experience these difficulties become easier to overcome.

INTRODUCING FLIXBUSTER ANALYTICS

Now seems like a good time to introduce the running DW/BI example that I'll be revisiting throughout this book to show you how the various Agile practices are applied. I use an imaginary video rental chain to demonstrate the Agile Analytics practices. The company is FlixBuster, and they have retail stores in cities throughout North America. FlixBuster also offers video rentals online where customers can manage their rental requests and movies are shipped directly to their mailing address. Finally, FlixBuster offers movie downloads directly to customers' computers.

FlixBuster has customers who are members and customers who are nonmembers. Customers fall into three buying behavior groups: those who shop exclusively in retail stores, those who shop exclusively online, and those who split their activity across channels. FlixBuster customers can order a rental online or in the store, and they can return videos in the store or via a postage-paid return envelope provided by the company.

Members pay a monthly subscription fee, which determines their rental privileges. Top-tier members may rent up to three videos at the same time. There is also a membership tier allowing two videos at a time as well as a tier allowing one at a time. Members may keep their rentals indefinitely with no late charges. As soon as FlixBuster receives a returned video from a member, the next one is shipped. Nonmembers may also rent videos in the stores following the traditional video rental model with a four-day return policy.

Approximately 75 percent of the brick-and-mortar FlixBuster stores across North America are corporately owned and managed; the remaining 25 percent are privately owned franchises. FlixBuster works closely with franchise owners to ensure that the customer experience is consistent across all stores. FlixBuster prides itself on its large inventory of titles, the rate of customer requests that are successfully fulfilled, and how quickly members receive each new video by mail.

FlixBuster has a complex partnership with the studios producing the films and the clearinghouses that provide licensed media to FlixBuster and manage royalty payments and license agreements. Each title is associated with a royalty percentage to be paid to the studio. Royalty statements and payments are made on a monthly basis to each of the clearinghouses.

Furthermore, FlixBuster sales channels (e-tail and retail) receive a percentage of the video rental revenue. Franchise owners receive a negotiated revenue amount that is generally higher than for corporately owned retail outlets. The online channel receives still a different revenue percentage to cover its operating costs.

FlixBuster has determined that there is a good business case for developing an enterprise business intelligence system. This DW/BI system will serve corporate users from finance, marketing, channel sales, customer management, inventory management, and other departments. FlixBuster also intends to launch an intranet BI portal for subscription use by its clearinghouse partners, studios, franchisees, and possibly even Internet movie database providers. Such an intranet portal is expected to provide additional revenue streams for FlixBuster.

There are multiple data sources for the FlixBuster DW/BI system, including FlixBackOffice, the corporate ERP system; FlixOps, the video-by-mail fulfillment system; FlixTrans, the transactional and point-of-sale system; FlixClear, the royalty management system; and others.

FlixBuster has successfully completed other development projects using Agile methods and is determined to take an Agile Analytics approach on the development of its DW/BI system, FlixAnalysis. During high-level executive steering committee analysis and reviews, it has been decided that the first production release of FlixAnalysis will be for the finance department and will be a timeboxed release cycle of six months.

WRAP-UP

This chapter has laid the foundation for an accurate, if high-level, understanding of Agile Analytics. Successive chapters in this book serve to fill in the detailed "how-to" techniques that an Agile Analytics team needs to put these concepts into practice. You should now understand that Agile Analytics isn't simply a matter of chunking tasks into two-week iterations, holding a 15-minute daily team meeting, or retitling the project manager a "scrum master." Although these may be Agile traits, new Agile teams often limit their agility to these simpler concepts and lose sight of the things that truly define agility. True agility is reflected by traits like early and frequent delivery of production-quality, working BI features, delivering the highest-valued features first, tackling risk and uncertainty early, and continuous stakeholder and developer interaction and collaboration.

Agile Analytics teams evolve toward the best system design by continuously seeking and adapting to feedback from the business community. Agile Analytics balances the right amount of structure and formality against a sufficient amount of flexibility, with a constant focus on building the right solution. The key to agility lies in the core values and guiding principles more than in a set of specific techniques and practices—although effective techniques and practices are important. Mature Agile Analytics teams elevate themselves above a catalog of practices and establish attitudes and patterns of behavior that encourage seeking feedback, adapting to change, and delivering maximum value.

If you are considering adopting Agile Analytics, keep these core values and guiding principles at the top of your mind. When learning any new technique, it is natural to look for successful patterns that can be mimicked. This is a valuable approach that will enable a new Agile team to get on the right track and avoid unnecessary pitfalls. While I have stressed that Agile development is not a prescriptive process, new Agile teams will benefit from some recipe-style techniques. Therefore, many of the practices introduced in this book may have a bit of a prescriptive feel. I encourage you to try these practices first as prescribed and then, as you gain experience, tailor them as needed to be more effective. But be sure you're tailoring practices for the right reasons. Be careful not to tailor a practice simply because it was difficult or uncomfortable on the first try. Also, be sure not to simply cherry-pick the easy practices while ignoring the harder ones. Often the harder practices are the ones that will have the biggest impact on your team's performance.

Chapter 2

AGILE PROJECT MANAGEMENT

In 2006, NBC launched a television series in the United States called *Studio 60*, a comedy/drama about the production of a weekly live variety show à la *Saturday Night Live*. The series gave viewers a behind-the-scenes look at the intensity with which each new weekly variety show is planned and executed. Unlike typical weekly TV shows, each episode of a live variety show is planned in a "just-in-time" fashion. The content must be adapted to current events, the decisions of producers must be responded to immediately, and the cast and crew must be highly adaptable to change. No matter what happens during the week, the show must be completely planned and ready to air at a fixed time. And it must be good enough every week to keep viewer ratings very high or risk cancellation. Imagine the pressure!

A live variety show team consists of people with a diverse set of skills, including studio executives, producers, writers, actors, stagehands, props and lighting crews, camera crew, and others. After an episode airs, the executives, producers, cast, and crew celebrate their success, monitor viewer ratings, and then immediately start planning for the next episode. The team must work fast and be highly collaborative to pull this off. There is absolutely no room in the schedule for superfluous meetings, ceremony, or formality. However, there must be sufficient attention to detail and rigor to ensure that the show is highly successful every single week.

This got me thinking. What if we developed DW/BI systems as if we were producing a live variety show every week? And what if we measured success with the same ruthlessness with which TV networks use viewer ratings? Agile Analytics developers work in short iterations delivering chunks of end-user functionality incrementally. What if we behaved as if the project's future were dependent upon high "viewer ratings" at the end of our current iteration? Not only had we better have new features for our "viewers," but these features had better be great!

As you read this chapter, I challenge you to think of each development iteration as the creation and airing of your own live variety show. What does your team need to do to keep its viewer ratings high every single iteration?

One of the first fundamentals of Agile Analytics is adopting a project management process that is tailored to support iterative, incremental, and evolutionary development of DW/BI systems. Traditional project management methods are insufficient for this purpose. This chapter will introduce you to some of the key practices of Agile Project Management (APM); it is not the final word on the subject. My good friend and colleague Jim Highsmith wrote the book on APM (Highsmith 2010a). In this chapter I will focus on some of the key APM principles and practices as they relate to building business intelligence systems.

WHAT IS AGILE PROJECT MANAGEMENT?

Historically, the methods we have used to manage IT and software projects have been adapted from the construction engineering and management industries. Building bridges and skyscrapers requires a highly sequential and phased approach in which architectural details are finalized and approved before construction can begin. After all, once the cement is set and steel girders are welded into place, it is very costly to change the design. Most of us know the phased/sequential systems development model as the "waterfall model," and we often use this term disparagingly. Many years and a lot of data points have shown us that the waterfall model isn't the best way to manage systems development projects.

Fortunately, software systems aren't built of concrete and steel. We have the unique opportunity to benefit from an approach that allows us to design a little, build a little, share it with users, listen to their feedback, and adjust accordingly, eventually converging on a solution that may be more desirable than what was first envisioned.

Agile methods recognize this, and some agilists suggest that projects should just get started and the solution will evolve one iteration at a time. Unfortunately, this rather extreme point of view is disconcerting to those who manage budgets, monitor return on investments, and allocate resources—senior management! So Jim Highsmith tackled the problem of balancing agility with sufficient rigor by introducing APM (Highsmith 2010a).

The following scenario is an example of how effective Agile Analytics project planning and management works:

Scenario

FlixBuster is a company offering video rentals received by mail, by visiting a retail store, or by instant viewing over the Internet. FlixBuster management has determined that the company needs a data warehouse and business intelligence system that will help them better understand customer rental patterns, studio DVD releases, order fulfillment bottlenecks, and opportunities to increase revenues and profits as well as customer satisfaction.

Software and Web site development at FlixBuster has been following Agile methods for a few years with great success, so management wants to use the same approach for the new DW/BI development project. They'll tailor the APM framework and technical practices to work for the DW/BI project.

Because these are big, loosely defined business goals, Pete, the VP of finance and primary executive sponsor for the project, decides to form a "FlixBuster DW/BI project community." Together with Allen, the CTO, he identifies the key technical team members and decides that Arlene, an experienced scrum master,[1] would be ideal as the project manager. Since Dieter has worked in both finance and customer management and has been advocating the project for some time, Pete and Allen select him to be the product owner. Pete also creates a "co-development customer team" consisting of five seasoned business professionals who will be users of the BI system and whose roles give them differing perspectives on the business.

The project community has been asked to participate in a three-day visioning and chartering session to kick off the project. Pete has learned from prior experience that project chartering is most effective off-site, where people are focused and away from workplace distractions. So, he reserves a meeting room at the nearby Regents Hotel where snacks and lunches can be catered in to keep the group well fed and happy.

Pete starts off the chartering session with a broad statement of the long-term vision for the DW/BI system. He emphasizes that he's not exactly sure which of the broad goals is most important, but he wants the team to work in 90-day "planning cycles." He charges the group with spending the next three days deciding what to build and deploy within the next three months, and to develop a release plan.

With Arlene facilitating, Dieter takes the floor and spends about 30 minutes sharing his ideas and discoveries with the group. He has done some preliminary research and analysis on the broad goals of the DW/BI system and has formed the opinion that getting a handle on customer rental patterns and behaviors is the most valuable goal and should be tackled first. FlixBuster doesn't have a good way to evaluate customer behavior across all three rental channels to get a whole picture of the customer. They currently don't have a reliable way to determine how profitable each customer is, and who their most and least profitable customers

---

1. The Agile method Scrum introduces the role of "scrum master" to replace the traditional project manager on a project team.

are. Dieter also points out that FlixBuster's customer support issues and customer satisfaction feedback aren't currently being tied to customers, and so they don't have a complete picture of their customers' experiences and patterns. It's hard to determine the impact of these issues on revenue and profit.

After some discussion and friendly debate, the group agrees to focus on customer analytics as the primary goal of the first project cycle. They also agree to schedule a strategic DW/BI road-mapping session for another time with the goal of identifying all of the big DW/BI goals and prioritizing them as future project goals.

With the general goal agreed upon, Arlene guides the project community in establishing a more detailed, shared vision of the customer analytics project. She leads them in some "serious games" to facilitate the *envisioning* process. They build product boxes, they create elevator statements, and in the process they have lots of conversations in which the end users describe the information they'd like to have and what they would do if they had it.

The technical team gets a chance to ask lots of questions and learn about the needs of business users. Already the technical team has started thinking about how hard, if not infeasible, it's going to be to accomplish all of these goals in only three months. As the technical team lead, Prakash shares some of these concerns with the group, and they begin *speculating* on the risks and uncertainties that are inherent in the project vision. Arlene guides them in setting a reasonable set of project boundaries and expectations. As the user community understands some of the technical challenges, they help out by lowering their expectations for this first release of the DW/BI system. They express their hope that future releases will include improvements to the features included in the first version. Arlene has the group complete a project data sheet as a preliminary agreement about the scope and boundaries of the project.

It's been a busy morning and everyone is ready for a lunch break. They agree to talk about anything but the project over lunch to give their brains a rest. Over lunch everyone gets to know each other better. Henry, a recently hired developer, learns that Andy, one of the business users, is an avid mountain biker like himself, and they agree to go riding together over the weekend. Allen is happy to see that everyone seems to be getting along.

After lunch Dieter facilitates the story-writing workshop with the project community. This is an important component of project chartering that will result in the product backlog that is populated with user stories in priority order. The project team knows that the product backlog is subject to change. New user stories can be added at any time. They can be removed or altered. And they can be reprioritized. It will be Dieter's job to continuously groom the backlog and keep it up-to-date. The team will plan each iteration with a story conference where they will select items from the top of the backlog, understand their details, estimate their effort, and commit to developing those new BI features.

It's the end of the day, and everyone is exhausted but thrilled to have accomplished so much in the first planning day. Javier, a business user who has been at

FlixBuster since its beginning, comments that it really feels like this project team is going to build a useful tool for his group to use. He's impressed with Prakash and the rest of the developers.

The next morning the group creates a release-planning calendar using butcher paper on the wall. The calendar divides the next three months into two-week iterations and identifies a few key milestones. One milestone the team identifies is that the FlixBuster budget-planning meeting for the 2011 fiscal year is scheduled at about the same time as the beginning of the team's iteration six. Kari wonders out loud if she will be able to use some of the new BI features to provide her boss with some of the information he needs for this meeting. The team notes that on the release plan and promises to try to do a preliminary deployment of features that Kari can use. The group also establishes a theme for each iteration that helps them think about the bigger capabilities that are being developed.

Because this project is the first in a series of FlixBuster DW/BI projects, the team agrees they need an iteration zero to set up the development and testing infrastructure, to install and learn some new development tools, and to develop a high-level system architecture and data model. So, the development team writes and prioritizes a set of technical stories that will be the focus of iteration zero.

While the development team is planning iteration zero, the user community meets with Dieter and Bob, as well as Jamal, the user experience designer, to begin sketching out the low-fidelity prototypes of the first set of user stories that are in the backlog. They will continue to refine these lo-fi prototypes during iteration zero to have them ready for developers at the start of iteration one.

The rest of day two is spent reviewing the user stories that the user community wrote yesterday. The stories are roughly divided into three priority groups (high, higher, and highest), allowing the team to focus on the highest-priority group first. The technical team asks clarifying questions and estimates the difficulty of implementing each user story. Team members identify the ones that are too big and work to simplify them or decompose them into multiple smaller stories. Then Dieter leads the users in rank-ordering them on the backlog so that the team can speculate on how they might be scheduled into the two-week iterations on the planning wall. This effort helps shape everyone's vision for the expected outcome of this 90-day planning cycle.

On the final day of the project-chartering session, Arlene has the group establish a shared set of core values and working agreements for this project. Developers commit to the importance of keeping their work highly visible to the whole community, and the business users commit to giving lots of feedback on working BI features and giving input on iteration plans. The technical team plans the details of iteration zero and makes a preliminary commitment to deliver the first three user stories in iteration one.

By now it's mid-afternoon on Friday, and Arlene asks if the participants have everything they need to start working on the project first thing Monday morning. Arlene will be helping the development team remain unblocked in their work, and Dieter continues to talk with users and to refine and groom the backlog. Bob will act as a bridge between developers and users, and Jamal will provide DW/BI developers with more detailed specifications for user stories along with acceptance criteria. Everyone is excited to start building, delivering, and deploying new BI features that will benefit the business units at FlixBuster.

PHASED-SEQUENTIAL DW/BI DEVELOPMENT

Data warehousing projects have traditionally followed some variant of the waterfall development approach (Figure 2.1). The waterfall (and related) approach is a *Plan → Do* model in which exhaustive planning is followed by comprehensive design, development, and testing.

The process is driven by a rigorous requirements analysis up front with an eye toward collecting and documenting comprehensive user requirements that establish a "contractual" agreement between the developers and users. The challenge in this stage is making sure that the users have an accurate understanding of what a system will and will not provide, and that they have a solid understanding of their own requirements.

Once agreed upon, these requirements drive a thorough and detailed systems design and data modeling effort. This is the core of the design cycle along with other design activities such as volumetric and network load analyses, report design, and ETL design.

By this time in the traditional approach the developers have minimal interaction with users because requirements analysis is allegedly done. Instead, their effort is spent on developing formal and detailed data models using modeling tools. The design document and data dictionary are typical artifacts that demonstrate progress during the design cycle.

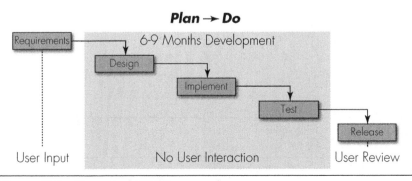

Figure 2.1 The typical DW/BI approach

The remainder of the development effort (often 12 months or more) is spent in implementing the design, developing ETL code, implementing data models, configuring cubes, developing data warehouse update scripts, and finally in integration and system testing. Final testing may even be handed off to a dedicated quality assurance team that verifies that all of the requirements are met without introducing new data anomalies.

Finally, when the developers, testers, and DBAs are confident that the data warehouse meets requirements (or more commonly when the schedule runs out), the users are treated to reviews and user acceptance testing. At this point it is common that

- Users have developed a bit better understanding of data warehousing
- Users are finally able to articulate their requirements
- User requirements have changed or become more refined
- Users' memories of early requirements reviews are fuzzy
- Users' expectations are very high in anticipation of having a new and useful tool
- Developers are still building the system based on the initial snapshot of user understanding and requirements definition

All of these factors lead to a natural gap between what is built and what is needed (see Figure 2.2). Scott Ambler examines the theoretical and practical implications of this gap and provides a compelling argument against "big requirements up front" in his Agile modeling article (Ambler 2009b).

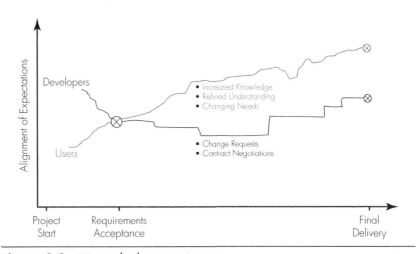

Figure 2.2 Mismatched expectations

ENVISION → EXPLORE INSTEAD OF PLAN → DO

Agile Analytics is marked by a highly iterative approach with a high degree of collaboration between developers, users, and stakeholders. Highsmith's APM framework is based on an *Envision → Explore* cycle rather than a *Plan → Do* model (see Figure 2.3). The significance of this paradigm shift is that it acknowledges that projects are subject to uncertainty and change, and good project teams seek to adapt to that change and uncertainty. The APM process (and Agile in general) is a highly collaborative one that encourages frequent interaction between developers, business users, and stakeholders throughout the project cycle.

Envision Phase

Envisioning is the process of figuring out what is going to be done on the project and how. Envisioning consists of establishing a *vision* of the project outcome, and then *speculating* about how to incrementally accomplish that goal. The objective of this phase is to answer these questions:

- What is the customers' vision of the project outcome (product, system, or solution)?
- What are the scope, boundaries, and constraints of the project?
- What is the business case supporting the project?
- Who are the right people to include in the project community?
- What will the solution development and delivery strategy look like?

The approach is a highly collaborative, low-fidelity, low-tech process. For most projects there has been some preliminary business case analysis prior to the envision phase. The business case has justified the allocation of

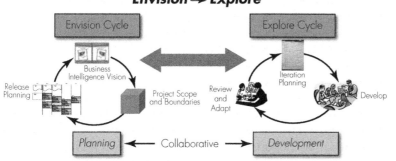

Figure 2.3 The Envision → Explore cycle

resources to start the project. Although the business case may include high-level business requirements or objectives, it does not need to be a comprehensive set of functional requirements.

For most projects the envision phase culminates in a two- to four-day project-chartering and release-planning session. Envisioning is most effective when the entire project community is involved in this kickoff—from end users to junior developers. This planning session often works best in a dedicated off-site setting such as a hotel meeting room, which helps eliminate the normal workplace distractions. It should be noted that Scott Ambler's Agile Model Driven Development (AMDD) lifecycle includes a more comprehensive envision phase, which encompasses requirements and architecture envisioning as well as other project preparation (Ambler 2004). On average this phase takes about four weeks.

New Agile teams sometimes resist this kind of time commitment. It may be perceived as a disruption that keeps people from their daily tasks and routines. I sometimes hear comments like "My gosh, you want all those people to give up their time for nearly a whole week." I have a few responses to this reluctance. First, you are about to embark on a project that will consume a lot of time and cost. If it isn't worth investing a few days to make sure that everyone is galvanized around a common vision, maybe this project is not worth doing. Second, in traditional projects the requirements analysis typically consumes months of calendar time and a large number of person-hours, and those requirements are often wrong. Agile Project Management replaces this protracted process with a weeklong envisioning workshop. It probably amounts to the same or fewer total person-hours, and the outcome is much more effective because it is a face-to-face collaboration among the entire project community.

Every team I've worked with that has been initially reluctant has ultimately been delighted with the outcome of this envisioning approach. They generally agree that the envisioning process leads to a much more effective project launch than traditional project kickoff meetings.

Explore Phase

Waterfall-type models include some variation of these phases: requirements, design, implement, test, and maintain. These are all important components of development, just not as organized in a phased/sequential manner as in waterfall. Instead, we need to do some analysis and enough design to get started, prove our design with working code, and do sufficient testing to convince ourselves that we did it right. Traditional development is task- or activity-driven (requirements, coding). Agile development is product-driven (small user stories).

We aren't going to build the entire system correctly in one iteration of this cycle. We must repeat this simple process many times as we nurture the evolution of a high-value, high-quality, working DW/BI system. At each turn of the cycle it is critical to seek feedback and acceptance, and then adapt.

Each iteration through the explore cycle takes two weeks[2] and results in one or more working business intelligence "features" that can be reviewed with the user community for feedback and possible acceptance. The explore cycle is so-called because it provides us with an opportunity to explore, experiment, test ideas, evaluate, and ultimately settle on the right thing to build and the right way to build it. One of the great things about working in these short iterations is that the development doesn't get very far off track before the need for course correction becomes evident.

Chapter 4, "User Stories for BI Systems," will introduce the concept of *user stories* as a representation of functional requirements, and a *product backlog* as a practice for prioritizing and managing the ever-changing collection of user stories. We will talk about backlog management and the fact that user stories are subject to change at any time, either in their definition or in the priority they are given. You will rarely hear Agile Analytics developers talk about "scope creep" or "requirements freeze." We know that requirements are going to change and expand—and we need techniques for adapting smoothly to those changes.

Each iteration through the explore cycle begins with an *iteration-planning* session. Depending on how well the story backlog is maintained, iteration planning generally takes anywhere from a couple of hours to one full day to complete. During this time the development team conducts user story effort estimation, moves one or more user stories from the top of the backlog into the iteration plan, commits to the completion of those stories, and defines the underlying tasks required to complete each story. In essence, the team does everything necessary to begin working.

Each iteration ends in a *feature review* or *showcase*, and a *retrospective* or *reflection*. The feature review is a collaborative session with end users to

---

2. As Agile development has matured, two-week iterations have become the preferred length on most Agile projects. Two weeks offers enough time to do meaningful work but is short enough to get the frequent feedback we seek.

demonstrate new working BI features such as a report or dashboard component. The goal of the review is to gain acceptance of the new feature(s) as meeting users' needs. The retrospective is a development team self-examination that provides an opportunity for continuous process improvement and maturation.

Figure 2.4 recasts the Envision → Explore cycle of the APM framework as a process flow. You can see the iterative nature that exists especially between the exploration and adaptation processes. The top half of the diagram conveys some of the important artifacts and outputs that are generated during various stages of the process. Although the majority of project time is spent in the explore/adapt cycle, the APM framework encourages the project team to return to the envision/speculate stage whenever necessary. This might happen when there is a substantial shift in the project vision, or whenever a significant risk is encountered that materially changes the course of the project.

CHANGING THE ROLE OF PROJECT MANAGEMENT

Traditional project managers commonly focus on planning based on a work breakdown structure (WBS) that boils a predetermined scope of work down

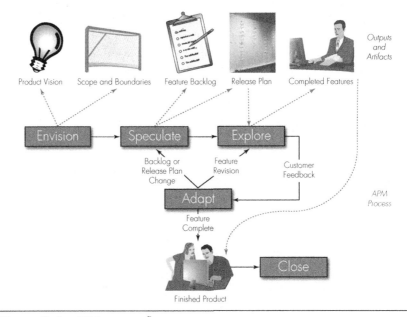

Figure 2.4 APM process flow

to a collection of scheduled tasks. Project managers develop project plans with input from developers, and they optimize those plans to maximize efficiency and productivity. The primary measure of success is how well the team completes the scheduled tasks according to the plan. The focus of the traditional project manager is on *task management* and ensuring that the project execution conforms to the plan.

I once worked with a team that was attempting to blend traditional project management methods (i.e., Gantt charts, PERT charts, and WBS) with Agile development practices (i.e., iterations, user stories, and backlogs). The project manager was very frustrated because he spent the vast majority of his time reworking the project plan to accurately reflect reality. It turned out that he had a Microsoft Project plan that consisted of more than 6,000 WBS tasks with a complex set of dependencies among them. Every change that impacted a single task had huge ripple effects throughout the project plan, and the poor project manager spent nearly all his time keeping the project schedule from exploding. Agile development requires Agile project management methods.

Agile project managers are focused on *team management* rather than task management. They ensure that the development team has what it needs to succeed. They help buffer the team from external pressures and disruptions. They work to maximize collaboration both within the development team as well as across the broader project community. Team managers are enablers. They enable teams to self-organize and to self-manage task completion. They enable teams to remain coordinated and effective so that they can succeed in their purpose. They enable teams to adapt to inevitable changes rather than forcing them to conform to a plan. After all, as the Agile Manifesto suggests, we value "adapting to change over following a plan."

The role of project manager is as important in Agile development as it is in traditional development. It is the relationship with the project team that is fundamentally different. An Agile project manager is a critical member of the team, not an overseer. The Agile project manager is involved on a daily basis with the development team. He or she attends daily synchronization meetings and sits in close proximity to the development team.

MAKING SENSE OF AGILE "FLAVORS"

If you've been around the Agile scene very long, you've undoubtedly heard terms like eXtreme Programming, Scrum, Crystal, Agile Model Driven Development, Lean Development, Adaptive Software Development, and others. These are all various Agile software development methods or "flavors." All of them have some common characteristics that make them Agile, and each introduces a unique and valuable set of practices that differentiate them.

Agile Analytics is largely a blend of practices chosen carefully from the various flavors and then adapted to the unique challenges of data warehouse and BI system development. These include technical development practices, daily and per-iteration coordination practices, team collaboration practices, value-delivery practices, and overarching project planning and management practices. So, it is helpful to understand existing Agile software development methods, some common terminology, and how they complement one another.

When Kent Beck, Ron Jeffries, and Ward Cunningham introduced eXtreme Programming, or XP, in the late 1990s, it was an immediate hit with software developers. Beck's *Extreme Programming Explained* (now in its second edition) was the first of a series of books on, or relating to, XP (Beck and Andres 2004). XP remains today one of the predominant flavors of Agile development. Its success is due in large part to the powerful technical and development practices that it introduced. Developers have long been hampered by methodologies, and XP offers a practical set of techniques that make sense. These include test automation, test-driven development, pair programming, refactoring, continuous integration, and more.[3] Agile Analytics relies on database test automation, test-driven database development, database refactoring (and ETL refactoring), continuous integration, and other practices that are adapted from XP innovations. These *development practices* are introduced in later chapters of this book.

Scrum is the other predominant Agile method in practice today. The term *Scrum* was first used to describe a style of developing software in 1990 by DeGrace and Stahl (1990). Meanwhile, Ken Schwaber was using an iterative approach at his company, Advanced Development Methods; and Jeff Sutherland, John Scumniotales, and Jeff McKenna introduced a similar approach at Easel Corporation. Sutherland and colleagues were the first to formally call the approach "Scrum." Sutherland and Schwaber jointly presented Scrum at OOPSLA[4] '95 in response to ". . . increasingly detailed and specific methodologies—overburdened with phases, steps, tasks, and activities

---

3. XP introduces 12 key practices, some of which are sound project management rather than development practices.

4. Object-Oriented Programming, Systems, Languages & Applications Conference.

(with documents to support each). . . ." (Highsmith 2002). Ken Schwaber and Mike Beedle wrote the first book on Scrum in 2001 (Schwaber and Beedle 2001). Scrum is based on the rhythm of working in two- to four-week iterations called *sprints* and short (15-minute) daily synchronization meetings called *scrums*. Many of today's Scrum practitioners have modified their sprint length to two weeks, and many other Agile methods have incorporated the idea of a daily scrum. Scrum introduces valuable project management practices. These practices include the *product backlog* and *sprint backlog* for requirements management and post-sprint demonstration of working features, among others. The project manager in a Scrum setting is called *scrum master*, and the scrum master's role definition is fundamentally different from a project management role. Agile Analytics relies heavily on a well-managed and prioritized backlog of user stories, short daily synchronization and planning meetings (scrums or stand-ups), a feature showcase at the end of each iteration, and the equivalent of a scrum master. These *daily/iteration management practices* have been adapted to Agile Analytics and are introduced in this and other chapters.

Alistair Cockburn introduced Crystal Methods in 2002. His guiding principle is that people, interaction, community, skills, collaboration, and communication are the factors most critical to the performance of effective development teams. Despite its name, Crystal Methods is not a software development methodology. A central tenet of Crystal is that the essence of any methodology is to describe the conventions of how people collaborate: If a convention helps people work together, keep it; if it doesn't, discard it. Synchronous collaboration (talking to each other) is preferred over asynchronous communication (e-mail threads). Face-to-face collaboration is preferred over physical separation. These principles are also central to Agile Analytics, which stresses team colocation, cross-functional development teams, and generalization over specialization, among other practices. Throughout this book various *collaboration practices* are introduced and discussed.

In the 1997–98 time frame Jeff De Luca, with help from Peter Coad, developed Feature Driven Development (FDD). FDD, as the name implies, is centered around planning, designing, and building in a user-feature-centric fashion, based on a master feature list. This goal of delivering working, granular, user-valued features frequently has become a common theme across Agile methods. However, FDD introduces some very powerful, and lightweight, practices that enable very large projects to be tracked, managed, and monitored in an Agile fashion. Specifically, you'll learn more about parking lot diagrams in Chapter 4, "User Stories for BI Systems." Moreover, the overriding theme of early and frequent delivery of high-valued BI features to end users runs throughout the Agile Analytics method (and this book). These *project-monitoring* and *value-delivery practices* are integral components of Agile Analytics.

Shortly after the formation of the Agile Alliance in 2001, Jim Highsmith observed that Agile methods tended to focus on the iterative and evolutionary nature of projects but didn't really address the need of management stakeholders to understand the bigger picture of project scope, schedule, and cost. So he developed the Agile Project Management framework introduced previously. The Envision → Explore cycle is separated into the more granular phases of *envision, speculate, explore, adapt,* and *close*. Each of these phases is defined by a set of objectives and specific practices to support those objectives. APM serves as an overlay framework that augments the other Agile methods previously introduced. Agile Analytics makes heavy use of APM for all project management practices, including project chartering, planning, and monitoring. Not all of the APM practices are introduced in this book, so I urge you to read *Agile Project Management* (Highsmith 2010a) to supplement your knowledge of Agile Analytics.

TENETS OF AGILITY

Although this chapter is not intended to completely re-present Agile Project Management, there is a set of foundational tenets of Agile Analytics that deserve some attention. These tenets lie somewhere between the 11 guiding principles introduced in the last chapter and the concrete practices that are introduced in the remainder of this book. In working with many Agile Analytics teams, and on my own Agile Analytics projects, I have discovered that these foundational tenets largely make the difference between "doing Agile" and "being Agile."

Just Enough Design

There are two common data warehousing design mistakes that are a curse to agility. The first is attempting to design the warehouse to accommodate anticipated (but not yet expressed) future business requirements. The second is attempting to completely design the data models before developing the rest of the warehouse to use them.

We are naturally tempted to anticipate, and design for, future business needs. While it is good to imagine future requirements, it is too costly to design and develop for these imagined requirements. Such gold-plating of your DW/BI system is costly for several reasons. It eats up development time that would be better spent working on necessary requirements. It increases the complexity and technical debt (see the section "Attention to Technical Debt" later in this chapter) of your current implementation unnecessarily; unnecessary features must still be tested, maintained, and supported just like the needed ones. In the Agile software community, this mistake is often referred to by the acronym YAGNI ("You Ain't Gonna Need It"). To paraphrase a quote by Ron Jeffries[5] as it relates to data warehousing: The best way to implement a DW/BI system is to implement less of it. The best way to have fewer defects in your DW/BI system is to have a smaller/simpler one. While it is important to design with an eye toward future requirements (i.e., adaptability), it is equally important to build only what is needed today.

There seems to be a mistaken belief in the data community that data models (and related stored procedures, ETL code, and other scripts), once implemented, are unchangeable, or at least too expensive to change. This belief triggers the tendency to complete exhaustive and comprehensive database designs up front, or Big Design Up Front (BDUF). BDUF causes a number of problems. Foremost is that we are likely to get it wrong, but we have no way of knowing until much later. Additionally, we are likely to incorporate more into a big up-front design than we really need or, conversely, omit design elements that are needed. The deeper you dive from logical modeling into physical modeling or conceptual design to detailed design, the greater your investment is and the more costly it is to change it. Our aim is to reduce the cost of database and data model changes through better technical practices such as database refactoring. Once we understand that database changes are not prohibitively expensive, we are free to practice "barely sufficient" data modeling.

We do need up-front database design in data warehousing—just enough to ensure that (a) the entire team is developing to a common architecture and (b) we are applying standards of technical excellence and adaptability. Agile Modeling and database development expert Scott Ambler recommends modeling in small increments and frequently validating the models with working code (Ambler 2002). Put into data warehousing lingo: Do just enough data warehouse design to get started, and then prove it with working BI features. Agile Project Management seeks to balance the need for some degree of up-front design against the goal of iterative, incremental, evolutionary development.

---

5. Ron Jeffries was one of the founders of eXtreme Programming in 1996.

Agile Analytics Practice: Work in Small Steps

The "waterfall" steps of requirements, specification, design, build, test are all relevant in Agile Analytics. But instead of applying these in big phases, we cycle through these stages over and over again, sometimes several times a day. The best proof of our requirements understanding and design is a working warehouse and BI feature.

Synchronize Daily

Agile teams operate as a cohesive unit, not a collection of individuals. The success or failure of the team to deliver on its commitments is shared by the entire team. For this reason Agile teams need daily synchronization so that everyone has a clear and accurate understanding of what has been accomplished, what remains to be done, and what issues may prevent the team from succeeding. However, frequent long meetings can be disruptive and counterproductive. Therefore, effective Agile teams hold a short daily stand-up meeting, scrum (in Scrum parlance), or daily coordination meeting.

Effective Agile teams hold these daily meetings to 15 minutes. In these, each team member answers these questions: "What did I complete yesterday?" "What do I expect to complete today?" "What problems am I having, or what help do I need?" When all is going well, everyone on the team gains confidence that they are on track. As soon as difficulties arise, the entire team is notified so that it can collectively decide how to address the problem.

Problems should not be solved during the stand-up meeting. Instead, a quick plan should be made about who the problem solvers are and when they will convene to address the problem. These meetings are often held next to the iteration plan so that team members can gain a sense of whether the entire team is on track for the iteration.

Agile Analytics Practice: Daily Coordination

Agile teams hold a 15-minute daily meeting to coordinate. Everyone briefly describes yesterday's accomplishments, today's expected accomplishments, and any problems they are having. Note the emphasis on accomplishments rather than ongoing activities.

Timebox Everything

Anyone with basic project management exposure has learned about the "iron triangle" of trade-offs among *scope, schedule,* and *cost.* You can't manipulate one of these variables without affecting the others, and it is not feasible to fix all three during project visioning. The Agile Project Management trade-off matrix insists that only one of these variables can be absolutely fixed, the next most important must be somewhat flexible, and the third is free to fluctuate as necessary to support the others.

By far, the most common tendency of data warehousing projects is for scope to be fixed. The guiding question during project planning is something like "Here are the project requirements. How long will it take *this team* to complete *this project?*" The question inherently implies that not only scope but also costs (or at least resources) are fixed. The only thing that is flexible (at least in the beginning) is the schedule.

The trouble with this, as I'm sure you have experienced, is that when the schedule is allowed to fluctuate to accommodate a fixed scope, it almost certainly will. But when the schedule fluctuates, cost is impacted. So fixing scope often causes both schedule and cost to balloon, and you wind up with a bulging iron triangle that is anchored by a fixed scope that was underestimated to begin with.

Agile Project Management turns the iron triangle upside down by constraining the schedule (see Figure 2.5). This is known as *timeboxing.* Timeboxing was devised by the founders of the Dynamic Systems Development Method (DSDM) Consortium in the late 1990s along with many other Agile techniques (DSDM Consortium 2002). By timeboxing the project you effectively control the project costs as well. By prioritizing requirements on the basis of value, you ensure that the most important ones will be completed on time, even if some of them do not get finished. Stakeholders love it when you deliver on time, even if a few features are left out.

Release cycles are timeboxed. These are relatively short, like three to six months—long enough to deliver high-value capabilities to customers, but short enough so that the expected scope is well understood. Large DW/BI programs may consist of multiple short, timeboxed planning cycles. The goal of the release cycle is to release whatever new BI features the team has finished into production for consumption by end users. Generally speaking, promoting features into production involves a fair amount of governance process. It is common in Agile Analytics to earmark the final iteration of a

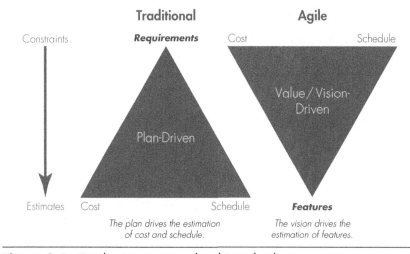

Figure 2.5 Timeboxing creates value-driven development.

release cycle for these activities rather than creating new features. Remember that we are doing production-quality development in every iteration, but that does not necessarily mean actually launching into production.

Iterations are also timeboxed. Agile teams plan each iteration by estimating the user stories at the top of the backlog and then committing to only those that will fit within the timeboxed iteration. Most Agile teams work in two-week iterations, but three or four weeks is not uncommon. I've even worked with teams that prefer one-week iterations. Shorter iterations don't make you "more Agile," but they do reduce the time between feature showcases and customer feedback.

Within iterations the work week should be timeboxed to 40 hours. Teams that work excessive weekly hours in order to accomplish more in a two-week iteration are not working at a sustainable pace. Agile project plans should provide for a sustainable development pace.

Even the daily stand-ups or scrums are timeboxed to 15 minutes.

Always remember the project management trade-off among time, scope, and resources (we don't sacrifice quality). The method I'm describing fixes time foremost and resources second-most. The scope is determined by team capacity and velocity. This technique has two major benefits:

- It helps avoid "surprise overruns." You can see what's left in the bank at the end of each release cycle and decide whether you can afford to continue or if you must stop or seek additional funding.
- It provides concrete and tangible results that the project community can use to make informed decisions about funding and sponsoring a next round of development.

Timeboxing offers a means of constraining the impact of activities that are uncertain or hard to estimate. By establishing a maximum amount of time that will be allocated to such an activity, the team can avoid letting that activity trample the other things that must be completed.

Finally, timeboxing forces the team and project stakeholders to make hard decisions early and frequently. By establishing an immovable project end date, the project community cannot entertain the option of "just running a little over schedule to get a little bit more work done."

Agile Analytics Practice: Timebox Everything
Timeboxing is a powerful tool that promotes agility. Effective Agile teams timebox everything from daily coordination meetings, to experimentation, to iterations, to release plans, and beyond.

Colocating Teams

The single most effective type of communication is face-to-face, and the most effective Agile teams are those that sit face-to-face. Team colocation is a significant contributor to project success (Ambler 2008a). It significantly reduces the overhead required to communicate through e-mail, chat, voice mail, and other impersonal means. Colocation promotes multimodal communication in which body language, whiteboard sessions, and hand gestures can augment verbal communication. Scott Ambler's essay on Agile communication provides excellent and compelling detail on the modes of communication and their impact on Agile teams (Ambler 2009a).

The ultimate colocation occurs when team members literally sit next to and across from each other during core team hours each workday. Cubicle walls and private offices are barriers to this degree of colocation. Many Agile teams rearrange cubicles or find a dedicated project room where they can sit face-to-face during work hours.

Teams that are geographically distributed have the added challenge of creating "virtual colocation" in order to eliminate as many barriers to collaboration as possible. Many good collaboration tools are available to assist in this, such as instant messaging, desktop-sharing tools, voice over IP (VoIP), and others.

Teams that are also separated by time zones must creatively overcome that barrier as well. A few time zones are surmountable, but team members who are on opposite sides of the planet face significant challenges.

There are many examples of Agile teams that are effective despite geographical and temporal separation. These teams are able to creatively minimize the collaboration barriers. However, teams whose members work in the same building but do not maximize collaboration and colocation stand to lose a great opportunity for maximizing effectiveness.

> ### Agile Analytics Practice: Strive for Colocation
> If it's possible to work face-to-face, do it. Even if it isn't possible to be physically together, Agile teams seek creative ways to eliminate the barriers of being a distributed team.

Attention to Technical Debt

Ward Cunningham uses the metaphor of fiscal debt to describe the natural entropy that occurs in systems over time (Cunningham 1992). He points out, "A little debt speeds development so long as it is paid back promptly with a rewrite. . . . The danger occurs when the debt is not repaid. Every minute spent on not-quite-right code counts as interest on that debt."

Technical debt is a common occurrence in data warehouse development. It occurs when time pressures cause us to take shortcuts. It occurs when we fail to make good design decisions. It occurs naturally over the course of time as we make revisions and fix bugs. Technical debt is the entropy that occurs in all systems over time.

Just like financial debt, a little technical debt is okay as long as we monitor it and don't let it accumulate. However, technical debt drives up the cost of making changes to the system. The problem occurs if technical debt continues to accrue unabated. A DW/BI system with high technical debt is costly to modify or enhance because we must navigate convoluted code, messy data models, sloppy designs, and other problems. In the extreme, technical

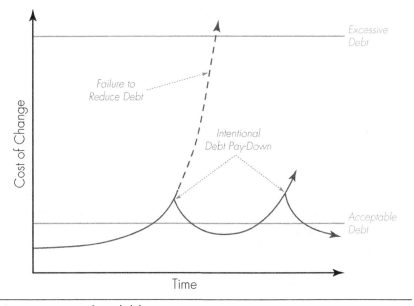

Figure 2.6 Technical debt management

debt has the potential to bury a system if the cost of change outweighs the cost of building a new system (see Figure 2.6).

Effective Agile Analytics teams keep track of known technical debt and work to pay down that debt on a routine and intentional basis. Such teams identify, track, and manage technical debt in much the same way they manage user stories or defects. They prioritize debt and allocate the necessary time during the project cycle to eliminate it. We will examine specific debt reduction techniques, such as code and database refactoring, in later chapters.

> ## Agile Analytics Practice: Track and Manage Debt
> When an aspect of the data warehouse or BI apps is uncovered that reflects unwanted technical debt, write it on an index card and prioritize it on your product backlog alongside user stories, defects, and other backlog items. Don't let it be forgotten.

Plan to Capacity and Monitor Velocity

Every project team, regardless of team size or project complexity, has a finite work capacity. Moreover, the very same team working on two different projects may have a different capacity on each project. Because Agile Analytics is a feature-driven approach, we define capacity in terms of the number of features that a team can complete at product quality during a single iteration. Features are not always equivalent in the effort required to complete them, so we use a story-point or feature-point estimation to differentiate them. Team capacity is a measure of how many story points the team can complete in an iteration. Story-point estimating is presented in much greater detail in Chapter 4, "User Stories for BI Systems."

It is important for Agile Analytics teams to assess their capacity and plan within that upper limit. A newly formed team on a new project will not know its actual capacity. So, the team starts the project in the first iteration by committing to one or more user stories based on the team members' best experience and judgment. At the end of the first iteration, when the team has completed its commitments (ideally) and the new features have been accepted, the total number of story points represented by those features is the team's demonstrated capacity. In other words, the team's performance has confirmed what the members' experience and judgment suggested.

When planning the next iteration, the team must not plan more than its demonstrated capacity from the previous iteration, even if their judgment tempts the team members to do so. If the team finishes its commitments early in the iteration and feels it can complete another feature, it may pull another story from the backlog. If the team is successful in this, it has a newer and higher demonstrated capacity and can plan to this new capacity in the next iteration. Agile Analytics teams boost their velocity by planning conservatively and then exceeding their own expectations. Figure 2.7 depicts a typical capacity growth curve on a new project. Over the first several iterations the team settles into its rhythm, and its capacity levels out, representing optimal performance.

Once optimal capacity is established, Agile Analytics teams track their velocity against that capacity. Velocity is also a measure of completed and accepted story points during each iteration. Velocity relative to capacity helps the team determine if it is working at peak effectiveness. For example, suppose the team has an established velocity of 30 points. During iteration eight it completes four new features for a total of 31 story points. However, the business owner rejects one 5-point feature, because of a flaw in the logic. In this case the team's velocity is only 26 points even though its demonstrated capacity remains at 30—the team did not perform at peak effectiveness. During iteration 11 two of the team's members are away on vacation. The team velocity drops as expected during this iteration, but the team

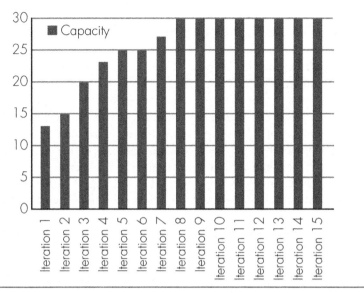

Figure 2.7   Team capacity in story points

capacity remains at 30 because this is a temporary dip in productivity. As Figure 2.8 shows, it is when team velocity exceeds previously demonstrated capacity that new, higher capacity is established.

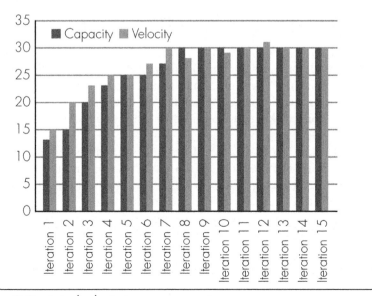

Figure 2.8   Actual velocity increases capacity.

Failure to plan within demonstrated capacity boundaries can cause unpleasant outcomes. In Chapter 5, "Self-Organizing Teams Boost Performance," we will examine team responsibility and accountability. If a team plans beyond its capacity, it must bear the responsibility for honoring its overcommitment. There are a variety of pressures that cause Agile teams to plan beyond their capacity. Some are caused by internal team optimism, and others are caused by external prodding. Jim Highsmith describes this as a shift from *capacity-based planning* to *wish-based planning*. The plan is based on how much work the project community wishes the team could accomplish rather than what it has demonstrated. Ultimately the team will accomplish the volume of work it is capable of doing. Wish-based planning generally leads to disappointment and a sense of failure, whereas capacity-based planning generally leads to a sense of joy and celebration. Personally, I prefer to celebrate!

Agile Analytics Practice: Capacity-Based Planning

Avoid wish-based planning by never letting an iteration plan exceed the team's demonstrated capacity. Increases in capacity should occur by delivering more than was committed, not by committing to more than is possible.

Track Daily Progress

Sometimes Agile Analytics teams with the best of intentions still find themselves scrambling at the end of an iteration to complete their commitments. In addition to daily synchronization and colocation to help teams work as a unit, Agile project managers (and teams) should explicitly track and monitor their daily progress. Doing so will help the team avoid eleventh-hour "uh-oh" moments. There are multiple practices and techniques that will assist the team with this daily tracking. We'll take a brief look at iteration planning, story tracking, and burn-down charts as a few of these.

In Chapter 4, "User Stories for BI Systems" you will be introduced to the effective creation of user stories for a DW/BI system and the management of a prioritized backlog of user stories. These practices provide the project community with a project-level or release-level view of scope. Assuming the backlog is properly managed, and the team has an established capacity, planning the next iteration is relatively simple. The highest-priority user stories are moved from the backlog into the iteration plan. The effort to complete these stories has already been estimated using story points (also covered in Chapter 4). The total points from all of the stories that are moved into the iteration plan must not exceed the team's demonstrated capacity.

Once the team has committed to completing the user stories that have been moved into the iteration plan, it identifies the detailed development tasks needed to complete each story. With the use of flip charts, index cards, and sticky notes, the iteration plan might end up looking something like Figure 2.9 (the details of this figure are not important at this point).

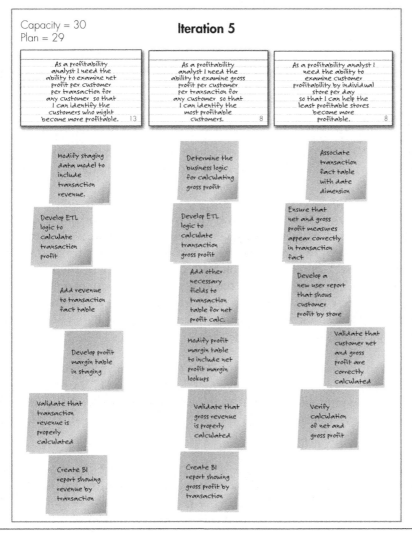

Figure 2.9 Iteration plan with task detail

Once the team launches into the iteration, it needs a method for tracking its progress. This serves two purposes: to give the team a visual cue as to whether it is on track for success, and to provide visibility into the team's progress for external community members. The card wall is an effective and highly visual tool for accomplishing this goal (see Figure 2.10). Although somewhat more jumbled, the card wall communicates much more than the iteration plan in Figure 2.9.

The card wall hangs in a visible spot in the team workspace, and the team holds its daily stand-up meeting in front of it. In this way the team members can see what tasks are left to be completed, and they should expect to see reasonable completion of tasks throughout the iteration. As team members commit to completing tasks, the task notes are moved from the "On Deck" column into the "In Progress" column. When tasks are finished, they are moved into the "Done!" column. When all of the tasks for a story card are complete, the story card is moved into the "Done!" column. As soon as a card is done, it is ready for review and acceptance by the business owner and/or the user representatives. When user acceptance is complete, the user story is "Done! Done!" If the team were just a few days from the end of iteration five and the card wall looked like the one in Figure 2.10, this team may have reason to be very concerned.

There are many other creative ways to track and monitor task and story completion on a daily basis throughout an iteration. Some Agile teams use different-colored dots or markings on a story card to denote the stages of "in progress," "complete," and "accepted." Although there are many ways you can track this progress, it is the highly visual nature of these that is key to their effectiveness. When the card wall is posted in a prominent place, the team members are continuously reminded of how well they are tracking toward completing their commitments.

The burn-down chart is another tool for tracking daily progress during an iteration. This project management tool is another visual control that many teams hang prominently on the wall. Burn-down charts track the completion of work from one day to the next and convey the team's trajectory toward its iteration goal.

Figure 2.11 depicts an example of a burn-down chart that tracks tasks remaining during a two-week iteration beginning on Monday and ending on Friday of the following week. In this example the team has completed 15 out of a total of 20 tasks as of the end of the second Monday of the iteration. A glance at this chart suggests that the team is on a trajectory to complete all of its tasks by the end of the iteration.

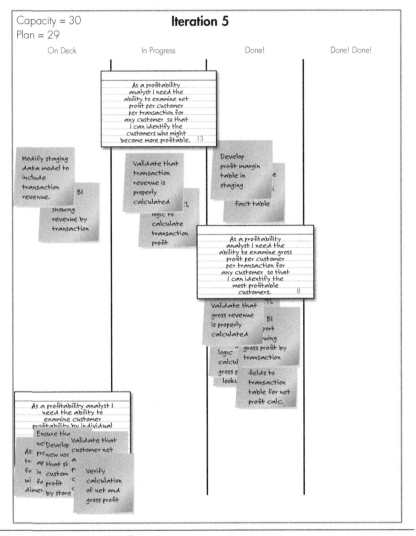

Figure 2.10   Card wall

Alternatively, burn-down charts can track estimated hours of work remaining, story points remaining, or some other comparison of work completed to work remaining. It is not uncommon for teams to identify new tasks after the iteration has begun, or to recognize that previously identified tasks can be eliminated. When this happens, the burn-down chart will show a sharper-than-normal drop in trajectory, a flattening over multiple days, or

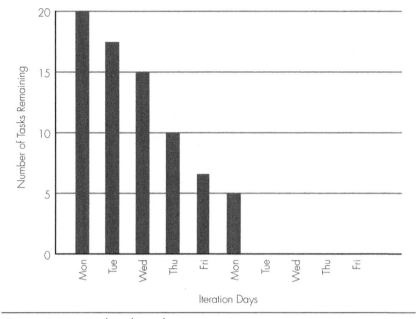

Figure 2.11 Tracking burn-down

even a temporary rise in trajectory. As long as the team understands and properly manages the impact of these anomalies, there should not be cause for alarm. Remember, the primary goal is the completion of working features. Task completion is simply in support of that goal.

Many Agile teams use electronic tools such as Microsoft Excel to manage their burn-down charts. At the time of this writing there are a number of fairly elaborate Excel solutions and tools for tracking burn-down, both free and commercial, available on the Internet. Likewise, most of the commercial and open-source Agile project management tools available provide a burn-down tracking feature. Whether you elect to use an electronic burn-down or a manual one like the example in Figure 2.11, this tool is most effective when it is updated daily and is made visible to the entire team.

Agile Analytics Practice: Team Self-Monitoring

Teams monitor their own velocity, burn-down, and card walls on a daily basis. These visible controls are ever present in the team's workspace. Outsiders can see them but should not use them as performance metrics.

Monitor Story Completion, Not Task Time

A brief observation about the tasks in Figure 2.10: Even though they are not particularly readable, you may have noticed that they do not include time or effort estimates. It isn't clear whether some tasks are more or less time-consuming than others. Although there is a temptation to estimate and track task completion time, doing so has the undesirable effect of taking the team's focus off of what is important: completed features.

Instead, the team should strive to define tasks that are small enough to be completed in less than one workday. Some will take less than an hour and others will consume nearly a full day of effort. Many teams establish the practice of defining tasks that are expected to take less than half a day to complete. Doing so enables the development team to self-manage their tasks as a simple to-do list. As with any to-do list, new tasks can be added to the list, and tasks that become irrelevant can be removed without a burdensome change procedure.

Also, you may have noticed that owners are not assigned to the tasks in Figure 2.10. As previously mentioned, effective Agile teams operate as a collective. By maintaining a collective set of tasks, any member of the team who is available can complete any task provided he or she has the necessary skills to do so. In practice it may be implied that the ETL developers will handle ETL tasks, data modelers will handle modeling tasks, and so forth. However, Agile teams work best when they behave like generalists rather than specialists. It is not uncommon on a healthy team to see a DBA stepping up to write a bit of ETL code, or an ETL developer stepping up to write some PL/SQL if needed. This promotes better cross-disciplinary understanding of the entire solution, and team members have the opportunity to develop new skills. During each daily stand-up meeting the team cooperatively decides what should be done, and team members volunteer for the tasks that they are best suited to complete. The project manager facilitates this process.

One Agile Analytics team of which I was a member established the practice of assigning an estimated effort of 1.0 hour to every task. It was our goal to define tasks smaller than half a day. Some took less than one hour, and some took more. We did not establish this practice until well into a multi-year, multirelease project. In the beginning our team estimated task effort in person-hours, and, like many teams, we tracked actual time versus estimated time. Like most effort estimates, ours were routinely incorrect. After shifting to the simpler practice of not estimating task effort and assigning 1.0 to every task, we discovered the following benefits:

- Our iteration-planning time became much shorter because we didn't have to estimate effort for every task.
- We were liberated from the previous impact of adding, removing, and modifying tasks once the iteration was under way. Prior to our simpler approach task changes messed up the burn-down chart and caused a bit of grief for the project manager.
- Our entire team shifted its focus more toward story completion and away from task completion.
- Tasks assumed their proper role as to-do items rather than measures of productivity.

Not long ago I was asked by a client to conduct an assessment of their Agile Analytics efforts. Although they were doing many things very well, they were experiencing a particular problem during iteration planning. Roughly 90 percent of their iteration-planning time was spent in task definition and estimating. The project manager was intent on aligning task time estimates with the personnel time allocated to the project. So, if Russell was allocated 25 hours per week to the project, all of the tasks assigned to Russell had to add up to 25. If Russell was overtasked, he had to lower estimates or eliminate tasks; if he was under 25, he had to account for how he would spend his available extra time. Surprisingly little attention was given to understanding the user stories, story acceptance criteria, or related business drivers.

I observed several interesting effects that this task-centric planning caused. First, the team members were frustrated because they didn't see the value in this type of planning. Second, the team tended to sandbag its task time estimates so that they added up to the "right" number. Third, it promoted individualism over team cooperation because individuals were assigned "their tasks" to fill their personal time capacity. Finally, it was not a collaborative team planning effort; it was a grilling of the team by the project manager to get the information he needed to plug into his planning tool. In the end the team left the meeting exhausted and frustrated—and that was on a Monday morning at the beginning of a new iteration. Not a good way to start!

However you choose to tailor your iteration planning and daily tracking practices, make sure that your team's primary focus is on the completion of working features in the DW/BI system. Keep in mind the first principle of Agile Analytics: "Our highest priority is to satisfy the BI user community through early and continuous delivery of working user features."

Agile Analytics Practice: You Get What You Measure

Agile Analytics teams and Agile leaders measure what is important. That is principally the delivery of high-quality, high-value, working BI features. Progress and performance metrics should be built around value delivery and quality rather than on such things as task completion and velocity.

WRAP-UP

Creating a weekly live television variety show requires a lightweight approach in which time is not wasted on things that don't directly contribute to the show. It requires lots of face-to-face teamwork among writers, actors, stagehands, and other people. It requires creative ideas and visions, followed quickly by the exploration of those ideas to see if they are good enough to keep. It requires adapting to the feedback of test audiences and to external events. Creating a live TV show requires airing at the scheduled time whether or not the creators need more time. And by the way, the show had better consistently get high network ratings to stay alive. This type of pressure quickly forces creative teams to abandon practices that don't help and to emphasize and fine-tune the ones that do.

This chapter on Agile Project Management lays the foundation and framework for a set of lightweight Agile Analytics practices that are introduced throughout the remainder of this book. Agile Analytics is formed of a blend of practices from XP, Scrum, Crystal, FDD, and APM. These practices have been adapted to the unique challenges of data warehousing and business intelligence. They require discipline and rigor but should never get in the way of the goal of producing high-value, working BI features every two weeks. Good Agile Analytics teams tailor these practices to meet their needs. They abandon practices that don't help, and they emphasize and fine-tune the ones that do.

In this chapter we have examined the core differences between phased/ sequential processes and iterative/incremental/evolutionary processes. We have explored the key differences between traditional Plan → Do cycles and the APM cycle of Envision → Explore. These key differences primarily reflect a mind-set shift in our approach to project planning and management. This mind-set shift is the foundation of Agile Analytics. Built on this foundation is a set of planning practices and execution practices that represent a significant change in the way we build data warehousing systems.

This approach embraces changing requirements. It seeks user feedback early and often. And it focuses on the early delivery of business-valued features.

This overview of Agile Project Management is not a substitute for a deeper study of APM as presented in Highsmith's book. APM introduces a well-defined collection of phases and practices for effective project visioning, speculation, exploration, adapting, and finishing. Agility requires a very different style from the project manager than traditional projects. The project manager becomes a team facilitator and enabler rather than a task completion manager. This chapter has highlighted the tenets of agility—those behaviors and attitudes that make the difference between a team that has Agile DNA and a team that does not.

In my experience working with numerous data warehousing groups in their Agile Analytics adoption, the most common problems I have observed involve project management practices. Although development practices, collaboration practices, and other practices are important, they do not seem to be as critical to Agile success as project management. Teams that are successful in adopting good APM practices have established the basis for rapid Agile maturation in other practice areas.

This page intentionally left blank

Chapter 3

COMMUNITY, CUSTOMERS, AND COLLABORATION

I occasionally am asked to describe Agile project failures and struggles. I haven't formally studied root causes of failure but have worked with enough struggling Agile teams to gain a qualitative sense of these causes. Agile struggles are commonly caused by non-Agile behaviors masked behind Agile trappings and terminology. Failure to collaborate is a common problem. People tend to revert to the asynchronous communication (e-mail and written documents) and "throw-it-over-the-wall" habits with which they've grown familiar.

Two of the Agile Manifesto's core values are focused on collaboration—one between team members and the other with customers. Another one focuses on responding to change. Fundamentally, responding to change requires collaboration and the continuous realignment of expectations among developers, customers, and stakeholders. Despite the apparent focus on budgets and schedules, projects are generally declared successful when the results meet the expectations of stakeholders and customers—even if those expectations have changed dramatically during the course of the project. This chapter is about how to facilitate interactions among team members and collaboration with BI "customers."

I also occasionally get asked what kinds of projects are not suitable for an Agile approach. After much thought, I've concluded that I would use Agile on every BI project, small or large, as long as I had the committed participation of stakeholders, customers, and developers. Not long ago I was asked to coach an Agile data warehousing group in a large company. They had recently adopted an Agile approach but were struggling to be effective. During the assessment phase of my coaching process I asked the team technical leaders to describe their collaboration with end users. I learned that the users were too busy to be involved in planning, story prioritization, and new feature review and acceptance. The same was true for many of the business experts and stakeholders, so I advised the team to halt the project. **A project that isn't worth the involvement of users and stakeholders is not worth doing**; time is better spent on other endeavors. This chapter is about how to effectively involve everyone in the project community, and how to ensure that their time is well spent.

On a positive note, the most gratifying and successful Agile projects I have experienced or witnessed have active project community involvement. The strong bond of trust that develops among users, team members, and stakeholders on such projects is a wonderful side effect of successful Agile projects. Because success breeds more success, these bonds carry forward to future projects.

WHAT ARE AGILE COMMUNITY AND COLLABORATION?

The very nature of traditional, phased, sequential (e.g., "waterfall") development methods tends to promote interaction between project leaders and customers early in the project lifecycle, during requirements gathering. This is followed by very limited interaction during design, development, and initial testing. Then customers are reengaged during final acceptance testing and release preparation. It isn't uncommon in this approach for developers never to interact with customers.

Similarly, under this model management sponsors and stakeholders are involved in early project inception, cost justification, and planning. Then throughout project execution they are kept informed about progress through periodic status reports and updates.

In fact, our industry has spent many years training developers not to bother customers during development, project managers to keep management happy with cursory status updates, and customers to be uninvolved after initial requirements analysis. These behaviors are anathema to the principal goal of Agile Analytics, which is the incremental delivery of working features and the evolutionary development of a DW/BI system by adapting to frequent customer feedback. Agile success requires that we change these traditional organizational habits and project community behaviors.

The project community includes those building the system, those who will use the system or benefit from its use, and those who understand the corporate benefits of undertaking the project in the first place. Agile development calls for regular and frequent interactions between these groups. While the builders are involved on a daily basis, the customers/users are involved weekly, and the management sponsors/stakeholders are involved every few weeks. Here is a glimpse at how the FlixBuster DW/BI project community practices healthy, effective collaboration:

Scenario

The FlixBuster DW/BI project has been progressing well since its inception. The team is now in its third two-week iteration. The end of this iteration will mark the midpoint of the 90-day project plan, so in addition to the normal feature showcase that the developers hold for the customers in their co-development group, they will also be holding a project showcase for the management stakeholder group.

Arlene, the scrum master for the team, will be coordinating these two showcases and has worked hard to ensure that the right people have committed to being there. She has discovered on past projects that when key people miss out on these important checkpoints, expectations can get out of alignment and misunderstandings can arise. She also knows that the key stakeholders on this project are extremely busy and expect their time to be used wisely. The project team trusts her to facilitate both showcases to ensure that they are effective and efficient.

It's Friday morning at 8:30 and all of the feature showcase participants begin arriving. Arlene arranged a continental breakfast to get everyone there early for a prompt start at 9:00. Pete, the VP of finance, and Allen, the CTO, are the executive sponsors of the FlixBuster project. They have been invited to observe the feature showcase along with key stakeholders Gary (VP of sales) and Marcus (VP of marketing). This group will be staying for the project showcase afterward.

The co-development team includes Beulah (finance), Andy (retail sales), Kari (marketing), Mike (operations), Jane (finance), Chuck (finance), Mack (operations), Samantha (marketing), and Javier (controller). Beulah has been with the FlixBuster finance division since the beginning ten years ago. Jane and Chuck are financial analysts who provide key decision support information to Carroll, the CFO, and Georgina, the CEO, along with other executive decision makers. Because Mike, Andy, and Kari are off-site in Reno, Nevada, Arlene has set up a videoconference bridge so that they can participate effectively.

Arlene wrangles everyone into the conference room at 8:55 and the showcase starts right on time. She kicks off the meeting by reminding everyone that the project is at the midpoint of the current 90-day planning period, and this is a key checkpoint. She emphasizes the team's desire to highlight any concerns, issues, problems, or unmet expectations now so that the group can make any course corrections that might be necessary.

Arlene reminds the group that the showcase is only for feature review and acceptance, and she reiterates the ground rules that they agreed upon at the beginning of the project:

Rule 1: This meeting is for the customer community to review completed work and give feedback.

Rule 2: Everyone except the product owner and customer community is a silent observer, including executive sponsors and stakeholders.

Rule 3: Developers shouldn't explain why features work the way they do or offer suggestions for how to fix problems.

Rule 4:   If a feature is not accepted by users, the reasons will be noted but no commitments should be made about when or how it will be corrected.

Rule 5:   The showcase is only for the features the team completed in this iteration. Feedback on previously completed features or new feature ideas should be given to the product owner outside the showcase.

The team has discovered that these guidelines keep the showcase focused and effective and prevent heading off on tangents.

Bob, the team's business analyst, will be the scribe for this showcase. His job is to capture all comments and feedback. Dieter, the product owner, will demonstrate the features and will talk about any deviations from the original iteration plan two weeks earlier. As the facilitator, Arlene creates a flip chart poster titled "Parking Lot" where she will capture any topics that come up that threaten to pull the group off track. She knows that these topics may be important, and the parking lot allows her to capture them while keeping to the agenda.

Alongside the parking lot poster is the team's card wall, showing team accomplishments during the past two weeks. Next to that are the project release plan and product backlog. Dieter references these during the feature demonstration.

He reminds the co-development customers that the team committed to three new stories in this iteration along with a requested revision of a feature from an earlier iteration. The team has had a productive iteration and has met all of its commitments. Dieter makes a list of the stories that he will demonstrate, which include top 10 percent of movie rentals by genre, release date, and studio; customer profitability analysis; seasonal profitability analysis; and a revision to the studio royalties feature from iteration one.

Dieter kicks off the demonstration by role-playing a business scenario. He pretends to be a profitability analyst after the winter holidays reviewing holiday sales figures. He has learned that these demonstrations are most effective when they follow a use-case scenario because that puts the demo into a meaningful business context.

Kari stops Dieter during the first story demo, saying, "What if I want to see the top 20 percent rather than the top 10 percent?" Andy adds, "How about the bottom 10 percent or 20 percent?" Dieter points out that this particular user story is just part one of a series of stories that are on the backlog. He points to a couple of other stories near the top of the backlog that call for giving users the ability to specify top or bottom N percent, where the user defines N. But he agrees to review those other stories later with customers to be sure they are still valid. Bob makes note of this agreement and everyone is satisfied.

As Dieter continues with his demonstrations, co-development customers stop him with questions, observations, or feedback. Bob takes notes. At one point Beulah says, "With our third quarter about to end, it would be really helpful if the finance department had these new features sooner rather than later. What would it take to put these into production right away, even though they are still relatively immature?" Without making a firm commitment, Dieter agrees to evaluate this with Arlene and the development team. He promises to have more information for Beulah and the co-dev group by Monday for the next iteration-planning session.

The co-developers accept all of the new features and the feature revision. It was a successful iteration and everyone is very excited. Javier comments, "It's amazing how much our team has done in only 45 days. The last BI project ran for nine months before they had anything to show us." Arlene finds it interesting that he said "our team" in the first sentence but used the pronouns "them" and "us" in the second. That's a good sign that he feels like part of the team.

After the feature showcase, Arlene kicks off the project showcase for management sponsors and stakeholders. It is only 9:50; they are ahead of schedule. She asks if anyone needs a break, and since nobody does, she proceeds. The goal of the project showcase is to highlight the team's progress toward the initial project vision and any deviations from the original release plan that was developed during project chartering. Her goal is to keep the conversation at a summary level, getting into the details only if sponsors and stakeholders ask her to.

Arlene is well prepared with iteration burn-down charts to show that the team has only missed its commitments on the first iteration. The team's velocity is currently 34 story points but seems to be increasing. She reminds managers that this just means the team is getting better, and that they should not use velocity as a productivity measure. She shows a project burn-up chart that shows how many value points and features have been delivered, and that the team is on a good trajectory, but the original 90-day plan might be a little too ambitious. She and Dieter will continue working with the co-development team to rein that in. Finally, Arlene presents a parking lot diagram (this is different from the parking lot poster and is introduced in Chapter 4, "User Stories for BI Systems"). The parking lot diagram gives sponsors and stakeholders an at-a-glance look at the project status. It shows capabilities delivered, capabilities still in progress, capabilities not yet started, and capabilities that are behind schedule. The profitability analysis capability is a little behind schedule, but Beulah pipes up and says, "That's because it took the finance group longer than expected to agree on how net profit should be calculated. We finally got that to the team and now they are on track." Arlene wasn't going to ascribe blame, but she's happy that Beulah was willing to accept ownership.

Arlene gives Prakash, the technical team leader, a chance to update everyone on the current known risks and uncertainties as well as plans for handling them. She also gives Dieter an opportunity to update the group on changes in the product backlog and BI features to be delivered. Marcus, the VP of marketing and a project stakeholder, wants to be sure that customer segmentation is still included in this project phase. His team needs this capability to meet some of its annual goals. After a few other questions from sponsors and stakeholders Pete, the VP of finance, comments on how great it is to see his staff working so closely with the development team. He is excited about the ongoing collaboration and what it means for the success of this and future projects.

It's now 10:30 A.M. and Arlene has promised to have everything finished by 11:00. It's time for the iteration retrospective, a chance for the team to reflect on and improve its performance. Arlene writes the following three questions on the flip chart: "What went well?" "What to improve?" "What are my questions or concerns?" She asks everyone to take a few minutes to write their answers to these questions, one per sticky note. When the writing seems to slow down, she asks someone to volunteer an answer to the "What went well?" question. Francisco, a developer, hands Arlene one of his answers and says, "The team did a much better job of testing during this iteration." Many of the other developers have a similar answer, so Arlene collects all of these and puts them in a cluster on the flip chart. She asks for another volunteer, and Dieter gives her a sticky note that says, "There's still too much problem solving during daily stand-up meetings," which many others agree with. In this way Arlene quickly gathers and groups everyone's answers to the retrospective questions. The team has learned not to use this time to resolve all of the areas for improvement or answer outstanding questions. Instead, Arlene commits to following up with the team on any new action items or process adjustments. She also promises to work with the team and sponsors to answer any of the questions or concerns. Allen, the CTO and project sponsor, commends the group on everything that has gone well and mentions how impressed he is by the synergy that is apparent between the developers and the co-development "customers."

It's now 11:00 A.M. and, as promised, Arlene adjourns the meeting on time and promises to follow up on the various action items and commitments that were made during the showcases and retrospective. She also promises to update the information radiators (the big visible charts and posters) in the team room so that they accurately reflect the decisions made today. She reminds everyone that the FlixBuster BI system is running on a demo platform with the latest accepted features and encourages everyone to regularly test-drive that system and give the team feedback.

THE AGILE COMMUNITY

Agile Analytics relies on a well-populated project community: the *planners*, the *doers*, and the *consumers* (see Figure 3.1).

The *planners* are senior management, project sponsors, and stakeholders. Anyone who has a vested interest in project success and its strategic importance to the business falls into this category. The project community relies on planners to prioritize the project and to act as executive champions and enablers when tough decisions must be made. Planners care about the project budget, schedule, and its ultimate value to the organization. They are not directly responsible for feature acceptance, but they care about the users' needs being met. Planners are involved in the project every few iterations and should be monitoring project status more frequently.

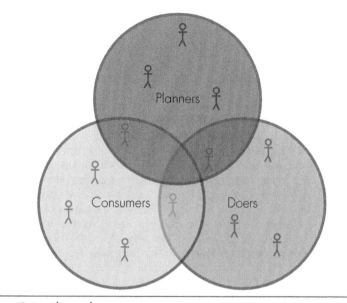

Figure 3.1   The Agile project community

Doers include those community members who are directly involved in executing the project plan. This group includes technical architects and developers as well as testers, business analysts, technical writers, and operations specialists. The Agile project manager is a doer as well as a planner. Doers are involved on a daily basis.

Consumers are anyone who is directly or indirectly involved in accepting the working BI system produced by the doers. This group includes "fingers on keyboard" end users, consumers of the resulting business intelligence, business managers whose staff members rely on the BI system to do their jobs, those making project funding decisions, and others. Anyone who cares about the functionality of the system falls into this group. Consumers are involved in the project on a weekly basis.

Some community members have multiple roles or are in more than one subgroup. The data warehouse technical lead may be both a planner and a doer, and the business analyst may be both a doer and a consumer. Furthermore, the interface between subgroups is generally facilitated by appropriate community members. The interface between planners and doers is commonly the project manager, and the product owner is typically the interface between doers and consumers, and between consumers and planners.

The members of a healthy Agile community are actively engaged in the project and committed to its success. In traditional plan-driven projects the planners complete their work, and the doers are expected to execute the plan and deliver it to the consumers. Agile communities work best when planners, doers, and consumers are actively involved from start to finish. Doers are directly involved in the project daily, consumers are involved weekly, and planners are involved several times per month.

Agile community members may have multiple roles, but each individual's purpose is well understood. Although Agile Analytics favors generalists over specialists, community members must still bring appropriate skills and talents to the team. Project success depends on having the right members in the community who are actively engaged and possess the right blend of skills.

Agile Analytics Practice: Self-Identify

During your project release-planning meeting draw the Venn diagram in Figure 3.1 on a flip chart. Ask the attendees to write their initials where they believe they fit in the project community. Ask them to write their roles as community members next to their initials.

This practice will help clearly define each team member's purpose for themselves and others.

All projects have a core group of *critical* community members without whom the project cannot succeed. They are the showstoppers. Peripheral to this core group are members who are *essential*. The project can succeed without them, but not optimally. Outside the essential group are other interested, and possibly contributing, community members. These *ancillary* members are not essential to success, but their involvement may become essential at any time. Figure 3.2 depicts this overlay of critical, essential, and ancillary members of the community.

Agile Analytics communities must carefully evaluate each project to identify the minimally sufficient critical, essential, and ancillary member roles. These roles include an executive sponsor who can champion and facilitate, a project manager, a product owner, a technical team leader, a lead business analyst, development team members, customer team members, DBA and systems support staff, and others.

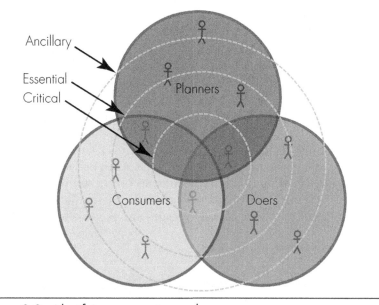

Figure 3.2 Identifying community members

Once identified, these roles must be filled with the most appropriate individuals—people with sufficient experience, expertise, and understanding to effectively perform in their respective roles. Once the roles are filled, these community members should be actively engaged early, during project planning, and periodically throughout the project. The initial goal of this collaboration is to provide early opportunities for input, risk identification, and expectation setting. Throughout the project, this collaboration serves the important goal of continuously realigning everyone's expectations.

A CONTINUUM OF TRUST

In *Coaching Agile Teams*, Lyssa Adkins differentiates *cooperation* from *collaboration*, explaining that group cooperation yields the sum of its parts, while collaboration yields a sum that is greater than its parts (Adkins 2010).

Cooperation between group members involves the smooth transfer of work in progress, work products, and information from one member to another. The team has a shared commitment to a common outcome, and individuals coordinate their activities in ways that support other group members. In a cooperative team, members interact in an egoless manner and understand their individual roles as they relate to the group's objectives.

Collaboration elevates groups beyond cooperation, adding an essential ingredient for emergent, innovative, and creative thinking. With cooperation, the properties of the group's output can be traced back to individuals, whereas with collaboration, the properties of group output exceed anything that could have been achieved individually. When a team is truly collaborating, its members build on top of each other's ideas, and the collective result is beyond what any one member could have envisioned. Cooperation is a prerequisite to collaboration.

Jim Highsmith builds on this distinction by adding a third aspect of group interaction: *compliance* (Highsmith 2010c). He describes a continuum of trust (see Figure 3.3) within a group that ranges from compliance to cooperation to collaboration, depending upon the level of trust that exists within the group.

A group relationship based on compliance is one where trust is limited. Groups lacking internal trust tend to compensate for the lack of trust by formalizing procedures and documents such as contracts, change control boards, and stage gates. Not all compliance procedures are bad, and many are beneficial. However, groups that are predominantly compliance-based cannot achieve the same levels of performance as cooperative and collaborative teams. Highsmith points out that that the level of trust that exists within a group is a critical factor in the group's ability to be cooperative or collaborative.

As one of the original Agile Manifesto authors, Jim Highsmith describes the 2001 gathering at Snowbird, Utah, and the resulting Manifesto, as an example of true collaboration. He points out that with very few exceptions, he isn't able to distinguish who contributed which elements to the Agile Manifesto. Furthermore, the Manifesto emerged as a result of a highly focused group of motivated individuals freely sharing good ideas with one another during an effective face-to-face gathering. It probably would not have emerged without the level of trust and respect that the Agile Manifesto authors had for one another.

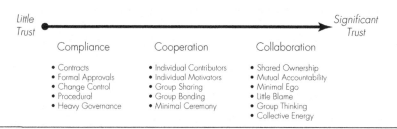

Figure 3.3 A continuum of trust

Every project community falls somewhere along this continuum of trust. It is important for an Agile project community to evaluate where they are operating along the continuum. Furthermore, there may be disparity within the Agile project community in this regard. For example, the development community may internally be highly collaborative, but their interaction with the customer community may tend more toward cooperation or even compliance until trust improves. When product owners fail to trust development teams, they often focus on pushing the team to be more productive. Agile project communities must work to smooth out these disparities in order to establish a shared level of trust within the community. Then the community can seek to progress toward a truly collaborative relationship. Lyssa Adkins offers many powerful coaching techniques to help teams and individuals become truly collaborative (Adkins 2010).

THE MECHANICS OF COLLABORATION

Collaboration is an essential ingredient in healthy Agile project communities, yet in my experience truly effective collaboration is perhaps the hardest thing to do well. We have become so adept at using e-mail, instant messaging, voice mail, and telephones to communicate that we have lost our preference for face-to-face communications. I once met a developer who said, "I prefer sending e-mail or leaving voice mail so that I don't get sucked into a conversation." I've heard other project team members say things like "All those face-to-face meetings—they keep us from getting work done." These are sad statements but somewhat understandable. Most organizations today have a meeting culture, and we've all been victims of time-wasting meetings at one time or another.

However, the avoidance of healthy collaboration is the wrong response to this prior conditioning. What we need are some principles for ensuring that our collaboration has high signal and low noise, that is, high-value collaboration that makes a difference. Jim Highsmith differentiates collaboration and coordination this way: ". . . collaboration can be defined as working together to jointly produce a deliverable (think pair programming as an example) or make a decision, whereas coordination is sharing information" (Highsmith 2010c). Here are some effective principles and mechanics for achieving this goal:

- **Don't call them "meetings."** Healthy collaboration is not the same thing as useless meetings. If you're like me, the invitation to a "meeting" raises those little hairs on your neck. Certainly not all meetings are useless, but often a request to attend a scheduled meeting is met with resistance or negativity. Our goal is for collaborative sessions to be perceived as enhancing project effectiveness.

If you need to have a collaborative session with other developers, customers, or stakeholders, it's helpful to give the session a descriptor that conveys its purpose, such as "object modeling session" or "requirements clarification roundtable." While this seems like a minor thing, it helps the participants get in the right frame of mind to make the session worthwhile.

- **Collaborate with a purpose.** Avoid scheduling collaborative sessions for ambiguous reasons. The best collaborative sessions are those with one or two well-defined purposes, such as "To develop a use-case model for customer profitability analysis" or "To modify the star schema to handle the invoice facts and dimensions." This practice serves two valuable goals. It ensures that everyone has a shared understanding of why they are at the gathering, and it clearly defines how everyone can know when the session is finished (when the purpose is achieved).

- **Get done quickly.** How often have you agreed to attend a one-hour meeting and left at the end of the hour thinking, "We could have done that in 15 minutes"? One hour is the default length of most scheduled meetings. However, the most rewarding collaborative sessions are the ones in which the issue gets addressed quickly and with minimal wasted time. An hour-long (or longer) session is fine if the issue really deserves that much time. But many issues can be resolved much faster than that. When you are collaborating with consumers or planners, they will greatly appreciate earlier-than-expected finishes.

- **Get the right people.** How many times have you been in a meeting wondering, "Why am I here? I have little or nothing to add"? The purpose of the collaborative session should dictate who needs to be involved. Every session participant should be involved because he or she can either add to the conversation or must be kept informed.

  Keep in mind Figure 3.2, and make sure that you include the appropriate critical and essential participants. Then decide if there are ancillary participants who can either add value to the session or who need to be kept informed. Additionally, participants should be invited to opt out of the session if they do not feel that they can contribute.

- **Limit the membership.** What is the minimally sufficient set of participants needed to achieve the purpose of the session? Avoid including participants who are superfluous to the purpose. But focus on the "sufficiency" aspect of minimal sufficiency. It can be very frustrating to make a collective design decision only to discover later that it violates database optimization protocols that you overlooked because your DBA wasn't involved.

- **Live in a glass house.** Sometimes people are hurt, offended, or bothered when they are excluded from collaborative sessions. This problem can be mitigated by holding collaborative sessions in an open space such as the team room. If others are interested in the conversation or the decisions, they can become silent observers of the process. If you aren't careful, this practice can conflict with the "limit the membership" practice. It is helpful to establish explicit working agreements for the entire project community about how people may observe without disrupting collaborative sessions.

  "Glass-house" collaboration extends beyond meetings and gatherings. Agile teams make project progress and issues easily visible to everyone. Alistair Cockburn coined the term *information radiators* to describe displays of useful information that people can easily see as they work or walk by (Cockburn 2004). These are often simple posters and flip charts with useful information. Good information radiators are easily understood at a glance, are easy to update, are posted in a high-traffic area, and are current. Agile team rooms are loaded with radiators that show current iteration progress, current work assignments, number of stories delivered, architecture decisions, and other information. Although they are used by the Agile team, they generally serve to inform people outside the team.

  More high-tech information radiators are the various Agile project dashboards that have emerged in recent years. Many open-source and commercial project management tools now support at-a-glance project metrics such as burn-down and burn-up charts as well as automated product and team performance metrics.

- **Eliminate distractions.** Laptops closed . . . cell phones off or on vibrate . . . and focus! The people in front of you are more important than the people who might be trying to call you, text you, or e-mail you. In my opinion this should be etiquette rule number one in today's corporate culture, but that's a topic for a different book.

  However, collaborative sessions are quickly derailed when participants are distracted by unrelated activities. The fact is that we stink at multitasking. Intensive corporate meeting cultures condition people to multitask as a compensation for low-value meetings, which reduces their focus at the meeting, which further reduces the value of the meeting, thereby creating a negative feedback cycle.

  Participants in a collaborative session must be singly focused on the purpose of that session for the agreed-upon duration of the session. If key participants are distracted, it's often better to cancel the session and find a time when everyone can focus.

- **Decide quickly.** When the purpose of a collaborative session is to make a decision, avoid getting stalled in the process. Group decisions that get made today can be changed tomorrow in light of new information. If the group doesn't have enough information to decide, then quickly identify the research that needs to be done to get enough information. If the group is split after everyone's input has been gathered, it may be the case that more information is needed.

- **Minimize ceremony.** The best collaborative sessions are not formalized meetings with agendas and meeting minutes distributed. Instead, they are the ones with the right people talking to each other until the goal is achieved. Often the best documentation is a digital photograph of the whiteboard or flip chart posted on the project wiki. The picture triggers memories of the conversations that took place, the decisions that were made, and the knowledge that was shared.

- **Synchronous is better than asynchronous.** Most of us have participated in e-mail threads that took a day or longer to reach a conclusion when a simple conversation would have allowed us to get there much faster. How many times have you waited several hours or more for a response to an e-mail request? How many times have you taken several hours to reply to someone else's e-mail request? Lost time caused by asynchronous communication can be very costly on a project. Real-time conversations are the most effective collaborative methods.

- **Face-to-face is better than voice-to-voice is better than. . . .** By far the most effective collaboration is face-to-face and in-person with a shared medium like a whiteboard (Ambler 2009a). This form of communication offers multimodal expressiveness that includes words, facial expressions, gestures, sketches, and other additions to meaning. Today's project teams are often geographically separated, thus making in-person collaboration challenging. Your goal should be to get as close to face-to-face/person-to-person communication as possible using whatever tools are required to facilitate that goal. This practice will greatly increase the likelihood that participants will have a truly shared understanding of the outcome of the session.

- **Avoid repetition.** If you can't get all of the right people involved in a collaborative session, postpone it until you can. This is preferable to having multiple repeats of the session with the same purpose and different participants, which can cause inconsistencies and conflicting outcomes. Similarly, once a session has resulted in a decision or outcome, avoid rehashing it unnecessarily unless there is new information that gives cause for reconsideration.

Poor collaborative practices can be a time sink for project community members and can adversely affect the project. Good Agile teams often make explicit agreements about their collaborative practices and include those in their team working agreements, which are discussed elsewhere in this book.

> ### Agile Analytics Practice: Frequent Reflection
>
> Agile project communities seek continuous improvement by frequently reflecting on and evaluating their performance. At the end of each iteration reflect on what went well, what needs improvement, and areas of concern. Also reflect on how well the community is maturing toward effective collaboration.

CONSUMER COLLABORATION

"Customer collaboration over contract negotiation"

It's one of the four values expressed in the Agile Manifesto, yet it is perhaps the hardest one to really practice well. Customers of business intelligence systems are a highly diversified group. They are diverse in their analytical skills, their analytical needs, their business responsibilities, their informational requirements, and so on. Furthermore, they are busy people who often balk at being asked for frequent review of and feedback on newly developed BI features. I was once on a smallish project to build a customer profitability data mart for the finance division of a midsize company. That project scope sounds pretty homogeneous, right? Well, between the needs of the CFO, the VP of finance, the financial controller, the forecasters, the predictive analytics group, the accountants, and others, the needs and perspectives of the user community were surprisingly diverse. It would have been inappropriate to consider only one customer type on that project. Scott Ambler prefers the term *stakeholders* to reflect this diversity within the consumer community (Ambler 2008a).

Customer collaboration in BI systems development is further complicated by the fact that users often don't know what to expect, or ask for, from a BI system. They need to experience using one before their wants and needs begin to jell (another reason why Agile Analytics makes sense). Furthermore, our customers have probably never been asked to actively and continuously collaborate during the development of any system, so they may not understand what we need from them. Sometimes we even sabotage ourselves by feeling apologetic about asking for time from our busy customers, and so we refrain from "bothering" them.

All of these challenges translate into an increasing likelihood that we will build the wrong thing as a result of insufficient customer involvement. These challenges cause many Agile teams to use easier, but less effective, alternatives to customer collaboration, such as heavy reliance on business analysts, choosing only one customer to represent the entire customer community, or relying solely on a "product owner" to be the proxy voice of the customer community. Each of these alternatives erodes the effectiveness of "adapting to feedback" and is a poor substitute for real and deep collaboration with our customers.

The fact of the matter is that, if our BI customers don't see the value of being actively engaged in helping us get it right, the BI system is not worth building at all. Our time would be better spent on other projects. That said, it is incumbent on us as an Agile project team to use our customers' time wisely and efficiently so that they will experience benefits that far outweigh the efforts.

Effective customer collaboration models have the following characteristics:

- All user types are sufficiently represented.
- Real users are actively engaged during every iteration.
- The user group is small enough to be manageable.
- There is a mechanism for prioritizing user input.
- There is a mechanism for resolving conflicting feedback from users.
- Customer collaboration quickly becomes a natural part of the process.

An effective model for customer collaboration is the *co-development user group*. The name itself suggests that users are in partnership with developers. This group contains carefully selected representatives of the various end-user types, organized into an actively involved extension of the project team. Good co-dev user groups have the following attributes:

- **Product ownership.** The group is often organized or led by a business analyst from the business domain who bridges the divide between the business domain and the technical team of experts.

Alternatively, co-dev user groups might be led by the business sponsor of the project who works directly with other members of the user community. A product manager serves this role when the BI system is a commercial product offering. In any of these cases, the user group lead acts as a filter and funnel from the broader user community into the project team. This group leader is responsible for feature prioritization, tie breaking, and resolving conflicting feedback so that the project team can take the right action and adapt appropriately to feedback.

- **Collegial membership.** Co-dev user group members should be supportive and "bought into" the Agile process and the BI project goals. Members who are cynical and/or antagonistic can do more harm than good as co-development partners. Similarly, co-dev partners should be confident in their roles, aware of their purpose on the team, and confident in the project's success potential. The co-dev user group is in a partnership with the project team, and they share the responsibility for project success. People who have a fragile or adversarial relationship with the project team do not make good co-dev partners.

- **Agile mentoring.** Co-dev user groups receive education about the Agile process, its reliance on customer feedback, its focus on high-value feature delivery every two weeks, its adaptive/evolutionary nature, and the roles and responsibilities of the user group. They are taught to view the Agile Analytics project as a "glass-house" activity that seeks frequent input and involvement from users. They are involved in the chartering and release-planning activities, the iteration commitments, and the end-of-iteration feature showcases. They may also be involved in conversations during the iteration to illuminate, explain, or make decisions with the project team.

- **Bilateral commitments.** Involvement in the co-dev user group is based on commitments on the part of both the user group members and project team members. User group members commit from 8 to 16 hours (one to two days) per month of active engagement, involvement, and availability, and the project team agrees to ensure that this time is well spent and effective. The user group members agree to provide timely and thoughtful feedback, and the project team agrees to evaluate and consider this feedback. The user group understands that its feedback is not guaranteed to be acted upon, but that it will be prioritized alongside other backlog items.

- **Retrospective involvement.** It is essential that the co-dev user group be involved in each end-of-iteration retrospective. Doing so enables the entire team to adjust its practices to ensure that user group members' time is well spent, that expectations remain in alignment, and that value is continuously being delivered.

Co-dev users quickly establish a sense of ownership in the BI project and pride in its outcome. When users share the responsibility for success with the project team, the outcomes are significantly more exciting. Not long before writing this I was asked to lead a BI project for an IT division in a large company. The company was relatively new to data warehousing and had no experience with the Agile style of development. My job was to introduce the organization to Agile Analytics and help them advance their technical data warehousing disciplines. I stipulated that the company needed to provide easy access to the user community as well as a "product owner" to bridge the gap between the technical team and customer community. The product owner turned out to be an energetic guy with deep experience in the business domain who was very knowledgeable about analytics and multidimensional reporting. He was initially reluctant to bother the very busy sales reps, customer service reps, and marketing executives—and they were reluctant to commit very much of their time. At first he made most of the feature priority and feature illumination decisions by himself. The user group first became involved at the first feature showcase, and their response was lukewarm; we had missed the mark on several of their user stories. In response we adjusted and involved the user group more frequently, and the feedback quickly became marvelous and insightful. Sales and marketing people love to talk about their world! Although we consumed significantly more of our users' time, they remained eager partners. During the first project retrospective (after six two-week iterations) the user group unanimously agreed that its involvement was a key in our ability to build what the users wanted. In spite of the project's demands on their time, these users felt that they wanted even more involvement in the next phase of development. They saw how their involvement translated into a BI system that made their jobs easier and better.

Agile Analytics Practice: Customer Commitment

Promise your co-development customers that you will not ask for more than two days per month of their time, and in exchange you need them to be wholly committed to partnering with you, test-driving new features, and providing valuable feedback. Make sure you use the customers' time effectively.

DOER COLLABORATION

"Individuals and interactions over processes and tools"

Another of the core values from the Agile Manifesto. This one is directed at the criticality of collaboration between delivery team members. Data warehouse delivery team members include ETL developers, data modelers, data architects, DBAs, business analysts, BI tool specialists, testers, project managers, and anyone else who is involved in the day-to-day activities required to build the BI system.

In an Agile Analytics project, these people need to be face-to-face as much as possible. Face-to-face communication is by far the most effective multimodal communication method. If I can see your facial expressions, hear your voice inflections, observe your gestures, and view what you are drawing on the whiteboard, I will much more accurately understand what you are trying to tell me. Furthermore, I can save a great deal of time if I can just talk directly to you about what I'm thinking rather than writing it in an e-mail or trying to explain it over the phone. When the entire team (or subgroup) is involved in collaborative whiteboard discussions, the result is a better-designed system that includes everyone's good ideas.

While there is no doubt that face-to-face communication is preferred, the realities of today's workplaces sometimes make this impossible. Geographically distributed teams are common, and the use of offshore developers is routine. If you are lucky enough to be in a BI team that is not geographically distributed, be sure to get your team sitting and working together face-to-face. While this may take a bit of getting used to, the benefits will be evident and the team effectiveness will increase greatly.

If geographic separation is inevitable, do everything possible to create what Jim Highsmith refers to as *virtual colocation*; that is, find ways to be as collaborative and "face-to-face" as possible. This includes the use of VoIP communications technologies, desktop-sharing technologies, instant messaging, Web cameras, and other tools. Not long ago I consulted with an Agile team that was separated into three remote locations. Each of the sites had a team room in which all project team members at that site sat together face-to-face. All of the developers wore headsets and had Web cams at their workstations. They made heavy use of Skype[1] to simulate face-to-face communications.

---

1. Skype is a voice-over-Internet application. For more information see www.skype.com.

They also used the desktop-sharing capabilities of Skype to enable pair pro-gramming and "whiteboarding" discussions. The ability to do multiway conference calling enabled this team to be highly effective despite its geographic separation. There are several remote collaboration tools designed to help geographically distributed teams achieve virtual colocation. These are constantly improving and offering more powerful capabilities.

Time zone differences are perhaps the greatest impediment to developer collaboration. When half the team is on the American continent and the other half is in Asia or Europe, the time separation is significant. While Agile teams can function under these conditions, true collaboration suffers. It is often best to separate the project into two subprojects with independent and noncompeting objectives. Each team can work autonomously on its user backlog and, with weekly synchronization, can evolve the BI system in parallel. The weekly synchronization is needed to ensure that both teams are making mutually beneficial design choices and working toward the same architecture.

PLANNER COLLABORATION

Undoubtedly your BI project is championed by people in the organization who are not users of the system but who recognize the project's value to the business. These executives, management sponsors, and stakeholders have a vested interest in the success of your project, and they care about budgets, schedules, and progress. They also care about whether the evolving system is on a trajectory to meet the needs of the consumer community, even if they have no direct input into user stories or priorities.

It's easy to overlook the criticality of collaborating with project planners, which can result in misperceptions about the health of the project. Project planners need to be kept aware of project risks and uncertainties. During project visioning and planning it is common for the planner community to set ambitious expectations about the project outcomes. As projects unfold, we must help the planners realign their expectations in light of the typical risks and challenges that we encounter on projects.

I was once involved in a high-exploration-factor[2] project. As the project unfolded over multiple iterations, the shared vision of the user and developer

---

2. Exploration factor is an assessment of project uncertainty introduced in *Agile Project Management: Creating Innovative Products* (Highsmith 2010a).

communities naturally morphed and adapted to the realities of the project. The expectations of both users and developers were in alignment, and both groups were satisfied with the project's trajectory. Unfortunately, the project sponsor and other stakeholders had not been involved in the various conversations that altered the course of the project. When they became aware that the project had deviated significantly from their initial vision, the stakeholders began to view the project as a failure. Effort was expended on root-cause analyses and assessing how to get the project "back on track." Eventually the planners came to realize that the needs of the consumers were being met by the doers. In fact, the planners acknowledged that the new vision was better and more correct than the original one. The lack of frequent collaboration with the planners had caused a significant mismatch in expectations, which resulted in substantial churn while those expectations were realigned.

The planner community should be encouraged to attend the feature showcase that occurs at the end of each iteration. In these showcases planners are passive participants. Their role is to observe the interactions between doers and consumers and the feedback and acceptance of new features. It is this flow of feedback that subtly and gradually shifts the trajectory of a project away from the original vision. It's much more difficult to track and document these subtle changes than to track the major explicit changes. Therefore, when planners are absent from the feature showcases, it is easy for them to lose track of the little course corrections that occur naturally on an Agile project.

We also need to hold intentional "stakeholder showcases" for the purpose of realigning everyone's expectations. These should be held about every third iteration, approximately every six weeks—immediately following the feature showcase. During these stakeholder showcases we review the status of the project relative to the latest release plan that was established by the entire community. We examine the things that have changed since the last planning session. We examine the current user story backlog and focus on new stories and newly reprioritized stories. We review the known risks and uncertainties and discuss our mitigation and exploration plans for resolving them. We talk about the team's development velocity and the rate of user acceptance of new features. And ultimately we talk about the project's current vision and expected outcomes as they have changed since the latest visioning or re-visioning session. Stakeholder showcases may or may not include users but should include the product owner or lead business analyst to represent the consumer community. Adjust the frequency of these stakeholder showcases as needed to ensure that the entire community's expectations remain closely aligned during the project.

Agile Analytics Practice: Regular Stakeholder Showcase
Hold a stakeholder showcase every third iteration (six weeks) to realign stakeholder expectations. Review current plans against the original plans; review risks and unknowns; review value delivered and changes in priorities.

PRECURSORS TO AGILITY

In addition to the mechanics of the project community and collaboration, there are some precursors to Agile Analytics—the "stuff" that must exist before an Agile project can achieve the high levels of performance often reported by mature Agile project teams. These precursors include

- **Solid tools.** You can't be Agile without reasonably solid tools. These include both the technical stack of products on which your BI system is built as well as the development tools used to produce high-quality working code.

    If the tools aren't solid, you end up dealing with a special class of problems. In addition to the uncertainty and "high exploration" associated with the actual BI system (what needs to be built), the team must also devote time to the high exploration factor associated with its tools. Unless the focus of exploration is on the actual tools, such as a proof-of-concept project, the team will be perceived as inefficient (at best) or incompetent (at worst).

- **Agile infrastructure.** Even if your tools are solid, you can't really be Agile without the proper infrastructure. This means such things as configuration management systems, testing infrastructure, and so forth. These topics are presented in greater detail in later chapters.

    In a new project adopting Agile, this is often not that difficult because you can build the infrastructure you need in an Agile manner. In an existing project adopting Agile, the retrofitting of an Agile infrastructure, including the retraining of the team to use existing tools in an Agile manner, can be significant. Adding a legacy code base into the mix can further complicate the Agile infrastructure planning.

- **Agile workmanship.** If you have solid tools and a solid infrastructure, you still can't be Agile if your team doesn't know this *specific* set of tools and this *specific* infrastructure. This result has been discussed by many people, including Fred Brooks (Brooks 1975), as well as Abdel-Hamid and Madnick (1991) with their human system dynamics models, and is crudely (but usefully) summarized by the rule of thumb that it takes between two and six months for a developer to become acceptably (not necessarily fully) productive on any project, Agile or otherwise.

- **Agile architecture.** There is, of course, the great debate about BDUF (Big Design Up Front). Aside from the silliness of the debate, with some proponents of Agile arguing that there is no need and others claiming that this traditional architectural design practice makes sense as is, there is a place for UFD. The "Big" part of it in an Agile project comes from leveraging proven architectures, often by applying one of many architectural patterns. The "UFD" means proving your architecture in your project as quickly as you can. The challenge here is that more than any other method, Agile needs architecture as the stable, unifying conceptual framework that enables developers to work urgently but without hurrying, and quickly but with minimal waste. We will cover this in greater detail in Chapter 6, "Evolving Excellent Design."

- **Customer commitment.** While the role of customers and your access to customers vary greatly from project to project, it is critical that your Agile project team have sufficient external input into project planning, capability definition, feature prioritization, product review, and feedback. The form that customer collaboration takes in an Agile project is widely varied, but its absence is a warning sign that you do not have the necessary precursors for Agile success. We will discuss the perils of customer collaboration in greater detail later in this book.

I don't claim that this is a complete list of the precursors required for a given set of developers to become genuinely Agile. I have also omitted certain precursors that seem painfully obvious, such as development computers. You may find the need to add others, and we are finding that different teams have different precursors that often must be addressed, ranging from "What is a unit test?" to "How do I prioritize feature requests from multiple customers?" However, this list is a solid start and should be considered as a jumping-off point for further Agile enablement.

The astute reader may argue that these precursors must be present on any project, Agile or not. This is true, but since a key Agile principle is the *frequent delivery* of a working BI system to users, the extent to which Agile projects require these precursors is far greater than for standard projects.

Agile Analytics Practice: Iteration Zero

Iteration zero is a regular Agile iteration but without the expectation of BI feature development. This gives the team time to ensure that the necessary precursors for success are in place. Team members can stand up new technologies, do some initial design, conduct some experiments, and perform other preliminary tasks.

WRAP-UP

This chapter frames many of the critical prerequisites for the successful adoption of Agile Analytics practices. Project success requires much more than just good technical skills and discipline or good project management methods. Unfortunately, many BI development efforts involve the users and the stakeholders looking passively toward the IT department or BI development team to "make it happen." Historically we in the development community have largely shouldered the burden and accepted the lion's share of responsibility for project success. When projects fail, users and management look to the delivery team and ask, "Why?" and "What went wrong?" That community model is a recipe for trouble.

This chapter is placed intentionally early in the book to clearly establish the necessity of a shared-responsibility community model. The *planners*, the *consumers*, and the *doers* each form essential and valuable subgroups within the project community. Each group brings a unique perspective about the vision, goals, scope, and boundaries of the BI project. The perspectives of these groups serve as a system of checks and balances that are needed to ensure that the right product is built.

A high degree of collaboration between these groups is required for this community model to be effective. Daily collaboration within the doer group is mandatory. Near-daily collaboration between the doers and consumers is required as well as formal feature review and acceptance activities near the end of every iteration. The planners must be actively kept in the feedback loop as well to ensure that their goals are met and their expectations remain realistic.

In addition to all of this community and collaboration, there is a set of precursors that are required for Agile Analytics projects to succeed. The tools and technologies used in development must be sufficient to their purpose, and the project team members must be proficient in the use of these tools and technologies. These tools and technologies must exist in the necessary infrastructure for developers to deliver production-quality features every few weeks. Too often I work with BI teams that do not have the right development and testing infrastructure to work effectively. Typically the reasons given are along the lines of excessive licensing or hardware costs; yet these costs pale in comparison with the cost of lost productivity and people time developing within an insufficient infrastructure.

This chapter introduced several collaboration practices. Upcoming chapters in this book will introduce specific engineering practices and project management practices that build on the precursors outlined here. Seasoned Agile practitioners know the value of looking for ways to be more Agile. These include adjustments in attitudes and behaviors as well as specific practices and techniques. The nuances of your project may dictate that you tailor these customer, community, and collaborative techniques and may even cause you to invent a new set of techniques to be more effective.

This page intentionally left blank

Chapter 4

USER STORIES FOR BI SYSTEMS

Contrary to popular opinion, the best business intelligence systems are not driven by the data or the operational source systems. I recently had a conversation with a group of data warehouse developers who were completely baffled by the notion of building a BI solution without first extracting all of the source system data into a single, normalized data model. They insisted that this was the necessary precursor to building BI applications for end users. I asked them what specific business problems the data warehouse was required to solve. They speculated on a lot of possible ideas but admitted that they had no business requirements. They explained that their project was an IT initiative, and their first job was to consolidate the data. After that, they planned to begin building BI applications against the warehouse. This was how this group had always worked. When I asked how often their customer/user community was completely delighted with the resulting BI applications, the team chuckled and reluctantly admitted that users had never been "delighted."

This story is too often the way data warehousing projects go. They fail to focus on the early delivery of business value and lose end-user trust and acceptance. We "*data* geeks" take a *data*-centric approach to building a *data* warehouse, and we convince ourselves that we have to solve lots of thorny *data* issues before we can build the applications for users. It's all about the data! Many data experts make the wrong assumption that if they get the data right, they can meet all possible future user requirements. Oddly enough, when you talk to the business users, it's not about the data. The data is just a means to the end goal of handling business problems and supporting business decisions. Users have *stories to tell*, and they are usually *not* about the data. The data merely plays a supporting role.

Agile Analytics is a feature-driven or story-driven approach. We are eager to produce user features that enable our customers to do their jobs better or more efficiently. The data just supports this goal. And it just so happens that the best way to deliver that data is via a data warehouse.

Story-driven development is a very gratifying way to work once you get the hang of it. In this chapter I will show you how to write good user stories for

BI systems, how to make your stories small enough and simple enough that they can be completed in short iterations, and how to prioritize stories and estimate effort. You'll pick up a few other tips along the way. By the way, Mike Cohn has written extensively about "user stories" among other Agile topics. You should read his book for a deeper dive into this topic (Cohn 2004). My focus in this chapter is to show how to do story-driven data warehouse development, and to help you wrestle with the common question "How can we build anything meaningful in only two weeks?"

WHAT ARE USER STORIES?

User stories offer a quick way to gather and organize project requirements without conducting a comprehensive requirements analysis up front. Stories capture the essence of features that users need in the BI system while deferring the details until later. Stories are gathered collaboratively during project chartering and then prioritized on a product backlog that is continuously groomed and maintained by the product owner. The backlog provides the basis for planning each development iteration in what Ralph Hughes calls the *story conference* where the detailed specifications are determined (Hughes 2008). The process might look something like the following scenario:

Scenario

An important element of project chartering is the story-writing workshop. In this workshop the development group works with the co-development customers to gather and organize user stories. The user stories will be managed on a prioritized product backlog by Dieter, the team's product owner.

Prakash, the team's technical leader, kicks off the story-writing workshop by facilitating a use-case discussion. He acknowledges that the co-development customers in the group are from various business units at FlixBuster. Beulah, Jane, Javier, and Chuck are from the finance department; Kari and Samantha are from marketing; Mike and Mack are from operations; and Andy is from sales. They also have some executives in the group, including the CFO, CTO, and VPs of finance, sales, and marketing.

Prakash draws several stick figures around the perimeter of a whiteboard and labels them Sales, Marketing, Finance, Operations, and Executive. The stick figures represent business user roles from each department. He points out that this is just a starting point, and the team can change role names, add more roles, or remove roles as the discussion ensues.

He starts by asking the members from finance to describe the big-picture goals they hope to achieve using the FlixBuster BI system. Jane mentions that she needs to analyze customer profitability; Chuck mentions operational cost analysis and reduction; and Beulah mentions channel profitability (stores versus online rentals). Prakash draws an oval in the middle of the whiteboard and labels it "Analyze customer profitability." He draws another and labels it "Analyze channel profitability," and so on for each of these goals.

He draws lines linking the Finance stick figure to each of these ovals, and Beulah points out that there are really different roles within the finance department. She recommends separating them into profitability analyst, operations analyst, and financial forecaster, which Prakash does. The discussion continues by adding roles from marketing, sales, and operations. More ovals, or use-case bubbles, emerge, and the FlixBuster BI vision is starting to take shape. Prakash helps the group avoid creating too much detail in this use-case diagram because its main purpose is to provide a conceptual understanding of the different types of users and the kinds of things they need to do.

When the group decides they have an accurate use-case diagram, Prakash shows them how to create more detailed use cases. He points out that each bubble on the diagram should map to one or more use cases. He uses Jane's need to analyze customer profit as a starting point and asks Jane to describe how she wants to do this analysis. She explains that she needs to be able to see net profit per customer per transaction, but she also wants to see average profit margin per customer, as well as the net profit margin for the top and bottom 10 percent of all customers.

Prakash writes Jane's description on the flip chart and then asks Jane to imagine that the BI system is working, and to describe the specific processes she wants to follow to accomplish these goals. As she describes them, Prakash adds them as *event flows* below the general use-case description. He asks the group to divide up into user types and asks the developers to partner with each of the groups to create detailed use cases for each of the bubbles on the use-case diagram. The developers are to be scribes, and the business users are to tell them what to write.

After about an hour, each of the groups has a pretty good collection of use cases written in detail. The whole group comes back together, and each small group presents its use cases to the larger team. Arlene, the scrum master, takes digital pictures of the use-case diagram as well as each of the detailed use cases. These will be published on the project wiki for future reference.

After a short break the project team reconvenes and Dieter, the product owner, takes over. Now that the group has a shared understanding of the conceptual use-case model and the more detailed use cases, he wants them to break these use cases into user stories. He explains that a use case represents a BI system capability that is made up of multiple features. Each feature may be fairly complex and is made up of smaller user stories. These stories should be small enough to be built in two weeks while still reflecting business value.

Jane suggests this story: "As a finance analyst I need the ability to analyze past transactional profit by month or season, by sales channel, and by customer region so that I can understand seasonal trends in video rentals." Natasha, an ETL developer, writes down Jane's story on an index card and starts asking clarifying questions about the business logic for calculating profit. Arlene intervenes and reminds the group not to dive into the details of each story. She encourages them to just capture as many stories as the users can think of.

Dieter asks the members of the group to return to their smaller groups to write as many stories as they can think of from the use cases they created earlier. He reminds them not to dwell too long on any single story; the goal is to quickly create a good collection of stories. They will refine these later. The technical team members in each group are experienced with user stories and story-driven development, so they help the customer community members in the story-writing process.

When the groups have finished this preliminary story writing, Dieter brings everyone back together. They review the stories and group the duplicate ones together. Dieter guides the group in prioritizing the user stories. Since the theme of the first 90-day planning cycle is "Finance Analytics," the finance-related stories naturally land in the highest-priority grouping. However, the team discovers that some of the sales stories are beneficial to the finance group and vice versa. Dieter acknowledges that some of Andy's requirements can be met during this first planning cycle even though the sales and marketing theme is scheduled for a later planning cycle. These stories move up in priority, which is on the basis of business value.

As the stories are prioritized, Dieter hangs them on the product backlog, which is posted on the planning room wall. In the first pass, the group roughly grouped the stories into thirds reflecting the first, second, and third highest-priority groupings. Such grouping allows the team to focus on refining the highest group and simplifies their task.

After the customer group rank-orders the stories in the top third, the team has an initial product backlog populated and prioritized. Now the team members can do enough estimating to make some projections for their 90-day plan. Arlene reminds everyone that the customer team drives prioritization and the technical team drives estimation. However, she points out that the customer group can help in estimating by shaping and simplifying stories.

In the first estimating pass, the team simply identifies the stories as small, medium, large, or extra-large. The extra-large stories are epics (too big for one iteration). The epics need to be split or simplified, but not all at once. The group grapples with the epics that will affect the first couple of iterations, and Dieter agrees to shepherd the others as part of his backlog grooming duties.

Arlene facilitates the process of moving stories from the top of the backlog into the release plan. For each iteration the technical team speculates about how many stories seem reasonable. The technical team members have learned to be conservative in their estimates. The purpose of this practice is simply to get an initial projection of what can be delivered at the end of the planning cycle. It isn't a commitment, but it helps level everyone's expectations.

It's now Monday morning of the first iteration. The team completed a successful chartering session last week and now has a high-level 90-day project plan divided into six two-week iterations. The team also has a backlog, which Dieter spent more time grooming after the chartering session. The group kicks off Monday morning with a *story conference* that includes both the customer co-dev and technical groups.

The aim of the story conference is to understand enough details of the stories to estimate them using story points, to move stories from the product backlog to the iteration backlog, and to commit to the iteration plan. The FlixBuster BI team uses relative sizing for its estimates. The team has chosen a scoring system of 0, 1, 2, 3, 5, 8, 13, 21, and 34 as for story-point values. After a few iterations the team will begin to establish its *velocity* for this project. The team's velocity will provide an upper limit for planning each iteration within the team's capacity. This way the team can avoid overcommitments and frustrations. The team can increase its velocity by accomplishing *stretch goals* that aren't part of the initial commitments.

The story conference takes up the better part of Monday morning, but by the end the technical team members feel they have all of the necessary details to get started working. Everyone feels good about this first iteration plan. If everything goes as planned, it will result in some good working BI features that the finance group can begin using and exploring.

User Stories versus Requirements

Agile Analytics takes a user-story-driven rather than a data-driven approach to building the BI system. This serves the first principle of frequently delivering high-value, working features. A user story is a statement that can be expressed from the point of view of the user and can be tied to a specific business need or goal. User stories should be able to fit into the following story template:

> As a *<role>* I need the ability to *<do something>* so that I can *<goal statement>*.

For example:

> As a financial analyst I need the ability to see net profit per customer per transaction over time so that I can identify upward or downward profit trends.

A well-written user story has the following characteristics:

1. It represents business value to the customer community.
2. When implemented, it can be demonstrated to business users as a working feature for feedback and acceptance.

3. It can be implemented in a single iteration as an *architecturally complete* and *production-quality* working feature.
   a. Architecturally complete: The feature spikes through the architecture from end to end. It is not a nonfunctional or disposable prototype.
   b. Production-quality: The feature is fully tested and ready for potential deployment.

Watch out for epics! An epic can be expressed in the same form as a user story, but it contains so much complexity that it must be decomposed into a collection of simpler user stories that meet the characteristics just listed. Users commonly think in terms of epics, since their needs are fairly complex. An example of a data warehousing epic might be the following:

> As a financial analyst I need to understand our cost of service per customer relative to the profitability of that customer, and I need to analyze customers by city, state, and region and evaluate their trends, so that I can identify opportunities for either reducing cost of service or increasing profits.

This is a great description of a BI feature, but it isn't a great user story because it is probably too complex to be completed in a single iteration. We care about these epics, and we will deliver them as user capabilities, but we need to deliver them incrementally.

User stories don't always translate into glorious, exciting features. Sometimes they are relatively mundane stepping-stones toward more powerful capabilities. For example:

> As a financial analyst I need the ability to open a previously saved report.

This is a valuable user story, but it doesn't have much sex appeal. Effective Agile Analytics developers know how to think in the smallest, simplest terms in order to chip away at delivering the right solution.

Also, watch out for *anti-stories*! These are statements that are expressed in the story template but don't meet all of the criteria. For example:

> As a financial analyst I need to know that the FlixBuster data model will correctly house all of the data I need so that I can conduct a wide variety of revenue and profit analyses.

This is an architecture story hiding in user story clothing. I've actually seen data modelers and architects write stories like this one to exempt themselves from a true customer-value focus. A good acid test is to pretend that you aren't building a BI system (or any software solution for that matter) and ask if the user story still reflects something that users need the ability to do in order to accomplish their business goals. Users don't need data models and system architectures; they need the solutions that data models and architectures support.

The great thing about user stories is that they enable the project community to quickly define the capabilities and features that the system needs to support without investing a huge effort in exhaustive requirements analysis.

User stories by themselves are *not* requirements; they represent requirements. Mike Cohn says user stories "are a promise to have a conversation about the requirements" (Cohn 2004). This conversation is the collaboration between developers and users to establish a shared understanding of what is needed. Stories work best when this conversation happens in a just-in-time fashion as the story is being scheduled into an iteration. The conversation produces the following residue:

- A description of the story
- Notes or low-fidelity sketches that detail and clarify what is needed
- Acceptance tests that add clarity and help determine when a story is done

As a user story is scheduled for development, this residue gives developers what they need to build the right thing. Scott Ambler describes just-in-time data modeling as a key component of iteration modeling in Agile Model Driven Development (Ambler 2006). This may be an additional artifact produced as a result of the story conversation.

I once worked with a company that had spent 18 months gathering detailed requirements for a large business intelligence system. They wanted to be sure to get input from everyone to ensure a complete set of requirements. During that 18-month period many of the original users moved on to other jobs, and there were new users. So, many of the original requirements were stale and obsolete. Similarly, the original project sponsor had been replaced by a new sponsor, so the vision and goals of the project had shifted. Additionally, the strategic direction of the entire organization had shifted, rendering many of the requirements irrelevant. Several of the original users told me that they had given up any hope of ever seeing a working system, so they had developed their own unsanctioned Microsoft Access databases and Excel workbooks to analyze the data. As is often the case, the user community was doing whatever it needed to accomplish its objectives in the absence of a working BI system.

As I reviewed the work of this requirements effort, I discovered that if they had conducted a collaborative story-writing workshop, the company could have identified at least 80 percent of those requirements in a couple of days (Ambler 2005b). With a bit more effort they could have prioritized the stories and quickly begun development on the highest-priority ones.

FROM ROLES TO USE CASES TO USER STORIES

When a BI project is well defined or relatively small in scope, it is often possible for the team to go directly to story writing. However, in more complex or broad-reaching BI projects teams need a process for accurately identifying user roles and decomposing the problem domain from the top down. Role definition and use-case modeling offer an effective means of decomposing the problem domain down to the user story level.

Not all users are created equal. Our FlixBuster data warehouse users are a diverse group of business experts in different areas who have different jobs to do. Jane, in finance, needs to understand revenue, gross profit, and net profit. Chuck, also in finance, needs to analyze and reduce operational costs. Carroll, the chief financial officer, needs to analyze trends and project the future profitability of FlixBuster. Mack, the head of operations, needs to manage a just-in-time DVD inventory to minimize a surplus of unrequested titles, while maximizing the ability to meet customer requests. Samantha, in marketing, needs to run an effective campaign to attract new customers and upgrade existing customers to the "Unlimited Movies" package. Kari, also in marketing, needs to analyze what movie genres customers prefer based on geography, age, gender, socioeconomic status, marital status, and a variety of other factors. Andy, in retail sales, needs to evaluate and forecast sales volume, revenue, and profit by retail store. Mike, in operations, needs to analyze and find ways to improve the average time it takes customers to receive movies by mail. Oh, yes, then there is Georgina, who reports to the CEO, needs to evaluate a wide variety of what-if scenarios and analyze whether the new strategic road map is helping improve the balanced scorecard key performance indicators (KPIs). This is just the beginning—there are a lot more FlixBuster business experts who need the data warehouse.

User Roles

Clearly we can't write user stories from just a single perspective. We need to consider each user story from the point of view of that user's role and goals. In fact, it's really useful to post a set of user roles on your team room wall where the team can use them to write stories, and developers can reference them to keep stories in the proper perspective. As new roles are identified, you can add to the collection, and as their goals change, you can modify the roles.

Keep in mind that the same person is likely to have many different roles at any given time or span of time. For example, I am in the role of author as I write this, but when my wife interrupts my writing by asking me to take out the trash, I am in the role of husband (and servant!). Official job titles are often insufficient as use-case roles. For instance, CFO is a title, but the CFO probably acts in a wide spectrum of roles during the course of business.

Start by brainstorming an initial set of roles and give each one a distinct title. Write the roles on index cards, a single role title per card (see Figure 4.1). Post these on the wall or on a flip chart. Brainstorming rules apply, and anything and everything goes for the first pass.

Next, organize the roles into logical groups of similar functions. If two roles have overlapping functions, overlap the cards to convey this (see Figure 4.2). Greater card overlap means more duplication between the roles.

Figure 4.1   Brainstorm initial user roles

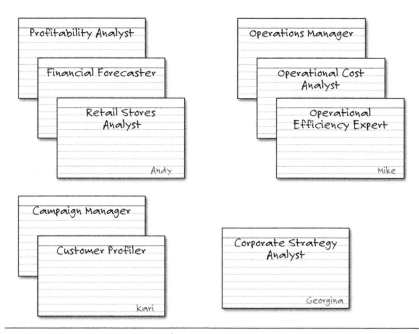

Figure 4.2   Organize user roles

Now consolidate the roles by eliminating the duplicates and clarifying the differences. When there is a high degree of overlap among multiple roles, replace them with a single role title that covers them all. When there is a minimal degree of overlap among roles, rename them to more clearly distinguish them from one another (see Figure 4.3).

Finally, refine the roles by defining the distinguishing characteristics, expected usage frequency, usage patterns, savvy in using data for analysis, domain expertise, usage goals, and other factors. Write this as a short, descriptive paragraph on each card (see Figure 4.4).

Sometimes it's useful to create a mock user persona to remind developers who their users are. A persona is an imaginary example of a user role with a name, a background, interests, hobbies, a family, and so on. Use magazine photos or online images to associate a picture with your personas. Personas are optional, but in complex environments they can help developers think about users in more concrete ways.

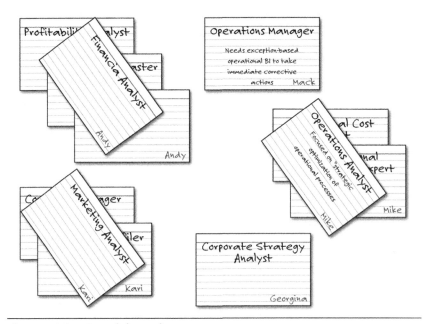

Figure 4.3   Consolidate roles

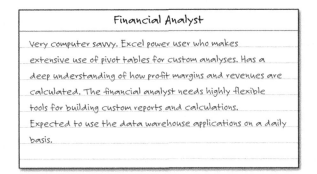

Figure 4.4   Refine and distinguish roles

Agile Analytics Practice: Create Personas

Taking time during project planning to create a persona for each of your identified user roles will help the DW/BI team continuously think in concrete terms about who the users are and how the development activities will benefit those users. Publish these personas on the wall in the team workspace where they can be referenced during development.

Use-Case Modeling

Now that you have a set of roles, you want to write a collection of user stories that, when developed as data warehouse features, will satisfy the needs of each role. When the scope of the BI system is small enough, you can often get straight to the writing of stories. However, sometimes it's helpful to decompose the problem domain incrementally so that you don't get overwhelmed. *Use-case modeling* is a great way to model the problem space in terms of user roles and goals.

Ivar Jacobson introduced the concept of use-case modeling in 1986, and *use-case diagrams* (one component of use-case modeling) are part of the Unified Modeling Language 2.0 (UML), which was introduced in the mid-1990s as a consolidation of popular software modeling methods from the 1980s and '90s. Alistair Cockburn has improved on use-case modeling techniques (Cockburn 2000). Use-case modeling describes *actors* who act on one or more *use cases* to accomplish *goals*. The user roles that we've identified work very neatly as actors in use-case modeling.

The first step in use-case modeling is the creation of a use-case diagram that provides a high-level identification of multiple use cases and the actors (roles) that interact with them. Figure 4.5 shows an example of a use-case diagram for our FlixBuster business intelligence problem domain. The use-case bubbles in the diagram describe the high-level actions that actors must perform to achieve their goals. Each actor is associated with one or more use cases, and use cases can sometimes use other shared use cases to perform their tasks.

You can do this simply on a whiteboard or flip chart. Although many UML software tools are available, I strongly advocate using low-tech tools such as index cards. The real value is in the conversations you have during the collaborative effort. Be thorough, but avoid getting overly detailed in your use cases.

Next, define the *use-case details* for each of the use-case bubbles in your diagram. Use-case details include the use-case title, a list of the actors involved, the goal or intended outcome of the use case, and a series of *event flows* that describe various interaction sequences and the outcome of each sequence. The *main event flow*, or "happy path," is the most common or expected event flow. Other event flows describe various exceptions to the main event flow. Figure 4.6 shows an example of the FlixBuster use case for "Analyze Customer Profitability."

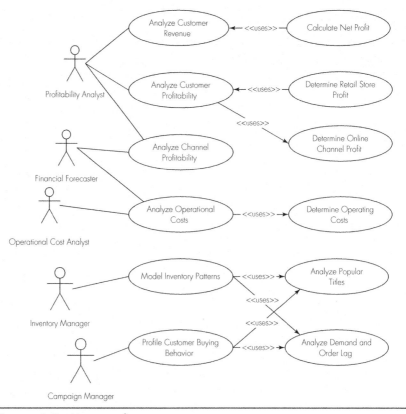

Figure 4.5 Use-case diagram

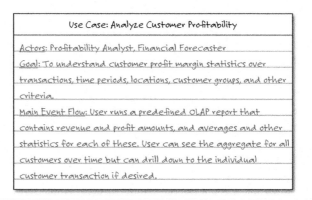

Use Case: Analyze Customer Profitability

<u>Actors</u>: Profitability Analyst, Financial Forecaster

<u>Goal</u>: To understand customer profit margin statistics over transactions, time periods, locations, customer groups, and other criteria.

<u>Main Event Flow</u>: User runs a predefined OLAP report that contains revenue and profit amounts, and averages and other statistics for each of these. User can see the aggregate for all customers over time but can drill down to the individual customer transaction if desired.

Figure 4.6 Use-case detail

Agile Analytics Practice: Big Visible Use Case

Post the project's use-case diagram on the wall in the team workspace to provide a constant reference for developers to the problem domain and the big-picture vision of the system.

Finding User Stories in Event Flows

A simple use case might translate directly into a user story. For example, the use case "Log In to BI System" might be simplistic enough that it becomes the user story "As an operations manager I need the ability to log in to the FlixBuster business intelligence application." However, most use-case details suggest a whole collection of user stories related to the various event flows. The use-case detail for "Analyze Customer Profitability" might generate the user stories shown in Figure 4.7.

Write each user story on a separate index card. Remember, a user story by itself is not a requirement. It is a promise to have a conversation about the requirements. We can defer that conversation until we need the detailed requirements for any given user story.

Use-Case Scenarios

One final word about use-case modeling and user stories, and *use-case scenarios*. A use-case scenario is a specific concrete path through a use-case

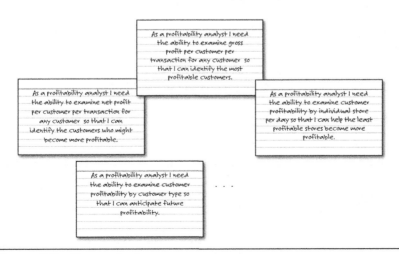

Figure 4.7 User stories from a use case

event flow. It is an example or instance of the use case in action. Use-case scenarios are often used to clarify the expected behavior of more complex use cases as well as to help ensure that all possibilities have been considered. Use-case scenarios are a natural outgrowth of collaborative sessions between developers and customers or users.

In Agile Analytics development we can take advantage of use-case scenarios to define *story-test cases*. User story testing and storytest-driven development (STDD) are introduced in depth in Chapter 7, "Test-Driven Data Warehouse Development." However, now is a good time to point out this relationship. Each use-case scenario should be recast as one or more story-test cases. These story-test cases become the acceptance criteria that developers need in order to know what it means to be done with a story.

Although it is important to be thorough as you write use-case scenarios, it isn't necessary to be comprehensive in one pass. Over time you can add more event flows, use-case scenarios, and storytests, and you can alter these based on user feedback or increased clarity of the user stories.

DECOMPOSING EPICS

Recall that one of the measures of a good user story is that it can be completed in a single iteration of no more than four weeks (preferably two). Although we aren't estimating user stories yet, it pays to do a quick pass through the stories to get a feel for whether they seem small and simple enough to pass this criterion. You will inevitably encounter some epics during this pass. Epics, in some ways, are close to use cases. They describe general functionality that may reflect various event flows and scenarios.

Epics should be decomposed into good user stories before they can be estimated or scheduled. The easiest epics to handle are those that naturally break down into multiple, simpler user stories. These often have a pattern of complex conjunctive phrases such as the following:

> As a sales forecaster I need the ability to see the daily revenue per store *along with* the number of transactions per day, *and* the demographic profile of customers near each store, *as well as* the historical revenue for each store over the past two years so that I can analyze and forecast revenue and buying trends.

This epic is clearly a collection of multiple related stories:

As a sales forecaster I need the ability to

1. See daily revenue per store
2. See the number of transactions per day (per store?)
3. See the demographic profile of customers near each store
4. See the historical revenue for each store over the past two years

Sometimes epics are not as obvious:

> As a financial forecaster I need the ability see profit and profit margin per customer per transaction for the top 10 percent of our customers so that I can identify the characteristics of the most profitable transactions.

In the eye of a user this looks like a reasonably atomic user story, but developers realize that profit and profit margin are based on a complex set of business rules. Furthermore, isolating the top 10 percent may involve complex processing in the presentation tier of the system depending on the presentation technologies. This is required in addition to the ETL coding, database development, and other architectural tasks.

Sometimes a seemingly reasonable user story is really an epic when the team forgets that the definition of done means production-quality workmanship. This includes writing all test cases, user documentation, and other ancillary but essential work.

Epics come in many forms, and with some experience the Agile development team is able to identify and decompose them before it is too late and they get scheduled into an iteration. While it is the right of the customer community to prioritize stories based on value, it is the right of the developers to estimate effort and identify epics.

Epics are either compound or complex (Cohn 2004), and there are two fundamental approaches to decomposing them. Compound epics should be split into a collection of separate user stories. The previous example with the complex conjunctive phrases is a good candidate for the splitting approach. The split lines for other epics may not be as obvious. Other epic-splitting approaches include the following (Cohn 2006):

- **Split on customer value.** An epic may represent a user story in its most glorious form. By separating out the highest-value aspects of the epic, and deferring the lower-value aspects, it is possible to shrink the epic to a story.

- **Split on data boundaries.** Data boundaries occur in multiple ways in a data warehouse architecture. By isolating a story to a single data source, to a single table, or even to a single column, it is possible to reduce a portion of an epic to a story. (See the anti-pattern sidebar on this approach.)
- **Split on operational boundaries.** When an epic represents multiple operations such as CRUD, split these into multiple stories in which each story provides a single operation.
- **Defer ancillary concerns.** Our typical goal is to incorporate issues like security, role-based access control, error handling, audit logging, and so forth into the completion of a story. While this is normally appropriate, if a story is too big it may be useful to defer these ancillary concerns until a later maturation story.
- **Defer nonfunctional requirements.** "Make it right before you make it faster" (Kernighan 1974). By deferring nonfunctional requirements, epics can be reduced to stories. The nonfunctional requirements can be addressed by a later card. Be forewarned, however, that these nonfunctional requirements are an important part of the definition of "Done! Done!" and should not be deferred for long. In fact, this technique for splitting epics should be viewed as an intentional choice to incur technical debt. That debt should be paid as soon as possible so that it doesn't accumulate.

Regardless of your epic-splitting approach, be sure to avoid splitting epics into tasks. Recall that a good user story is architecturally complete and represents business value; the resulting feature can be demonstrated to users; and the story is doable in a single iteration. Sometimes when an epic is difficult to split, it is tempting to start slicing it into tasks such as "Develop the ETL to populate the fact table." This should be avoided.

The Anti-Pattern of Splitting on Data Boundaries

Remember that Agile Analytics is a feature-driven approach rather than a data-driven approach. Our primary goal is to deliver business value irrespective of from where, or from how many sources, the data comes. The technique of splitting an epic on the basis of source data is contrary to this guiding principle. If we aren't careful, this strategy may cause us to shift into the traditional data-centric thinking that we are trying to avoid. However, if used sparingly and judiciously, this technique offers a useful tool for decomposing epics.

Complex epics should be made smaller and simpler so that they become good stories. The latter story example is well suited to the second approach. By temporarily removing the "top 10 percent" and the "profit margin" components, this story becomes smaller and simpler:

> As a financial forecaster I need the ability see profit ~~and profit margin~~ per customer per transaction for ~~the top 10 percent of~~ our customers so that I can identify the characteristics of the most profitable transactions.

This story may now be much more realistic for completion during a single iteration. If not, we may need to seek ways to simplify it even further. This approach requires that we create additional stories to mature the feature to its completion. For our example we may create two new stories, one for adding profit margin and another for presenting the top 10 percent of customers.

Luke Hohmann describes these small/simple stories as being like a baby. It is physically whole and complete with all the working parts, but it is immature and will grow over time. A feature must be architecturally whole and complete (and of production quality), but it may require incremental maturation over successive iterations before it is finished.

Finally, some stories are epics simply because they have a high degree of uncertainty or risk. These epics may require an exploratory or experimental "spike" to shake out the uncertainty or mitigate the risk. Experimental spikes should still result in something demonstrable but may be prototypical rather than production-ready. Sometimes these exploratory spikes may be for the purpose of comparing multiple technology or architectural alternatives to select the best one. In that case the work is demonstrable but disposable. In any case, the goal is to remove uncertainty and risk so that the stories that follow are well understood.

Agile Analytics Practice: Handle Epics Just in Time

Avoid worrying about all of the epics during initial planning. Some of them may be low enough on the prioritized backlog that you can defer them until later in the project. Grapple with the most important ones so that you can get busy planning the next few iterations. But flag the remaining epics so that you don't forget about them.

WHAT'S THE SMALLEST, SIMPLEST THING?

Data warehouse practitioners often have a difficult time envisioning how a user story can be completed in a single, short iteration. The goal of creating a production-quality working feature that is architecturally complete and is potentially releasable can be daunting. I sometimes work with data warehouse developers who declare every story an epic because they cannot imagine how it can be simplified enough to fit within an iteration.

Experienced agilists develop a variety of techniques for creatively simplifying a user story while still maintaining their focus on feature-driven development and production quality. Although developing this skill requires practice, one method that helps is to examine and simplify the specific tasks associated with the story.

Underlying every user story is a collection of implementation tasks that must be completed to deliver the completed feature. Tasks include both technical (data architecture, ETL development, etc.) and nontechnical (user documentation, quality assurance, etc.) activities for the team to accomplish. Tasks are the "to-do list" used by the implementation team to manage the details.

If your team is having difficulty envisioning how to complete a user story within a single iteration, try this: Sketch the conceptual architecture for your BI system on a whiteboard or flip chart. This is just a conceptual block diagram but should depict all of the essential architectural elements from the data source systems all the way through the data warehouse to the end-user application. You can decide later if you need more, or less, detail. Your diagram might look something like the one shown in Figure 4.8.

Now, select a user story that seems daunting. Starting with the end user in your diagram, work your way backward through the architectural diagram. At each block or transition in the diagram ask the question "What is the smallest, simplest thing that is needed here to complete this story?" Write the answer as a task on a sticky note, and stick it in the appropriate place on the diagram next to the corresponding component.

Now that you have identified the critical technical tasks, make another pass through the architecture asking, "What additional quality assurance tasks or nontechnical tasks need to be completed?" Be sure to add the necessary

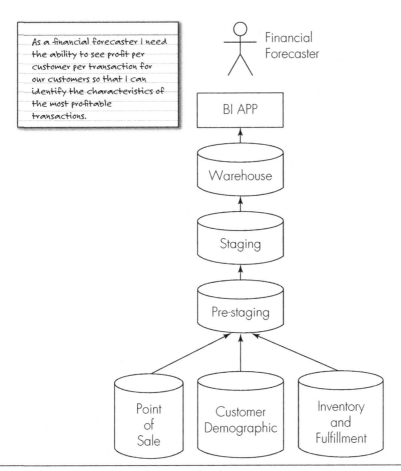

As a financial forecaster I need the ability to see profit per customer per transaction for our customers so that I can identify the characteristics of the most profitable transactions.

Financial Forecaster

BI APP

Warehouse

Staging

Pre-staging

Point of Sale

Customer Demographic

Inventory and Fulfillment

Figure 4.8 Conceptual architecture sketch

task notes for testing, documentation, training, and so on. Now your diagram might look something like what is shown in Figure 4.9.

Once the team has created all the task notes it can think of, the group should answer the question "Working collaboratively and in parallel, can our team complete all of these tasks within a single iteration?" If the answer is no, you should identify the tasks that appear problematic and seek to further simplify them. Generally only one or two tasks are the culprits, allowing the team to focus on those problem areas. Now it's time for the team to think creatively about how to further simplify these time-consuming tasks.

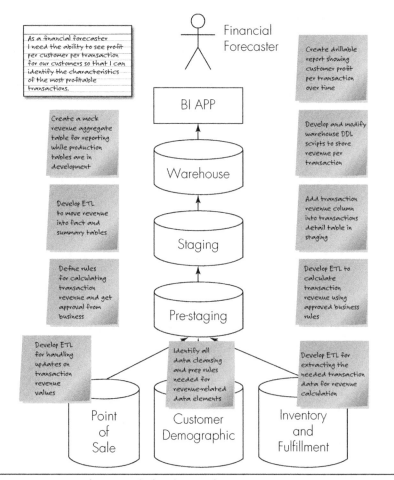

Figure 4.9 Overlaying task detail on architecture

Example

As an example, I recently worked with a data warehousing team that was wrestling with the challenges of calculating online advertising revenue as part of completing a user story. The business logic for calculating revenue was relatively complex and involved the use of an ancillary ad rates table. Populating a rates table was itself challenging, based on complicated business rules in which ad rates are different for different advertisers and subject to monthly changes. Finally, this was further complicated by the fact that the revenue calculation business logic was not well defined and agreed upon. All of these complexities were affecting a couple of ETL development tasks needed to properly populate the ad rates table and the revenue measures in a fact and summary table.

The team members decided to simplify the problem in a few creative ways:

- First, they chose to use a simpler (and initially incorrect) set of rules for calculating revenue. They would design their ETL so that they could easily and quickly replace the simple/incorrect rule with the more complicated/correct rule. This decision caused them to make better overall ETL design decisions because they realized that all business rules need to be easily modified. The team also added a task for the business analyst to determine, finalize, and confirm the revenue calculation logic so that it could be ready to plug in during the next iteration.
- Second, the team chose to start out by using a simplified ad rates table in which the rates didn't initially change monthly. The team made plans to incrementally mature the revenue-reporting feature by updating the ad rates table to include varying monthly rates. This decision caused the team to develop more modular ETL code to make it easier to incrementally add code to handle the monthly rate changes.

These two simplifying steps enabled the team members to craft an early, and admittedly immature, user story. They agreed that they could demonstrate the revenue-reporting feature to their users by explaining their simplifying assumptions. They created a second user story for maturing the initial feature to include the correct revenue logic and the changing monthly ad rates.

So, did this team cheat? The team members developed a feature that was demonstrable to end users; they needed to explain their simplifying assumptions to end users; they did production-quality work; and they planned to correct their simplifying assumptions in the very next iteration. Their simplification decisions also motivated them to create a better implementation design that enabled them to more easily adapt to changes. They didn't cheat; they judiciously and creatively identified the smallest, simplest thing that still satisfied the spirit of feature-driven development.

Often the problem is not the magnitude of any single task, but instead the dependencies between tasks. Teams say things like "We can't create the BI report until the rate and revenue summary tables are ready. We can't create the rate and revenue tables until the ETL code is written to pull the necessary data from the source systems; and we still need the business logic for how revenue should be calculated." None of these tasks takes the full iteration by itself, but completing all of them in sequence will take longer than the iteration length.

In these cases the team must think creatively about how to keep team members from being blocked waiting for one another. This is often done by creating disposable "scaffolding" or "mock" components. For example, if the MicroStrategy report developer needs the rate and revenue summary tables, he or she might manually mock up disposable replicas of those tables so that the reports can be built while the ETL and database developers are creating the real tables. The ETL developers might mock up the revenue logic while the business analyst confirms the real logic. Application developers use these mocking and scaffolding techniques as a normal part of their development methods. We can do the same things in database and data warehouse development.

It should be emphasized that this activity of sketching your conceptual architecture and evaluating the underlying tasks is not a routine Agile planning practice. Identifying all tasks for each story during project planning is too inefficient. However, it is an effective technique for learning how to think about stories in their smallest, simplest form. It can also be an effective technique for better understanding user stories that are somewhat vague or ambiguous to the team. Once you've developed this skill, you can more accurately identify true epics and move faster during story writing and planning. Generally speaking, task detailing is done in a "just-in-time" fashion during iteration planning. Effective Agile teams are able to think implicitly about task detail as they estimate effort, but the concrete identification of tasks occurs later.

Agile Analytics Practice: Do Less

Agile teams seek ways to deliver something smaller and simpler, sooner. This practice shortens the customer feedback loop and helps developers build the things that matter and avoid wasting time on things that don't.

STORY PRIORITIZATION AND BACKLOG MANAGEMENT

User stories are managed on a prioritized product backlog. The backlog is simply a visible chart or dedicated wall space where the story cards (index cards) are hung in priority order from the next most important user story to the least important one in top-to-bottom order. The backlog should hang in the collaborative team workspace where any community member can review it or work with it at any time. It is a highly dynamic artifact that is the basis for ongoing iteration planning and release replanning.

A word of caution: New teams (with the best intentions) often move their backlog into an electronic form such as a Microsoft Excel workbook, a relational database, or one of the various Agile project management tools available on the market. There is a lot of value in keeping the backlog visible and accessible in a way that enables the team to gather around it for conversations. Much of this value is lost by moving the backlog into electronic formats. I strongly encourage Agile data warehousing teams to keep their backlog in a low-tech medium, such as index cards, on the wall unless there is a compelling reason to store it electronically (e.g., Sarbanes-Oxley compliance, geographically distributed teams, etc.). Don't be too eager to go high-tech with your backlog management, even though it may be tempting to do so.

Scott Ambler introduces three models for prioritizing requirements in *Agile Best Practice* (Ambler 2005a). These include the Product Backlog approach from Scrum, the Work Item List from the Disciplined Agile Delivery method, and the Option Pool from Lean/Kanban development. Each of these is a powerful method for requirements prioritization. In this chapter we will focus on the Product Backlog approach from Scrum.

Value-Based Prioritization

Agile Analytics development is about the frequent delivery of high-value, working software to the customer/user community. Doing so requires the prioritization of user stories and the continuous monitoring of the prioritized story backlog. The primary driver for prioritization is customer value. However, it is insufficient to simply say that the highest-value stories are the highest priority. Product owners must also factor in the cost of development. An extremely valuable feature quickly loses its luster when it is also extremely costly to implement. Additionally, there are other secondary drivers such as risk and uncertainty. These should be resolved early. There may also be experimental stories that are worth developing early to find out whether customers see value in further development along those lines. For example, a wireless company's user community may need a basis for determining the value of a data mining model that profiles the top five predictors of customer churn. It may be beneficial to conduct an early experiment on this capability to provide the user community with the information they need to value the feature. There may be other prioritization drivers, but business value should always be foremost.

While each project is different, a good model for value-based prioritization is as follows:

1. Complete the high-value, high-risk stories first if the cost is justified.
2. Complete the high-value, low-risk stories next if the cost is justified.

3. Complete the lower-value, low-risk stories next.
4. Avoid low-value, high-risk stories.

In their book *Stand Back and Deliver* (Pixton et al. 2009), the authors introduce the Purpose Alignment Model for prioritizing on the basis of aligning project requirements with organizational strategy. The Purpose Alignment Model considers decisions along two dimensions. The first is the extent to which the activity differentiates the organization in the marketplace, and the second is the extent to which the activity is mission-critical. This yields four categories:

- **Differentiating activities:** market-differentiating and mission-critical. These are the "game-changing" kinds of activities.
- **Parity activities:** mission-critical but not market-differentiating. These are the activities that are essential to remaining competitive.
- **Partnering activities:** market-differentiating but not mission-critical. These are opportunities to find a partner with which you can combine efforts rather than bear the total cost of ownership internally.
- **Who cares activities:** neither market-differentiating nor mission-critical. These activities deserve minimal time and consideration.

The Purpose Alignment Model is very relevant to data warehousing, business intelligence, and data management projects. An example of this is enterprise data modeling. Enterprise data models offer value when they accurately model the business domain, and they highlight optimization opportunities or inconsistencies. These discoveries can reflect mission criticality and/or market differentiation. However, when enterprise data models simply parrot all existing and legacy systems, they can become overly complicated and overbuilt, adding little value and incurring significant cost. Replacing the term *activities* in the Purpose Alignment Model with *user stories* can help the product owner prioritize the backlog in alignment with organizational strategy.

Whether you adopt these guidelines or some other one, ensure that the entire team understands the prioritization guidelines. Otherwise the prioritization process will suffer from conflicting perspectives.

Capability-Based Prioritization

For very large or complex projects with a high volume of user stories it is often beneficial to group stories into themes or capabilities such as "Customer

Profitability Analysis" or "Operating Cost Analysis." This enables you to prioritize the aggregate collections of stories and avoid becoming mired in the sheer number of stories. Prioritizing on the basis of capabilities may also help constrain various release themes. For example, the first 90-day release of the BI system may deliver customer value analytics; the second release of the system may add retail store analysis; and so on. Then the stories that support the theme of the current release can be prioritized separately from those that are deferred until later.

Prioritization Process

As with other Agile practices, prioritizing is an incremental and iterative process. The process begins with coarse-grained prioritization and moves incrementally toward detailed prioritization.

The first pass is a coarse-grained "bucketing" of user stories into thirds—the highest-priority group, the middle-priority group, and the lowest-priority group. It is sometimes hard for the customer community to assign stories to a "low-priority" category because everything is important. Therefore, I prefer to label these priority bins *high*, *higher*, and *highest*. While this doesn't trick anyone, it conveys the important message that we intend to develop all of the stories; we just need to know which one to develop first.

The project community should conduct this coarse-grained prioritization around a table by creating three stacks of story cards. The process should move quickly, and the team should avoid overanalyzing whether a card belongs in one group rather than another since prioritization is not final and cards can be moved. Ensure that the three priority groups are equally balanced.

The next pass is a fine-grained prioritization of the top third. Focusing on this top tier helps the team avoid spending too much up-front energy on the wrong thing. Fine-grained prioritization follows these steps:

1. The technical community estimates the top-tier user stories using story-point estimating (see the next section of this chapter).
2. The technical community identifies stories with high technical risk or uncertainty.
3. The customer community applies prioritization guidelines to rank-order the top-tier stories according to priority.

The ultimate goal of backlog prioritization is to establish a clear under-standing of the next most important thing to develop. However, getting to this state is almost never easy. It requires evaluating cost-benefits, analyzing trade-offs, compromising, and collaborative bartering. It is the right of the customer community to set priorities, but the technical community must provide input and guidance in the process.

Backlog Management

Once the backlog is established and prioritized, it must be continuously maintained and managed. User stories move off the backlog in priority order as they are scheduled into an iteration for development. When they are completed and accepted, they are marked as such. The product owner and customer community have the responsibility of continuously reviewing and refining the backlog. As new knowledge about the BI system and the business needs unfolds, the priorities may change. As the project community gains clarity on certain stories, they may become obsolete or change. At any given moment, the backlog should reflect the most current understanding and prioritization of user features. Whenever the development team has an opportunity to work on something new, there should be no debate that the next most important thing is the story card that is at the top of the backlog.

The identification of user stories is never absolutely complete. During release planning we strive to identify a comprehensive set of the most important stories, but during the project stories will be redefined or eliminated, and new ones will be written. I've worked on many BI projects in which story definitions evolve as users' understanding of BI solutions matures. Don't be afraid to tear up a story card if it no longer seems relevant. If it turns out to be important, it will resurface later.

> **Agile Analytics Practice: Continuous Backlog Grooming**
>
> The product owner, in partnership with the co-development customers, should pay continuous attention to the product backlog. Grooming the backlog includes shaping the user stories, reprioritizing them, and adding new details as they are discovered. Doing this will ensure that the backlog is an accurate reflection of what is planned.

STORY-POINT ESTIMATING

In addition to writing *the* book on user stories, Mike Cohn is the authority on Agile estimating and planning, and his methods apply very appropriately to Agile Analytics development (Cohn 2006). This section serves as an introduction to Mike's techniques but is not a substitute for reading his more comprehensive treatment of this complex topic.

First let's acknowledge that we aren't very good at accurately estimating development effort and complexity. Traditional phased project management focuses on breaking down work into tasks and activities (work breakdown structures), estimating the person-hours required to complete each task, parallelizing wherever possible, then adding it all up to get an overall project time estimate. The success of the project is measured in terms of how well the team executes to the plan.

There are numerous reasons why this approach doesn't work. Each task estimate has error built in, and all that error gets added into the project total. Estimating is done up front when project uncertainty is greatest. It doesn't incorporate frequent replanning and re-estimating opportunities to make adjustments and corrections in light of new knowledge. Estimates become contractual obligations, so they get artificially padded at each step in the process. Estimation is often in terms of developer hours per task, which doesn't account for multitasking, distractions, and other external influences.

One of the biggest reasons work breakdown structure estimating doesn't work is that you cannot estimate tasks without really understanding the "product." Stories force you to understand the product and the customer value it represents first.

Imagine that you are asked to estimate the distance from your workplace to your home in centimeters. Assuming you live a reasonable distance from work, it's going to take you a lot longer to evaluate the distance in centimeters than it would in kilometers or miles. In fact, you'll probably start out estimating in a coarser-grained unit like kilometers and then converting to centimeters. (If you live in the United States you may take even more conversion steps.) It isn't appropriate to estimate large, uncertain things like long distances in fine-grained units like centimeters; nor is it appropriate to estimate project lengths in fine-grained time units like developer hours or even days.

Painters use square feet of space to estimate the cost of a painting job. For years software developers have looked for a similar unit of output to estimate. Both the early use of lines of code and later use of function points attempted to be this "unit." Unfortunately, both can be estimated only late in the development process—they were developed to complement a waterfall lifecycle process. Agile developers needed something new.

Story points are a nebulous unit of effort that enable us to avoid using clock time or developer time. Story points are relative. A 100-point story is expected to take twice as much effort as a 50-point story and half as much effort as a 200-point story. The actual point values are irrelevant so long as the development team uses its point scheme consistently.

To illustrate the concept, consider how you might select a car at the ACME Car Rental agency. They offer economy, compact, midsize, standard, full-size, and minivan classes of vehicles. Now it isn't really necessary to estimate the precise differences in the bumper-to-bumper length or interior volume of each car class to decide which class you need. Let's start with the standard car class and assign it an arbitrary value of 10. Since a minivan is about twice as large, we might assign it a point value of 20. The economy class gets a 6 since it isn't fully half as large as a standard but still significantly smaller. We'll assign the compact class 8 points, and the full-size class 14 points. Now we have a set of "car points" that describe the relative differences among these car classes. As long as we understand and agree upon our "car points" scheme, these numbers are relevant and meaningful.

We can do the same thing with user stories since some of them are relatively simple and straightforward while others are complex, risky, and uncertain. The numbering scheme you select for story points should reflect the notion of relativity. Two good numbering schemes are {1, 2, 4, 8, 16} and {1, 2, 3, 5, 8, 13}. The first one works because each number is simply two times the prior number. The second one is the first six numbers in the Fibonacci sequence starting at 1. This is meaningful because the gaps in the sequence become larger as the numbers get larger. This supports the goal of clearly separating bigger story estimates while allowing smaller ones to be a bit finer-grained. Numbering schemes like {1, 2, 3, 4, 5, 6} aren't a good idea because they promote unnecessary debate about whether something is a 5 or a 6 since these numbers sit so close together. If you really want to appear impressive, choose large numbers like {100, 200, 400, 800, 1,600} which will give the impression that the team is very productive.

To bootstrap the estimating process we must have a starter story to establish a point of reference. First, let's agree to use a {100, 200, 400, 800, 1,600} story-point scheme. Second, let's choose a moderately complex story and assign it a baseline reference value of 400 (see Figure 4.10). The reference story doesn't have to be one of the new user stories. If there is a story available that has already been implemented, and the team is familiar with it, this is a good candidate for the baseline reference. Ideally this reference story is not overly simplistic or complex. It should be of relatively moderate complexity.

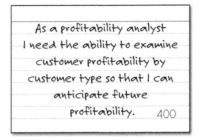

Figure 4.10   Story-point reference baseline

From this reference we now have the ability to assign story-point estimates to other stories by asking the questions "Is this harder, easier, or about the same as our reference story?" and "How much harder or easier?" Now in relative (and approximate) terms we can assign point values to the other user stories (see Figure 4.11).

The beauty of estimating in story points is that it keeps the team thinking in coarse-grained terms, which is akin to estimating long distances in kilometers rather than centimeters. There will be times when a team member might say something like "This is more than a 200 but less than a 400." Avoid the temptation to use point values between your agreed-upon values.

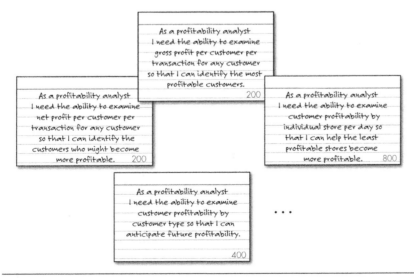

Figure 4.11   Relative story-point estimates

Restricting estimates to a small, discrete set of point values will help the team avoid overthinking these estimates. When in doubt on a point value, take the more conservative estimate to allow for the unknown tasks. If it turns out that a story is easier than you originally estimated, you can celebrate the earlier completion of a feature.

It is the right (and job) of the development team to estimate effort in story points. It is essential that the entire development team be involved in the estimating process. This practice has two distinct benefits. First, it ensures buy-in and ownership by the entire development team. Team buy-in and ownership are critical components of the success of self-managing teams. Second, it injects a sort of "checks and balances" into the estimating process. When everyone agrees on an estimate, the team quickly moves on to the next story. However, disagreement on the estimate suggests that either team members have differing understandings of the story or there is a high degree of uncertainty or risk in the story.

Don't be tempted to expedite the planning process by having the project manager, technical lead, or chief architect handle the estimating single-handedly. When the entire team is involved in planning and estimating, there is tremendous value in the conversations that ensue. Collaborative planning generates questions whose answers lead to greater clarity of understanding by all team members. It creates early opportunities to identify risk and uncertainty. And team planning ultimately leads to a galvanization of the product vision. These gains are well worth the time required for collaborative planning.

Development *velocity* is the key to the effectiveness of story-point estimating. Velocity is the demonstrated number of story points a team is able to complete and have accepted in a single iteration. A team's *capacity* is its steady-state velocity after the team establishes its sustainable development pace or rhythm.

Suppose a team commits to the completion of four user stories at the beginning of an iteration. The point values of these stories are 100, 400, 200, and 200 for a total goal of 900 points. If the team finishes all four stories, but the customer community accepts only the last three stories based on the acceptance criteria, the team velocity for that iteration is only 800, not 900. The remaining 100-point story is not finished until user feedback is addressed and the customer community accepts the feature. This highlights the importance of developer-customer collaboration and the clear definition of acceptance criteria. Nonetheless, user expectations are always subject to change, and we must embrace and adapt to that change.

Monitoring velocity establishes the basis for the next iteration plan. A development team should not commit to more points than its demonstrated velocity. Even though our hypothetical team did more than 800 points worth of work, it should commit to only 800 points for the next iteration. Now suppose the team commits to finishing the 100-point story plus three additional stories with point values of 100, 200, and 400. The effort required to finish the "hangover" story is minimal, and the team finishes all 800 points of work at the beginning of the second week of a two-week iteration. It now has the option of plucking one or more additional stories from the backlog (or the next iteration plan). The team collectively agrees to commit to an additional 200-point story. At the end of the iteration the features are showcased to the user community and are all accepted. The team's new demonstrated velocity is 1,000 points, so it can now make the next iteration commitments based on this velocity.

Another benefit of tracking velocity is that it enables the project community to anticipate the *cut line* on the prioritized backlog. The cut line is an imaginary line on a theoretically infinite backlog of user stories. The cut line represents the volume of story work that can be completed by a development team during a timeboxed project cycle. Since the team's capacity is finite, the project timeline is bounded, and the backlog is prioritized according to business value—the project community can anticipate which, and how many, stories will be delivered during the project cycle.

When an Agile team begins a new project, or a new team is forming, it may take several iterations for the team to match its velocity to its true capacity. During this time it is important that the team base its current commitments on the previously demonstrated velocity. This supports the well-known principle of undercommitting and overdelivering. I have worked with many new teams that succumb to the pressure to overcommit during early iterations. When they don't meet their commitments, they are demoralized. It is much more gratifying to celebrate a boost in velocity through overdelivery than to be discouraged by overcommitment.

Over time every team will establish its steady-state capacity. Capacity and velocity should not be used as productivity metrics for comparing one team with another, or one project with another. Capacity and velocity should be used only within a project to monitor whether the team is operating at peak efficiency. Planning should always be capacity-based. A project community should base project plans and expectations on the actual capacity of the team. Avoid the temptation to do what Jim Highsmith calls "wish-based planning." Business intelligence projects almost always have the natural tension between the desires and wishes of the customer community and the finite capacity of the development team. While the development team should work to maximize its capacity, the entire project community must maintain a realistic set of expectations. Because the focus is on the highest-value user stories, it is sometimes the case that developing the top 20 percent of user stories addresses the vast majority of the business needs of the user community.

PARKING LOT DIAGRAMS

Agile Analytics projects are primarily focused on delivering the next highest-value set of user stories in the current iteration. However, this should not imply that an Agile Analytics project simply shuffles from one iteration to the next without any clear understanding of when the current release cycle will be complete. We've spoken about release planning as the mechanism for establishing a release date and estimating the set of user capabilities and stories that will be completed within that timebox. The parking lot diagram provides a way of monitoring the overall health and status of a complex data warehousing project.

The parking lot diagram was developed by Jeff DeLuca and Peter Coad as a Feature Driven Development (FDD) practice (Palmer and Felsing 2002). FDD is distinguished by its business domain decomposition approach in which the domain is decomposed into functional *subject areas*, which are made up of *business activities* that contain a categorized *feature list*. Features are synonymous with user stories. Business activities may stem from complex use cases or epics. Subject areas may stem from capability cases.

Figure 4.12 depicts a parking lot for the first release of the FlixBuster Analytics system. This project represents a six-month release plan running timeboxed from January to July of 2008. A look at the example parking lot quickly conveys that the project is mostly on track, with the exception of the red business activity box, which is slightly behind schedule. This helps focus project monitoring on the delayed business activity and triggers a conversation about the impact of the delay and plans for getting it completed. Parking lot diagrams can easily be created in Excel workbooks or in a graphical tool like Visio.

Figure 4.13 describes the key elements in a parking lot diagram. The outermost boxes outline the project's major *business subject areas* using boxed groupings of *business activities* (capabilities). The business activities contain status information, including color[1] to represent the stage of work in

---

1.. Although Figures 4.12 and 4.13 are shown in gray in this book, parking lot diagrams are typically color-coded using red to indicate activities that require attention and green for those that are complete.

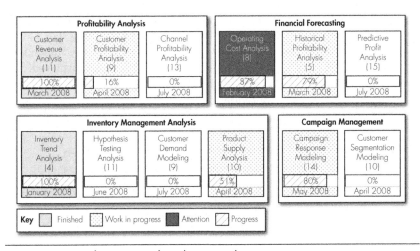

Figure 4.12   FlixBuster parking lot example

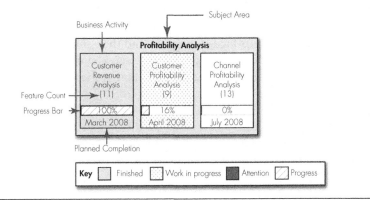

Figure 4.13   Parking lot elements

progress, a status bar to convey the percentage of completeness for each business activity, a date when each activity is expected to be completed, and the number of user stories or story points that are required for completion. Other relevant information can also be included.

The parking lot is intended to provide at-a-glance project status, not detailed status. Community members and stakeholders should use it as a starting point for deeper exploration and monitoring as needed. Note that the dates on the business activity boxes are at the month level, and the feature count does not convey any of the story detail. Alternatively this number can represent the estimated story points rather than feature count.

The parking lot should be used frequently to realign the project community's understanding of project health and status. It should be updated at the end of each iteration and used as part of status reporting to the stakeholder community. The parking lot is a powerful tool that can be displayed on a project wiki alongside other project residue that supports the goal of high visibility into development activities.

> **Agile Analytics Practice: Publish the Parking Lot**
>
> Publish a project parking lot in the team's workspace and keep it up-to-date to clearly communicate the health of the project at all times. This gives the team a big-picture sense of its progress, as well as an at-a-glance status for people outside the development team.

WRAP-UP

One of the most fundamental shifts from traditional DW/BI development to Agile Analytics development is the explicit focus on delivering working features to end users. Our focus is on *users* and their *stories* about what they need to be able to do. Our goal is to capture those stories, prioritize them, and deliver features that satisfy the highest-value stories as early as possible.

This chapter introduced user stories as an alternative to more traditional functional requirements. A user story is distinct in that it represents a demonstrable feature that can be completed in a single short iteration. It is written from the point of view of a specific user role, and it describes the goal of that user.

We have examined how to identify all of the user roles that should be considered and mapping those roles into imaginary personas to help us understand them better. Use-case modeling is a valuable language for evaluating how different user roles need to interact with the business intelligence system. This chapter showed how to begin with user roles, personas, and use-case diagrams—and then incrementally flesh out more detail by moving to use cases and then teasing out user stories.

One of the challenges with user stories is that they are sometimes too large to be completed in a single iteration. These stories are called epics, and several techniques were introduced to show how to decompose epics into smaller, simpler stories.

Once the lion's share of stories have been identified and written, the next step is to prioritize them onto a well-managed backlog of stories. Prioritization is primarily based on user value, but we also seek to give higher priority to risky and uncertain user stories. A two-pass method for quickly prioritizing user stories was introduced. The first pass is a coarse-grained grouping of stories, and the second pass is a more detailed assessment of the highest-priority group.

Chapter 5

SELF-ORGANIZING TEAMS BOOST PERFORMANCE

Agile data warehousing teams are self-organizing. The fifth guiding principle behind the Agile Manifesto (see Chapter 1, "Introducing Agile Analytics") says, "We value the importance of talented and experienced business intelligence experts. We give them the environment and support they need, and trust them to get the job done." This principle has a lot of implications, including that there is no substitute for having the right people on the team, and that there is much value in enabling the team to self-organize and self-manage.

The problem with self-organization lies in the potential for improper or sloppy behaviors. Self-organization and self-management do not imply no organization and no management. Instead, they imply that the locus of leadership and decision making is housed within the Agile team, not externally. In some Agile circles the term *self-management* has become synonymous with anarchy—no defined leaders. However, effective Agile Analytics teams have leaders; they have project managers, technical leaders, product managers, and others. Those leaders are integral members of the Agile team; they do not manage from on high. Moreover, such teams are self-organizing within the context of appropriate corporate governance. They still must adhere to organizational standards and align their performance with the goals of the company.

Most of the Agile failures that I have witnessed (fortunately very few) happened not because Agile methods don't work, but because the Agile project community failed to be disciplined, focused, rigorous, and intentional in its practices and behaviors. The early chapters of this book were focused on Agile core values and guiding principles. Most of the other chapters are focused on introducing specific Agile practices. This chapter is focused on another consideration, the behaviors and habits that are required for a self-organizing/self-managing team to succeed. These Agile Analytics behaviors lie in the nooks and crannies between values, principles, and practices. They are about teams adopting the right attitudes and habits as they implement the practices.

Failure to intentionally incorporate these self-organizing team behaviors can cause project delays, inhibit teams from maximizing productivity, lead to internal conflict or unrealistic external expectations, and be generally disruptive to the success of a project. This chapter is devoted to many of the hygienic behaviors that are essential to running an effective Agile Analytics project.

WHAT IS A SELF-ORGANIZING TEAM?

In his book *Drive: The Surprising Truth about What Motivates Us* (Pink 2009), Daniel Pink distills a significant body of psychological and sociological research to analyze the factors that contribute to personal and professional high performance. A key conclusion of his analysis is that people are motivated by three factors:

- **Autonomy.** People want to have control over their work.
- **Mastery.** People want to get better at what they do.
- **Purpose.** People want to be part of something that is bigger than they are.

Furthermore, he points out that people are not motivated by traditional management "carrots and sticks" such as bonuses or performance reviews.

These key factors are also key ingredients of highly effective Agile teams. High-performing Agile teams manage their own processes, techniques, and outcomes; they seek to continuously improve; and they are excited about their contribution to the greater good. The following FlixBuster BI team scenario demonstrates the characteristics of a high-performing and self-organizing team.

Scenario

It's 10:00 A.M. on Thursday morning in the first week of iteration five in the Flix-Buster Analytics project's 90-day (six-iteration) planning cycle. The project has progressed nicely through the first four iterations, and the DW/BI system is expected to be deployed into production in about three weeks.

Unfortunately, this iteration is not going smoothly. On Tuesday Natasha, the lead ETL developer, had to take a sudden leave of absence for a personal emergency. It is uncertain when she will return.

In addition, the team arrived this morning to discover that many of the continuous integration tests were suddenly failing. Apparently FlixTrans, the company's transactional system, was upgraded to version 4.0 overnight. This new version has significant data model changes, causing some of the ETL code to stop working. The FlixBuster Analytics team members were unaware of this upgrade. Had they known about the upgrade plans, they could have been prepared to handle the changes. Now they are caught off guard without their lead ETL programmer.

Arlene convenes the technical team to assess the situation. Prakash has already gathered some information about the FlixTrans upgrade, including the new data model. But he hasn't had much time to analyze it yet. Francisco, the team's release manager and sometime developer, reminds the team that he has been pair programming a lot lately with Natasha in his effort to become a better Informatica developer.

Francisco and Prakash agree to spend the next hour together to evaluate the ETL code that is impacted by the new transactional data model. They commit to sharing their findings with the team within an hour.

At 11:00 A.M. the team reconvenes, and Francisco and Prakash present their findings. Apparently, several of the core tables in FlixTrans have been revised. In some cases the changes are superficial, such as column name changes. However, in other cases they are more significant structural changes, such as data type changes and the addition of new columns, and in one case a single table was split into two new tables. Their conservative estimate is that it will take the entire team one day to fix all of the broken ETL code and get all the tests passing again.

Adriana points out that the team has committed to an ambitious backlog for this iteration and, with the loss of Natasha, is already stretched to meet those commitments. Henry, the team quality assurance expert, reminds everyone about the team agreement that a broken build is a top-priority "showstopper."

Arlene suggests that the team work through lunch to develop a plan of attack for mitigating these new problems. Everyone agrees with Arlene, and Bob, the team's business analyst and sometime developer, comments that this would be a good time to use the "Six Thinking Hats" method (de Bono 1999) for group decision making that he's been learning about. He's been telling the group about this for several weeks now, and everyone is intrigued. They agree to give it a try.

Bob goes to the team room whiteboard and creates six vertical columns. At the top of the first column he draws a white top hat and writes "Facts/Information" below it. He draws a red hat above the second column and labels it "Emotions/ Feelings." Above the third he draws a yellow hat labeled "Benefits/Positives." The fourth hat is black, labeled "Drawbacks/Negatives." The fifth is green, labeled "Creative/Unconventional." And the sixth is blue, labeled "Facilitation."

Bob explains that the process involves everyone figuratively wearing the same hat at the same time and suppressing the urge to switch hats without the whole group doing so. For example, if the group is wearing the green "unconventional thinking" hat, that is not the time to be critical or negative about outlandish ideas because criticism is reserved for black hat thinking. He also points out that there's nothing bad about black hat thinking, when the group is in that mode, and that the blue hat is for summarizing a discussion and switching group hat colors if needed. Anyone at any time can request a blue hat period to keep the discussion productive.

Bob asks the team to start in white hat mode and asks for all of the facts and information they have. As team members verbalize these, Bob writes them in the white hat column. This doesn't take long, and Jamal requests a blue hat switch. He summarizes the white hat discussion by pointing out that it is almost certain that the current iteration's workload exceeds the team's normal capacity. Everyone agrees.

Jamal is frustrated and calls for a switch to red hat to vent in a constructive way for a bit. Bob writes down the team's frustrations in the red hat column: They weren't notified of the FlixTrans upgrade; these problems are too late in the 90-day project cycle to absorb easily; the project has been on track until now, but the team may look bad anyway; nobody should blame the team because these problems are outside its control; and others.

Henry calls for the blue hat again and suggests this summary: "We're frustrated with the circumstances but don't want to let this derail our project." The team agrees with that sentiment, and so Bob suggests switching to the green hat to figure out what to do.

Arlene thanks the team for not blaming the FlixTrans surprise on her. It's part of her role to be aware of external factors that might impede or block the team. Unfortunately she hasn't spent much time with the FlixTrans project leaders, and so she wasn't aware of the upgrade. She commits to better collaboration with all of the source system team leaders in the future.

In green hat mode the team considers solutions to the problem. Team members come up with working over the weekend, working long days for the rest of the sprint, hiring a temporary ETL developer until Natasha returns, shrinking or simplifying user stories, eliminating stories from this sprint backlog, or turning the problem over to the broader project community for a decision.

When green hat ideas stop emerging, Bob suggests switching to yellow hat thinking—the benefits of these ideas. Francisco asks who is willing to work weekends and/or late nights. Most members of the team say they could, but Adriana has her kids this weekend so that won't work for her. Bob has a few evening obligations that may be a problem. Other members of the team are understanding of this and reassure Adriana and Bob that there are no expectations of them. Adriana also mentions that she has a friend who is an Informatica developer and an independent contractor. He may be available to help out on short notice. Finally, Prakash points out that shrinking or eliminating user stories has the benefit of getting the rest of the project community to share the burden.

Bob suggests that the team shift to black hat thinking before making any action plans. They agree and quickly come up with a set of drawbacks: Working long hours may affect quality and may set a bad precedent for the future; it would take time to get a temporary ETL developer up to speed; it may not be possible to shrink or eliminate stories and still have a minimally complete feature.

After reviewing the discussion, the team quickly agrees to take three actions. The technical team will first focus on fixing the broken ETL and failing tests. Second, the team will make plans to work long hours and through the weekend to bridge. Third, Arlene will convene a brief meeting of the entire project community to share the current issues and ideas for mitigation, and to ask for additional input and support. When the team is finished, the whiteboard looks like Figure 5.1.

WHITE HAT	RED HAT	YELLOW HAT
FACTS / INFO	EMOTIONS / FEELINGS	BENEFITS / POSITIVE
NATASHA IS ABSENT FOR THE FORESEEABLE FUTURE.	WHY DIDN'T THE FLIXTRANS TEAM NOTIFY US?	MOST OF TEAM WILLING TO WORK WEEKEND
ONE WHOLE DAY TO FIX ETL	THE PROJECT HAS BEEN ON TRACK UNTIL NOW.	
THERE IS NO TEAM CAPACITY BUFFER BUILT INTO THIS ITERATION.	WHO UPGRADES PRODUCTION SW MIDWEEK?	PROBLEM SHARED BY WHOLE COMMUNITY
ITERATION FIVE IS OUR LAST BIG CHANCE TO COMPLETE FIRST RELEASE STORIES.	WE CAN'T BE BLAMED FOR PROBLEMS OUTSIDE OUR CONTROL.	ADRIANA KNOWS AN ETL DEVELOPER WHO MIGHT BE AVAILABLE.
	ARLENE IS GRATEFUL THAT THE TEAM DOESN'T BLAME HER.	

BLACK HAT	GREEN HAT	BLUE HAT
DRAWBACKS / NEGATIVES	CREATIVE / UNCONVENTIONAL	FACILITATION
QUALITY MAY SUFFER.	WORK THROUGH THE WEEKEND.	CURRENT WORKLOAD EXCEEDS TEAM CAPACITY.
MAY SET A BAD PRECEDENT	WORK LONG DAYS FOR THE REST OF SPRINT.	FRUSTRATED WITH THE CIRCUMSTANCES BUT DON'T WANT THIS TO DERAIL PROJECT.
CUSTOMERS ALREADY FEEL THAT STORIES HAVE BEEN SIMPLIFIED.	NEGOTIATE SMALLER & SIMPLER VERSIONS OF STORIES.	TEAM WILL PLAN TO WORK OVER THE WEEKEND.
FINAL STORIES ARE NEEDED TO COMPLETE THE FEATURE.	ELIMINATE STORIES FROM SPRINT BACKLOG.	PROJECT COMMUNITY WILL BE ASKED TO SHARE DECISION.
TEMP ETL DEV. MUST BE BROUGHT UP TO SPEED.	HIRE TEMPORARY ETL DEV. UNTIL NATASHA RETURNS.	
	LET PROJECT COMMUNITY DECIDE.	

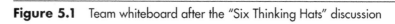

Figure 5.1   Team whiteboard after the "Six Thinking Hats" discussion

As Prakash and Francisco get started refactoring the ETL code to adapt to the revised data model, Arlene manages to get some time from the project sponsors, most of the co-development group, and a couple of the management stakeholders. The meeting is scheduled for 3:30 the same afternoon.

At 3:30 the project community gathers in the team room where Arlene quickly outlines the recent challenges that are plaguing the team. She reviews the Six Thinking Hats ideas and decisions that are still on the whiteboard, and she asks the group if they have any other thoughts or ideas to add. Allen, the CTO, says that he will immediately begin working with other IT leaders to avoid these types of problems in the future. Pete, the VP of finance, says that he will happily pay the cost of hiring Adriana's ETL developer friend if the team thinks that would help. The technical team agrees to discuss this further to determine whether it would be beneficial. As expected, the co-development users have a difficult time shrinking or eliminating any current user stories from the backlog. But they agree to spend time with Dieter after this meeting to think creatively about how they might reduce the scope of the current iteration.

Gary, the VP of sales and a stakeholder whose department will benefit from the first release of the system, comments on how impressed he is by the way the team handled these current circumstances. He likes the fact that the team has made these issues immediately visible to everyone, and that everybody is focused more on solutions than on blaming others for the problem. Pete seconds this sentiment and also points out how impressed he is by the Six Thinking Hats approach that the team used to handle the challenge. He can see a lot of places to use that technique in his own finance department.

By 4:00 P.M. the action plan is solidified, and Dieter and the co-development customers gather at the sprint backlog to talk about simplifying the scope. Adriana thanks Bob for introducing them to the Six Thinking Hats technique and suggests that they add it to their working agreements as a preferred decision-making method. Everyone agrees. Arlene also suggests adding a working agreement that calls for routine collaboration with other project teams and IT support staff to avoid future unwanted surprises.

At the end of the iteration the team is exhausted but happy. They've managed to meet all of their commitments despite the issues that arose in the previous week. Natasha returned to work on the following Tuesday, and by then Prakash and Francisco had resolved the broken ETL problem. They reviewed the ETL changes with Natasha, who pointed out a few techniques for avoiding this sort of problem in the future. She committed to reviewing all of the ETL code to make it more immune to source system data model changes. Although Dieter managed to get the customer team to shrink the user story scope, that turned out not to be necessary. At the feature showcase the customer team was delighted to find out that the team delivered everything that was on the original iteration backlog. The customers are especially happy because they had reduced their expectations and the team exceeded the new, lower expectations, rather than the other way around.

Arlene commends the team on a crisis narrowly averted. They decide to quit early on Friday and spend the weekend reenergizing before the final iteration, which will involve final system "hardening" and deployment.

SELF-ORGANIZATION REQUIRES SELF-DISCIPLINE

People and teams tend to work in ways that maximize how their performance is measured. Agile Analytics teams whose performance is measured on the frequent delivery of high-quality, working DW/BI system features will naturally respond accordingly. This phenomenon is the basis for the guiding principle of enabling *self-organizing* and *self-managing* teams by giving them the environment, support, and trust they need to succeed.

When this principle is put into practice effectively, it is a beautiful thing. Teams establish their own internal governance system; they adapt quickly to the changing nature of the project; they rapidly identify shortcomings and work together to overcome them; they freely share information and skills; and they don't wait to be told what to do next. While there is still the "storming and norming" that any new team must undergo (Tuckman 1965), effective Agile teams naturally do this more quickly and less painfully than command-and-control-managed teams.

Self-organizing teams must exhibit self-discipline. Team members must hold themselves and one another accountable to the norms and agreements of the team. Self-organizing teams must seek to continuously improve their practices and performance. They must strive to identify and correct areas and behaviors that are insufficient or problematic. Individual team members must be committed to the frequent delivery of high-quality business intelligence features.

It's difficult to pinpoint a set of specific practices that constitute team self-discipline. Rather, self-discipline is a set of group and individual behaviors and attitudes that a team embraces. It means individual compliance with group standards, or responsible efforts to change those standards. As in societies in which members have certain rights, they are expected to be good citizens, and members agree to be held accountable to citizenship standards.

When there is a breakdown in team self-discipline, the symptoms are often internal chaos or confusion, failure to develop production-quality software, failure to meet all commitments, and other inhibitors to success. In general, the performance of undisciplined teams falls below a minimally acceptable threshold.

As with many Agile team behaviors, self-discipline is often tested when the going gets tough. When teams overcommit or face unforeseen technical complexities, when mid-sprint disruptions occur, when personalities clash— these can disrupt team discipline. Some teams tout "self-organization" but then fail to comprehend the accompanying self-discipline required to be an effective self-organizing team.

> ### Agile Analytics Practice: Team Accountability
> Agile team members should agree on how to hold one another account-able to the commitments of the team. This includes how issues can be addressed without personally offending individuals.

SELF-ORGANIZATION REQUIRES SHARED RESPONSIBILITY

Too often the traditional data warehouse development team gets the short straw when the project begins to run late, requirements change, or users are unsatisfied. It ends up being the development team that pulls long nights and works weekends trying to deliver according to the original plan and timeline. And it ends up being the development team that receives the lion's share of blame for lack of user acceptance or project success. Similarly, if the development team dumps responsibility for a failing project on the management stakeholders without any input, guidance, recommendations, or alternatives, the management team cannot make sound and informed decisions.

In a healthy Agile Analytics project the entire project community shares the successes, failures, and challenges that occur on the project. Recall that an Agile project community consists of planners (management sponsors and stakeholders), doers (delivery team), and consumers (customers/users). Each of these groups has corporate responsibilities that are tied to project success, and each is accountable under organizational governance to perform those responsibilities. The planners are responsible for enabling the team to work unimpeded and uninterrupted. The consumers are responsible for defining, refining, prioritizing, and clarifying scope and for reviewing finished work and providing feedback. The doers are responsible for delivering high-quality, working features and providing the necessary support for ongoing development and maintenance. These are the three "legs" that hold up the project "stool." Without continuous involvement, buy-in, and support from all three groups, the stool will teeter and the project will suffer.

Agile or otherwise, project outcomes often vary from the vision at inception. Although sometimes this variance is an indication of failure, it is commonly a reflection of the changing and uncertain nature of building complex systems. Sometimes what is envisioned and planned for is the wrong thing, and the project community doesn't discover this until well into the project.

Other times what is envisioned and planned morphs into something else in light of the dynamic nature of business needs.

If you've been involved in systems development for any length of time, you have likely experienced this variant nature of project requirements. It doesn't happen in one instant. Rather, small changes occur incrementally, and uncertainty is uncovered gradually. This naturally occurring phenomenon is not, by itself, a problem. After all, we embrace change and seek to adapt quickly. The problem lies in the potential for an impedance mismatch between the expectations of the three groups that make up the project community.

Effective Agile communities frequently resynchronize and revalidate their project visions, assumptions, and expectations. As the customer community adds or revises user stories and reprioritizes the backlog, these changes must be shared across the entire project community. As the technical team uncovers technical risks and issues, the impacts of these on the project plan must be communicated to the entire community. As business strategies change stakeholders' project visions and goals, these new visions must be communicated across the entire community.

Problems and project difficulties tend to increase dramatically as the expectations of the subcommunities become more disparate. A feature showcase every iteration is critical for the proper alignment of customer and developer expectations. It's impossible to have a feature showcase without users. Their involvement is essential and should be a high priority.

Equally important is a periodic stakeholder review. The stakeholder review is held every few iterations. It provides visibility into the project and enables governance by presenting accurate information to decision makers. It addresses these questions:

- What has been accomplished to date?
- How have the initial project vision, scope, and boundaries changed?
- What are the key risks and issues?
- What is needed from the stakeholders to enable the development team to be successful?

When the project deviates significantly from the initial vision, scope, and boundaries, it may be necessary to revisit and revise the project charter. In this case, it's each community member's responsibility to plan, attend, and actively participate. The entire community comes back together to "restart" the project with a revised set of visions, expectations, and understanding.

As important as shared responsibility across the entire project community is the sharing of responsibility within the development team. A self-organizing technical team makes a collective commitment at the start of each iteration. Healthy Agile development teams establish a pattern of helping one another complete tasks to ensure that the team commitments are met. When one team member fails to honor his or her commitments, the entire team shares responsibility for that failure.

SELF-ORGANIZATION REQUIRES TEAM WORKING AGREEMENTS

Effective Agile communities collaboratively establish and commit to a set of core values and working agreements that establish the "playground rules" for the project. Core values and working agreements are posted on the wall in the collaborative team workspace and are refined and revised as needed. While these values and working agreements are self-imposed by the Agile team, they must be consistent with organizational values and guidelines.

Core values establish the criteria for decision making and community behaviors. A team's core values also establish the basis for a set of concrete working agreements. While the core values may mirror those of the entire company, it is valuable for the Agile community to establish and commit to its own set of values. I've seen Agile teams establish such values as "Pride in workmanship"; "Continuous focus on high quality"; "Respect, trust, and honor between team members"; "Have fun." Note that values are broad-brushed statements about what is important to the team. They are not rules. Even when these value statements are similar to company statements, teams that develop their own, with their own wording, become more committed to them.

Working agreements are the rules established by a self-organizing team. They are not imposed by external forces; they are the set of specific guidelines and behaviors that the team establishes to be highly effective. Working agreements can cover such issues as problem solving, decision making, team meetings, accountability, responsibility, and civility. I've seen teams establish such agreements as defining a set of core team hours, when the development team commits to being together and focused on the project. I've also worked with teams that establish agreements about timely responses to requests and preference for face-to-face communication whenever possible.

The development team may establish an additional set of technical practice working agreements such as "Pair programming is required for all story development activities" or "Tests will always be written before the code is written to pass the tests."

It is important that community members give one another permission to hold each other accountable to the values and working agreements. It can be challenging and sometimes daunting to call a teammate out for violating an agreement. To avoid this discomfort the team should establish a light-hearted and friendly technique for handling violations. Agile teams have been known to throw Nerf balls at the offender or shout out a silly code phrase to highlight the offense.

The power of a good set of core values and working agreements should not be underestimated. I've worked with teams that initially downplay these as "fluffy" or unnecessary. These teams typically arrive at some sort of impasse or difficulty in their early iterations that highlights the importance of a common set of values and agreements. I once trained a team that was to be the first to "go Agile" in the organization—the pilot Agile team. Team members were hand-selected from a pool of talented and interested employees. The team was provided with all of the best physical resources (team room, high-end workstations, etc.) needed to succeed. The team was assigned a modestly scoped project so that its primary focus was on learning agility. In spite of these success factors, the team foundered during its first four or five iterations. I was flummoxed: great people, great working environment, formal training, management support. How could they possibly fail? After closely examining the team dynamics and analyzing the challenges they were facing, I realized that they had not really committed to the working agreements I had them develop during the training workshop. The team members thought this was just a workshop exercise and that the working agreements didn't move with them into the team work environment. I gave them some general guidelines for team core values and working agreements and asked them to create their own (ones to which they were willing to commit) without me in the room. Improvements were apparent almost immediately. The team scrum master (project manager) later told me that the working agreements were key to solving the team's problems. It became clear that the team members' individual standards were inconsistent with one another, causing team strife.

Agile Analytics Practice: Establish Working Agreements

Taking the time during project chartering to establish a set of working agreements will boost team performance. These agreements should be published visibly in the team workspace.

SELF-ORGANIZATION REQUIRES HONORING COMMITMENTS

Self-organizing and self-managing development teams are given the freedom to make their own commitments during release planning and during iteration planning. They have the right to estimate the effort required to develop the desired features (and complete other tasks), and they are encouraged to plan within their limited capacity. Effective Agile teams plan to their capacity, make commitments that are within reason, and then take responsibility for ensuring that those commitments are met. Without commitments like these, the "we're just responding to change" mantra becomes a ready excuse for always missing targets.

The catch is that business intelligence practitioners, like programmers, are eternal optimists. Occasionally our estimates are overly optimistic, and we commit beyond our capacity. In a traditional phased project plan these underestimates tend to accumulate over time and create a large pile of work in the project's eleventh hour. You've probably experienced these projects. They are the ones in which the entire development team starts working 60, 70, and 80 hours per week near the project deadline. Quality of life suffers as does quality of work product.

In an Agile environment, these overcommitments put undue stress on the team's ability to complete everything before the iteration's end. A new iteration marks a fresh beginning, with a fresh set of commitments along with the lessons learned from the last overcommitted iteration.

Although establishing a sustainable pace is a key Agile principle, it is incumbent on the team to do whatever is required to meet all of its commitments during an iteration. There are two key reasons why honoring commitments is essential to a healthy Agile project. First, development teams that fall short of their commitments soon lose the trust of other project community members and in turn the right to be self-managing. Second, a team that allows itself to fall short of commitments stands to create a pile of eleventh-hour work as in waterfall projects. In *The Mythical Man-Month*, Fred Brooks wrote the oft-quoted rhetorical question "How does a project get to be a year late? One day at a time" (Brooks 1975). An Agile variant of this quote might be "How does an Agile project get to be late? One iteration at a time."

Effective Agile development teams bend over backward to meet their commitments, and when they get burned by overcommitting, they self-correct in the next iteration. This sometimes means late nights and long hours if the team has committed beyond its capacity. While this may not sound like a long-term sustainable pace, it is sometimes necessary in the short term to maintain the overall health of the project.

Watch Out for Hangovers

A hangover is a backlog item (typically a user story) that is scheduled into an iteration but remains unfinished at the end of the iteration. It hangs over into the next iteration. Hangovers are related to, but are different from, the unmet commitments we've been discussing. A hangover is a backlog item whose engineering tasks are all completed, and that the team believes is complete, but it fails to meet the minimum acceptance criteria to be considered finished.

While there are a variety of specific types of hangovers, they can be generally classified into two categories: those that are not "Done!" and those that are not "Done! Done!"

Recall the introduction of "Done! Done!" in Chapter 1, "Introducing Agile Analytics." The first "Done!" refers to all technical work being completed, passing all functional tests, and being of production quality. The second "Done!" refers to user review and acceptance.

The first type of hangover occurs when a development team completes all of the requisite technical tasks but falls short of creating production-quality output. Either there are tests that are not consistently passing, or there is insufficient testing, or there is unacceptable technical debt or rework required for the work product to be considered production-quality. In a data warehousing application, the focus may be less on functional testing of the presentation and more on the quality and accuracy of the data presented. Whatever the case, the project community (and probably the enterprise) has an established expectation of what constitutes production quality, and when additional work is required to meet this baseline, a hangover occurs.

The second type of hangover occurs when the development team has completed all work, and the work product meets the production-quality baseline, but the work product (feature) fails to meet user/customer expectations and acceptance criteria. These types of hangovers reflect the need for better or more frequent collaboration between developers and users. They also reflect the need for earlier, preliminary showcasing of features as they become available. One Agile data warehousing team I worked on established a working agreement that every user story required a low-fidelity prototype (generally a simple user interaction or wireframe sketch). This agreement eliminated much of the ambiguity that was formerly present in the interpretation of narrative user stories (and corresponding requirements).

Note that it is expected that feature showcases with users may trigger the identification of further enhancements and improvements to an existing feature. These should be captured as new user stories and should not be considered hangovers. It is natural in a business intelligence system for the answer to one question (a user feature) to generate several new questions and needs (user stories). These simply get incorporated into the backlog and assigned the appropriate priority.

Healthy Agile Analytics teams develop processes and methods that minimize hangovers. Test automation and test-driven development will be introduced in Chapter 7, "Test-Driven Data Warehouse Development." These technical practices are significant factors in reducing hangovers.

SELF-ORGANIZATION REQUIRES GLASS-HOUSE DEVELOPMENT

Have you ever worked on a project that wasn't going according to plan? Perhaps the plan was unrealistic to begin with, or maybe the plan was disrupted by a series of unanticipated difficulties. How did the team present project status or task completion? Was everyone open, honest, and realistic in delivering the bad news, or were efforts made to put the most positive (and maybe unrealistic) spin on the situation? If you're like me, you've probably worked on projects where bad news is suppressed or downplayed, and the project is presented as being "on track."

Historically the bearers of bad news are punished, so we naturally tend to avoid being the messenger with bad news. One good friend of mine tells of a large, high-exploration-factor software project he was part of. The gremlins were ever present on this project: Things that could go wrong did, risks became realities, and the project was not going according to plan. After a series of weekly status meetings in which the software engineers truthfully reported the problems they were having, a senior director in engineering became frustrated and pronounced that he "no longer wanted to hear any bad news. Only good news was to be reported!" This unfortunate Dilbertesque story reflects a behavior that occurs far too often on large projects. The suppression of bad news is bound to catch up with us sooner or later. The later bad news is discovered, the greater the negative impact and the cost of course correction.

Healthy Agile data warehousing teams make extra efforts to operate in a glass house. That is, they strive to make it easy for anyone who is interested in the project to gain an accurate and honest insight into the project. Fundamentally this glass-house nature is in the team's DNA. Good Agile teams adopt a variety of behaviors that promote this glass-house development environment—even when it is difficult and appears to be unappreciated. Additionally, there are some specific practices that Agile data warehousing teams should incorporate.

Foremost, the Agile data warehousing team that operates in a glass house uses *visual controls* liberally. Visual controls include all of the butcher paper, index cards, flip charts, sticky notes, and other things that we post on our team room walls to promote collaboration. When I walk into an Agile team room, I expect to see core values and working agreements posted on the wall, the current iteration plan, the prioritized backlog of user stories, the overall release plan, a collection of known technical debt (each item on its own index card), a bug-tracking chart, a risk management chart, and any other information that should be radiated to the project community. These are primarily for use by the team during development, but anyone visiting the team room can easily review the visual controls, ask questions about what they convey, and point out areas of concern. Additionally, disciplined Agile teams use automated dashboards populated with metrics culled automatically from development and testing tools directly. In essence, this is BI for use by BI developers.

The glass-house environment also includes a demo of the working BI system that includes all of the features that have been developed and accepted to date. This system is always up and available for anyone who wishes to see the work that has been completed. Nothing conveys the status of a data warehousing project more accurately and honestly than the working system. The demo system is probably based on a static snapshot of operational data and is not necessarily running in production, but it is available for others to explore. This practice is supported nicely by the preproduction or demonstration sandbox that is discussed in Chapter 7, "Test-Driven Data Warehouse Development."

In addition to the demo system, the glass-house environment should provide access to work in progress. Features that are in development, features that are finished and awaiting review, and any experimental or exploratory work should be available frequently. Chapter 9, "Project Automation," discusses the mechanics of establishing an integration sandbox that is routinely updated to include new features and enhancements. Establishing a continuous integration sandbox also enables others to see that tests are passing and the build is successful.

Project wikis are a powerful mechanism for making supporting artifacts and discussions available to others. Many teams use a wiki to present design documents, data models, domain models, use-case diagrams, business analysis documentation, and other project residue.

Finally, feature showcases and executive showcases provide further visibility into project status and any issues that might disrupt the plan. Many Agile teams also produce weekly status reports that convey accomplishments, agreements, issues/risks, and other useful information.

Agile Analytics Practice: Big Visual Controls

Having team plans, progress, decisions, as well as project and iteration status visible on the walls will boost team performance by keeping everyone aligned and communicating with others. When visual controls become outdated or obsolete, be sure to take them down or update them.

SELF-ORGANIZING REQUIRES CORPORATE ALIGNMENT

Effective Agile teams have a high degree of flexibility to determine the best ways to work within the boundaries of corporate governance and compliance mandates. The principle of self-organization does not invite teams to reject corporate conventions and standards. Tempering self-organization with appropriate corporate governance is a critical success factor for sustainable enterprise agility and sustainable data warehouses and BI systems. Jim Highsmith refers to this as "balancing flexibility with structure."

Typical organizations have IT infrastructure standards, technology standards, and IT protocols. Agile DW/BI teams must be in alignment with these. Oftentimes the larger the organization, the more rigorously these standards are enforced. When project teams attempt to circumvent the standards, they risk becoming organizational outsiders and their project is viewed as out of compliance. This outcome is undesirable for both the organization and the project team.

Moreover, many companies face other regulatory mandates such as Sarbanes-Oxley,[1] ISO 9000[2] and/or CMMI[3] certifications, FDA[4] requirements, and other external compliance constraints. Such external constraints impact the balance between flexibility and structure in much the same way that nonfunctional requirements impact the balance between technical flexibility and design structure.

By ensuring appropriate alignment with corporate governance and external compliance requirements, Agile teams establish themselves as responsible citizens within the enterprise. Effective Agile teams possess a deep understanding of these governance and compliance guidelines so that they can satisfy the requirements as simply and efficiently as possible.

WRAP-UP

Team self-organization and self-management can go badly wrong without attention and diligence on the part of the entire project community. A proper self-organizing team behaves in ways that establish and promote

- Self-discipline
- Shared responsibility
- A common set of core values
- Team working agreements
- Honoring commitments
- Glass-house development
- Corporate alignment

While there are probably many other desired behaviors and attitudes that we might identify, these are essential to Agile team effectiveness. Healthy Agile data warehousing teams benefit greatly from intentional and explicit focus on these characteristics. They monitor these behaviors during iteration retrospectives and self-evaluation periods. These behaviors, attitudes, and mind-sets mark the difference between practicing Agile "by the numbers" (doing Agile) and practicing Agile in accordance with the values and guiding principles (being Agile).

---

1. Financial regulatory requirements established in the United States under public law 107-204, 116 statute 745.
2. Family of quality standards maintained by the International Organization for Standardization.
3. Capability Maturity Model Integration.
4. U.S. Food and Drug Administration.

This page intentionally left blank

PART II

AGILE ANALYTICS: TECHNICAL METHODS

This page intentionally left blank

Chapter 6

EVOLVING EXCELLENT DESIGN

Design excellence is critical to the success of Agile Analytics. The right design choices will help minimize technical debt, facilitate adapting to changes, improve quality, and provide the Agile team with a cohesive technical framework. The wrong design choices can lead to overbuilt systems and high technical debt, severely hindering the team's ability to be Agile. This applies to the design of data models, system architectures, ETL code, BI applications, and other components of the data warehouse and business intelligence solution.

Agile Analytics presents a difficult paradox: The ability to quickly respond to change and frequently deliver new features requires excellent data models and system design, yet excellent design takes time to develop. How do we deliver business value early and frequently without doing a lot of the design up front? Not long ago I had a conversation with a DW/BI practitioner that went something like this:

Practitioner: "Agile makes sense for DW/BI systems already in production. It's not applicable to new data warehouse development."

Me: "Why do you say that?"

Practitioner: "Because it is important to have correct and complete data models and a populated data warehouse before we can start developing BI applications. It's not practical to keep changing the data models."

Me: "Why is changing the data models impractical?"

Practitioner: "Because it means a lot of rework. It's better to do it once and do it right the first time."

Me: "Has that approach worked well for you in the past? Do you typically get the model right on the first try?"

Practitioner: "We get pretty close, but of course some adjustments are always needed."

Me: "How much unused data is in your warehouse, for example, unused tables or unused columns of data?"

Practitioner: "We have quite a bit of data that isn't used. Some of it we expect to use in the future. Plus there is probably some data that we'll never use, but we felt it was better to include it just in case."

Me: "How long did it take to build your current data warehouse?"

Practitioner: "After we had the requirements, it took about two months to finalize the data models, and another six months to implement and test everything."

Me: "Assuming the BI application development started after that, how long was it before the first BI features could be reviewed by business users?"

Practitioner: "We were able to build a few reports in about a month after that, but it took two months before we had the first BI apps ready for production."

Me: "Were the users happy with those first available BI applications?"

Practitioner: "They were reasonably happy, but they asked for several improvements and new features, which will be in the next phase of development."

Me: "So, business users didn't receive any value for about ten months. What did they do while they waited for the system to be built?"

Practitioner: "They kept using the spreadsheets and pivot tables that they had been using. These were populated using some custom queries on the operational databases."

Me: "Sounds like they needed some support from the IT department while they waited."

Practitioner: "Yes, we had some DBAs helping run those custom queries weekly or monthly to produce the spreadsheets."

Me: "Suppose you could *safely* evolve your design while delivering continuous business value to the users. Would that be beneficial to the DW/BI team?"

Practitioner: "Sure, it would be nice to hear what users have to say earlier in the project. Plus, I suppose the system would be more refined and tailored to serve its purpose rather than too complicated and overbuilt. That would certainly be easier to develop, understand, and maintain. We could also move faster if we only had to deal with the data we need rather than all the extra data. But we still need an enterprise data model."

Me: "An enterprise data model is an important part of your master data management strategy. But evolutionary development lets you prove out your enterprise data model by putting it to use early."

Practitioner: "But it's too difficult and risky to change the data model once it is populated with data. Also, if the system doesn't conform to the master data management strategy and enterprise data model, we'll just have one more data silo in the company."

Me: "That can be true. So it's really important to have a disciplined approach to evolving the design toward, not away from, the corporate data standards. Better yet, evolutionary BI development can help shape the enterprise data model and master data management strategy to become more useful to the enterprise."

Practitioner: "I'm skeptical that it'll work without making a mess of things, but I'd like to learn more about the approach."

I have variations of this dialogue with seasoned DW/BI developers a lot. Fortunately, this practitioner was open-minded to a different approach. Initially the idea of incrementally evolving a complex system design and corresponding data models seems risky and prone to problems. Anyone who has worked with any sort of legacy database system has likely seen how data models naturally evolve over time, and it isn't pretty. Ad hoc tables get added as stopgap measures. Columns whose original purpose is long forgotten get reused on the fly to serve some other purpose. Pretty soon the whole model becomes like a bowl of spaghetti, with no clear and understandable design and lots of disconnected tables floating around the periphery. It's easy to see why the idea of evolutionary design is initially disturbing to some.

At the same time, most experienced BI developers have also encountered models and designs that, however well thought-out they seemed initially, fall short in practice and must be tweaked and adapted to achieve their purpose. We don't get the real validation that our design decisions are correct until we see them in action. This is true for system design as well as data models.

So, we are better off if we can do a little design, validate it in a working system, and repeat the cycle many times. But if we fail to do this with a high degree of technical excellence and discipline, the results can be fragile, overly complex, and hard to understand and maintain. Good evolutionary design is based on having a good conceptual model as a starting point and requires continuous refactoring toward design excellence. With good discipline evolutionary design often results in a better implementation than designing it all up front. The aim of this chapter is to introduce the set of practices required to evolve high-quality, effective, and maintainable models and designs.

WHAT IS EVOLUTIONARY DESIGN?

A common misconception among Agile critics is that Agile development involves zero design up front and therefore has a high risk of resulting in a poorly designed product. Conversely, agilists dislike the BDUF nature of plan-driven development, preferring instead to begin building something sooner that customers can evaluate and to which they can react. Uncertainty early in a project makes BDUF too costly and risky. However, experienced Agile developers also know that no up-front design leads to poor quality and high technical debt. What is needed is sufficient design up front (SDUF)—enough to galvanize developers around a shared understanding of problem domain, architecture, user experience, and data. Agile development doesn't require a whole new set of modeling techniques. What is required is a new way of applying good modeling methods in an incremental, iterative, and evolutionary manner. Establishing a minimally sufficient conceptual model up front, and then incrementally evolving the physical model as the system is built, helps limit technical debt and increase design quality.

However, good evolutionary design requires team discipline, design expertise, and technical excellence. In other words, Agile Analytics is not a magic alternative to proper training, techniques, and experience. In practice, evolutionary design looks something like this:

Scenario

The FlixBuster DW/BI system was first deployed into production at the end of iteration six with a couple of high-value BI capabilities. The users were amazed at how quickly the development team delivered the first release and were delighted at how useful those first simple BI features were. Now, after 28 iterations, the development team has established a steady rhythm of releasing enhancements plus a few new BI capabilities into production every month and a half. The user community is ecstatic at how fast the development team is able to build useful BI applications for them to use.

As the lead data modeler, Prakash has helped the data warehousing team follow two key principles: First, never implement anything that isn't necessary to support the current work in progress. Second, all data model modifications must be consistent with the reference (conceptual) data model.

With Prakash facilitating during iteration zero, the technical team collaboratively developed a relational reference data model for the integration tier of the warehouse and a multidimensional reference data model for the presentation tier. Originally these were simple whiteboard sketches that gave the team a shared understanding of the database designs. Even though there were lots of unanswered questions, the team had learned enough during project chartering and planning to feel confident in these high-level conceptual models.

Prakash initially documented these reference data models and published them on the project wiki so that team members could easily reference them during development. As aspects of the data model get implemented during iterative development, Prakash updates the wiki documentation to show this detail. This is how conceptual models gradually evolve into logical models. Also, the documentation always matches the physical implementation of the data models.

Each iteration, as soon as the iteration plan is finalized, the team collaboratively reviews the reference models to evaluate how the new user stories will affect the design. Sometimes the new stories don't require any new data. Other times the new stories require new data that has already been anticipated but is not yet populated in the model. And every now and then a new story requires data that Prakash and the team did not anticipate. When that happens, the team modifies the reference data model to handle the new data requirements, and it evaluates possible side effects or other impacts that the changes will have on the version of the warehouse that is in production.

As the team plans iteration 29, it runs into the third, more complex scenario. This iteration includes the story "As a FlixBuster financial analyst I need to determine cost of sales down to individual transactions so that I can more accurately calculate profit."

The FlixBuster team faces three problems. First, the formula for calculating *cost of sales* (CoS) is not well defined by the business but is expected to include elements such as studio royalty, handling costs, shipping costs, inventory overhead, loss and damage costs, among other variables. Some of these components are complex by themselves, such as the handling costs. Second, the components that constitute CoS come from a variety of sources, including some syndicated third-party sources. Finally, CoS is an aggregate value covering all sales for some time period. The business logic defining how to allocate CoS down to singular transactions must be developed by business experts.

Additionally, the team expects to add the CoS measure to the already populated **F_Transaction** fact table, which includes transaction revenue and net profit. This poses two challenges: how to backfill historical facts with values for the CoS measure (the production fact table contains billions of records) and how the new CoS measure affects the previously developed net profit measure. The team agrees that there may be other issues in addition to these.

The development team shares these challenges with Dieter, the product owner, who brings business users Javier, Beulah, Kari, and Andy, as well as Bob, the business analyst, and Pete, the VP of finance, into the conversation. The group quickly recognizes that completely maturing the CoS story will take a few iterations. So, to simplify the first iteration they agree upon a rudimentary formula for CoS that will give developers a chance to collect the necessary data while business experts develop a more accurate and permanent formula before the start of iteration 30. They also agree upon a simplistic CoS allocation scheme for developers to use until the business experts can agree on a better one. Finally, the group agrees that integrating CoS into the net profit formula is a separate user story. So they write that story and turn it over to the product owner to add onto the backlog. For the time being, CoS will not be included in net profit calculations.

The development team reviews the reference data models, working backward from the star schema in the presentation tier to the relational schema in the integration tier. The F_Transaction fact table already exists, and the team agrees that this is where the CoS measure belongs. So, a task card is written to reflect this modification of the data definition language (DDL) script for F_Transaction. The integration schema is more complicated because it involves multiple values, some of which are calculated. However, after some discussion the team agrees to add studio royalty as a new column in the Product table; add a loss_damage field to the Transactions table; create a new Studio table, which will be used to populate the D_Studio dimension in the presentation schema; and make some other data model refinements. The team creates task cards for each of these implementation decisions, and Prakash commits to updating the reference models to reflect the team's decisions.

Because there is already a version of the data warehouse in production with live data, the team must consider the impact of these new database changes on the existing warehouse and all BI applications that rely on it. The team recommits to using disciplined database refactoring techniques (Ambler and Sadalage 2006). Henry, the database developer with the most experience in database refactoring, commits to reviewing the other developers' refactoring plans and corresponding code.

The development team quickly reviews the expected work for iteration 29 and agrees that it is reasonable and fits within the team's capacity. The team formally commits to the iteration plan and begins working with the knowledge that there will be more changes in the upcoming iterations.

This example offers a glimpse of how an Agile data warehousing team takes a highly disciplined approach to evolutionary design to avoid overbuilding the data models while also limiting technical debt and continuously improving the design through careful refactoring. Effective evolutionary data warehouse design has the following benefits (Ambler and Sadalage 2006):

- **Minimal waste.** By evolving the warehouse design in a just-in-time fashion, you build what is needed, adapt to requirements changes as they arise, and avoid working on irrelevant elements.

- **Minimal rework.** By making small incremental changes in the warehouse design, you avoid sweeping overhauls of the design. Rework efforts serve the purpose of making improvements to, rather than replacements of, existing elements.
- **Continuous confidence.** An evolutionary approach results in a working system early and the frequent addition of new working features and enhancements, giving you continued confidence that you are building the right system and are building the system right.
- **High quality.** Refactoring is the discipline of improving your warehouse design a little bit at a time, continuously.
- **Reduced effort.** By working only on what you need today, you eliminate unnecessary efforts.

Evolutionary design involves the following key developer practices (Ambler 2003):

- **Database refactoring** to make safe changes that improve quality a little at a time without changing the semantics
- **Evolutionary data modeling** to ensure that the data model provides exactly what is needed to support the BI applications
- **Database regression testing** to ensure that new changes don't break preexisting components of the system
- **Configuration management** to manage the version history of the entire system as well as the change history of every artifact that makes up the system
- **Developer sandboxes** to give developers a place to safely experiment with ideas and develop and test their work before integrating it into the system

The following sections offer insight into practices that, when taken together, enable teams to effectively evolve the design of their DW/BI solution. Evolutionary design begins with making a series of decisions about the balance between up-front design and evolving design and how a design evolves toward excellence through the use of Agile Modeling, database refactoring, and design patterns. A key constraint to keep in mind during the evolutionary design process is minimizing technical debt in the design and implementation. Finally, the adaptive architecture section presents an in-depth example of how many of these practices were used to build a complex, hosted DW/BI product for enterprise customers. References are made in these sections to topics such as regression testing, developer sandboxes, and configuration management that are covered in detail in later chapters of this book.

HOW MUCH UP-FRONT DESIGN?

Evolutionary design strikes the right sufficient-up-front and just-in-time balance. Jim Highsmith compares this to trekking in the desert. If you're trekking in the desert, you'll benefit from a map, a hat, good boots, and a canteen of water. You aren't likely to survive if you burden yourself with a hundred gallons of water and a pack loaded with every imaginable piece of survival gear; nor are you likely to survive without a minimum of important supplies (Highsmith 2000). The goal of Agile design and modeling is to strike the right balance between too little and too much. Our objective is to model just enough up front to ensure that all developers have a shared understanding of the solution approach and can commence building the working components in a common and cohesive way.

We can take a lesson from Stewart Brand's observations in *How Buildings Learn* (Brand 1995). Brand identifies six layers that exist in any building:

- **Site:** the location where the building sits
- **Structure:** the foundation and frame
- **Skin:** the outer shell of the building
- **Services:** water, electric, sewage, and other systems
- **Space:** the interior layout and configuration
- **Stuff:** lighting, colors, flooring, decor, and other cosmetic elements

The order of this list of layers is important. Each successive layer is increasingly easier and less costly to change than the one before it, with site being the hardest to change and stuff being easiest. Like buildings, systems have these layers as well. The underlying hardware and technology infrastructure is much like the *site*; the systems architecture is the *structure*; and so on up to the look and feel of BI applications, which is the *stuff*.

While it is not impossible to change a DW/BI system's infrastructure or systems architecture after it has been built, it is difficult and costly to do so. Therefore, it is important to get these layers right as early as possible. Note that getting it right is not the same as getting it finished. In other words, we need to design these layers to a sufficient level of detail to convince ourselves that our design choices are viable, sustainable, robust, scalable, and flexible. We do not need a complete and comprehensive detailed design before we can start building the warehouse. During the early stages of design on a new project, before development has started, I like to continuously ask the following questions:

1. What is our design objective—to improve our own understanding or to communicate the solution to others?
2. Have we accomplished our objective yet (i.e., have we done enough for now)?
3. If so, what's keeping us from getting started developing?
4. If not, what is the smallest/simplest thing we can do to accomplish our objective?

Continuously asking this sequence of questions will help the Agile Analytics team avoid the temptation to spend too much time doing up-front design while helping ensure that they don't start developing without the important prerequisite design decisions.

Agile Analytics Practice: Architecture Envisioning

During iteration zero seek to develop a minimally sufficient up-front design. Look for opportunities to do less up-front design without falling below the "minimally sufficient" threshold. This will leave the development team with more empty canvas to work with as you adapt and evolve the design.

AGILE MODELING

An Agile approach to modeling is essential to evolving excellent designs. An Agile model is one that is minimally sufficient. This means that it conveys just enough to be useful while remaining malleable and adaptable. Agile Modeling is an iterative, incremental, and evolutionary approach that calls for a repeating cycle of modeling in small increments, proving your model with working code, and inspecting and testing the results. An Agile model has the following traits (Ambler 2002):

- **It fulfills its purpose.** We model for one of two reasons: to *communicate* a design to others, or to better *understand* what we're working on. Agile Modeling is done with clarity of purpose. When modeling to communicate, know who the audience is and what is being communicated. When modeling to understand, know what the question is, who should be involved, and when the goal is reached.
- **It is understandable.** Agile models are developed with the intended audience in mind, using the correct "language" for that audience. If we are modeling to understand the business domain, use-case

diagrams and business lingo are appropriate. For data modeling, a modeling notation such as an entity-relationship (ER) or UML 2.x class diagram is more appropriate.

- **It is sufficiently accurate.** Agile models don't need to be 100 percent accurate, but they do need to be accurate enough to serve their purpose. For example, if I am drawing a map to show you how to get to my house for a party this weekend, a simple sketch with street names and directions will suffice. It doesn't matter if it isn't precisely to scale.

- **It is sufficiently consistent.** Agile models don't need to be 100 percent consistent, but they do need to be consistent enough to serve their purpose. For example, a logical data model with a "Customer" table may be inconsistent with a use-case model that refers to a "Client" actor, yet this doesn't result in major misunderstandings of the two models.

- **It is sufficiently detailed.** The degree of detail in an Agile model depends on its purpose and audience. Drivers need maps that show streets and intersections; building contractors need maps that show civil engineering detail.

- **It provides positive value.** The more formal the model, the more costly it is to maintain. A digital picture of a conceptual model on the whiteboard is inexpensive compared to a formalized model drawn in a data modeling tool like ERwin, Rational Rose Data Modeler, IBM (InfoSphere) Data Architect, or some other professional modeling tool. An Agile model's value outweighs its cost of creation and ongoing maintenance. If a model is worth formalizing, it is worth keeping updated. Formalized models that are out-of-date have negative value.

- **It is as simple as possible.** In Agile models the level of detail is limited to only what is needed to serve their purpose. Furthermore, the notational symbols are limited to only what is necessary.

Note the recurring theme of *purpose* in these Agile model trait descriptions. Too often DW/BI practitioners fall into the trap of creating and formalizing models without a clear sense of purpose. When that happens, the models and corresponding documentation often become bloated and overdeveloped, and correspondingly more costly to create and maintain. The most accurate documentation of a DW/BI system is the system itself. Supporting documents are always at risk of being out of sync with the actual implementation. The best design documentation is a self-documenting implementation.

Agile Modeling is driven by these guiding principles:

- **The working solution is your primary goal.** Model just enough to get back to the business of building a working DW/BI system.
- **Enabling the next effort is your secondary goal.** A DW/BI system must be built with an eye toward the future, but it doesn't need to be built to handle all future possibilities. Part of fulfilling the needs of stakeholders is designing a system that is robust and extensible over time.
- **Travel light.** Create just enough models and documentation to get by.
- **Assume simplicity.** The simplest solution is usually the best solution. Don't overcomplicate the design.
- **Embrace change.** Change is inevitable. Anticipate it and design for it. Don't expect to get the design exactly right once and for all time.
- **Make incremental changes.** Work in small steps and avoid big sweeping changes.
- **Model with a purpose.** If you can't identify why you are modeling and for whom, don't do it.
- **Create multiple models.** There are a variety of modeling techniques and notations. Be sure to use the right tools for the intended purpose, and develop multiple models in parallel if it helps.
- **Ensure quality workmanship.** If the model is worth formalizing, it's worth formalizing with high quality. Like high-quality code, high-quality models are elegant and rich with useful information. They are not sloppy and incomplete.
- **Obtain rapid feedback.** Share your models with others early and frequently to avoid heading too far off course. Publicize stable models and invite input.
- **Maximize stakeholder investment.** Involve stakeholders in the modeling process whenever possible. This will help avoid modeling in a vacuum and will shape the models to more effectively meet stakeholder needs.

Agile Modeling is an attitude and style, not a prescriptive process. It is not a replacement methodology. Instead, it supplements and complements existing modeling methods. Agile Modeling is a way for developers to collaborate and evolve excellent designs that meet the needs of project stakeholders. There is nothing magic about Agile Modeling, but it is a cornerstone of evolutionary design. Scott Ambler's book entitled *Agile Modeling* offers a more comprehensive coverage of the values, principles, and practices that make up this approach (Ambler 2002).

Agile Analytics Practice: Prove It with Code

Avoid the temptation to model in large steps with lots of design revisions. Instead, model in small increments and prove out your ideas by implementing them. And don't forget to test as you go.

DATA MODEL PATTERNS

Designs evolve toward excellence when we take advantage of tried and tested existing solutions. The use of design patterns enables us to benefit from the mature solutions that have previously been developed.

Software design patterns were first introduced in 1994 in recognition that many of the problems programmers solve look very much like other previously solved problems (Gamma et al. 1994). The authors of *Design Patterns* (commonly called the "Gang of Four") sought to identify and catalog a set of reusable object-oriented design patterns and provide guidelines for when and how to use them. Later, Martin Fowler extended this catalog in his book *Analysis Patterns* (Fowler 1997). Since that time the software community has embraced other pattern books such as Kent Beck's *Implementation Patterns* (Beck 2008), Josh Kerievsky's *Refactoring to Patterns* (Kerievsky 2004), and others.

The 1990s patterns movement together with the explosion of object-oriented programming methods revolutionized software development. Design patterns give programmers a springboard for implementing high-quality software designs. They enable programmers to move more quickly because they don't have to design every solution from scratch.

Data modelers and data warehouse architects can also benefit from the effective use of design patterns. David Hay first introduced *Data Model Patterns: Conventions of Thought* shortly after the Gang of Four book was published (Hay 1996). More recently Hay produced a catalog of enterprise data model patterns in *Data Model Patterns: A Metadata Map* (Hay 2006). Even more recently, respected data modeling expert Michael Blaha published his catalog of data model patterns called *Patterns of Data Modeling* (Blaha 2010). These resources offer a solid set of tools for the evolution of excellent data warehouse designs.

Patterns are different from standards and conventions. Standards provide general guidelines on capabilities that must be part of the solution.

Conventions provide specific stylistic guidelines for developers. A pattern, however, provides an abstract and generalized design template that can be used to model a class of similar problems or scenarios. Using a data model pattern involves tailoring and specializing it to fit the specific situation you are modeling. You can think of a pattern as a half-baked model that requires you to bake in the remaining ingredients so that it best models your domain.

The *adaptive data model* is a good example of the use of data model patterns (see Figure 6.1). It is designed using an aggregate of simpler data model and object model patterns. The adaptive data model is based on Adaptive Object Modeling (AOM) principles (Yoder and Johnson 2002). The use of adaptive

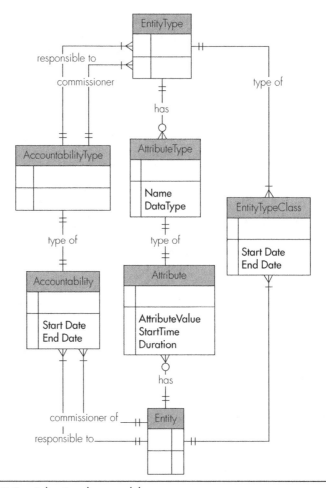

Figure 6.1   Adaptive data model pattern

data modeling (ADM) for data warehousing was first introduced at a Data Management Association (DAMA) meeting in the UK in 2005 (Longman 2005). Both AOM and ADM are strongly rooted in a collection of earlier architectural patterns. ADM is a domain-independent model that represents all entities in the domain, their attributes, their relationships to one another, and the duration of those relationships. The power of an adaptive model is that the definition of the domain model and the rules of its integrity are stored in a metadata base and are easily configurable by domain modeling experts without structural database changes.

Evolutionary data warehouse design calls for the appropriate use of patterns in data modeling. At present the majority of cataloged patterns for data modeling are focused on normalized ER modeling. However, an initial catalog of dimensional modeling patterns was introduced at the 2005 international ACM workshop on data warehousing and OLAP (Jones and Song 2005). This catalog includes temporal, action, location, object, stakeholder, qualifier, and combination patterns. Moreover, many of the dimensional modeling ideas introduced by Ralph Kimball, Margy Ross, and others have a distinct patterns flavor (Kimball and Ross 2002). ETL patterns also hold a lot of promise for future data warehouse design and development. At the time of this writing there were no published catalogs of ETL patterns. However, Bob Jankovsky has a Web-based collection of metadata-driven ETL patterns that deserve consideration (Jankovsky 2008).

Agile Analytics Practice: Gentle Application of Patterns

Patterns are powerful tools for developing excellent data models and code. Become knowledgeable about patterns and familiar with pattern catalogs, and then use them judiciously. Avoid treating everything as an opportunity to use a pattern. Some things are simpler.

MANAGING TECHNICAL DEBT

The topic of technical debt was introduced in Chapter 2, "Agile Project Management." Identification and proper management (and pay-down) of technical debt are integral aspects of evolving toward excellent data warehouse and BI design. In 1992 software development expert Ward Cunningham compared technical complexity in software code to fiscal debt. He pointed out that sometimes it's useful to take development shortcuts or less-than-ideal approaches in order to move quickly. But these shortcuts are like financial debt; if they aren't paid back, the complexities in the system will accumulate, eventually reaching unmanageable levels. Every minute spent on not-quite-right code counts as interest on the debt.

Since Ward introduced this concept, the term *technical debt* has become widely accepted in the software development community to describe the inevitable entropy that occurs in any system. Sometimes this entropy occurs by design when developers make trade-offs to optimize for speed. Other times it occurs unintentionally through suboptimal design choices, design decisions made in the absence of important information, multiple revisions made without discipline, developer mistakes, and other causes. Whatever the reasons, technical debt is an unavoidable consequence of systems development—and this includes data warehouses and business intelligence systems.

As technical debt increases, so does the cost of change (CoC). In fact, Jim Highsmith describes technical debt as the gap between a system's actual CoC and its optimal CoC (Highsmith 2010a). As a DW/BI system grows in essential complexity (multiple data sources, increasing capabilities, increasing data volumes, etc.), its optimal CoC is expected to increase. More complex systems are more costly to change than simpler systems. However, technical debt is a nonessential source of complexity that further increases the CoC beyond its optimal levels. As the CoC increases, customer responsiveness decreases. In other words, technical debt is anathema to agility.

One challenge with the technical debt metaphor is that it is difficult to quantify and prioritize. Everyone seems to be in agreement that it exists in all systems and should not be ignored. But when push comes to shove on a project, attention to technical debt routinely takes a back seat to new feature development.

Recently Israel Gat has introduced a model for monetizing technical debt by evaluating existing code and estimating the cost of repairing problematic code (Gat 2009). For instance, suppose that the FlixBuster DW contains 50,000 lines of stored procedure code and it is estimated that eliminating all known technical debt in the stored procedures will cost $100,000; FlixBuster will have to spend $2 per line of code to eliminate all technical debt.

Such monetization allows us to establish a "credit limit" on technical debt. When technical debt reaches a certain level, say, $0.25 per line of stored procedure code, new feature development is put on hold while the team focuses on aggressive refactoring to reduce technical debt to an acceptable level.

An additional benefit of technical debt monetization is that it can be listed as a liability line item on the balance sheet. Therefore, the net value of a DW/BI system is measured as the monetized business value of working BI features and capabilities offset by the monetized liability of existing technical debt.

Israel outlines the following transformative aspects of monetizing or otherwise quantifying technical debt (Gat 2010):

1. The technical debt metric enables *Continuous Inspection* of the code through ultra-rapid feedback to the software process. . . .
2. It shifts the emphasis in software development from *proficiency* in the software process to the *output* of the process.
3. It changes the playing fields from *qualitative* assessment to *quantitative* measurement of the quality of the software.
4. It is an effective *antidote* to the relentless function/feature pressure.
5. It can be used with *any [development] method*, not "just" Agile.
6. It is applicable to *any amount of code.*
7. It can be applied at *any point in time* in the [development] life-cycle.
8. These seven characteristics of the technical debt metric enable effective *governance of the [development] process.*
9. The above characteristics of the technical debt metric enable effective *governance of the . . . product portfolio.*

Highsmith says this about technical debt: "It's expensive to fix, but much more expensive to ignore. Technical debt reduces future earnings, but even more critically, it destroys predictability which in turn impacts market capitalization in the near term, not in the future" (Highsmith 2010b).

When a team allows technical debt to accumulate unabated, the system will eventually reach a point of stagnation. Defects are prevalent and increasing. It becomes too costly and risky to add new features. And fixing bugs becomes a full-time effort. When a system is referred to as a "legacy system," you can be sure that it is mired in technical debt. Nobody wants to touch those.

Agile Analytics Practice: Prioritize Debt

Agile teams intentionally identify, track, prioritize, monitor, and pay down their technical debt. Technical debt stories should be prioritized alongside user stories to balance new feature development against debt reduction.

Effective Agile Analytics teams seek to identify, monitor, and pay down technical debt. Whenever developers make choices that incur technical debt, or when they discover preexisting technical debt, they log it into the team's debt-tracking system. The debt-tracking system, like the defect-tracking system, need not be complicated or high-tech. A simple chart on the wall using index cards to capture "technical debt stories" is an effective way for a colocated team to manage its technical debt.

Unlike for the valuation and prioritization of user stories, it is the technical team that prioritizes technical debt stories and estimates the value of eliminating each one. It is important for the product owner to ensure that the priority of new user stories does not always trump the priority of technical debt stories. Technical team leaders must advocate for opportunities to schedule debt stories into development iterations. Some Agile project teams agree to allocate 15 to 20 percent of team capacity in each iteration to debt reduction, leaving 80 to 85 percent for user story development. Other Agile teams occasionally designate explicit debt reduction iterations that eschew user story development in favor of debt reduction work. Still other Agile teams find ways to eliminate technical debt in the course of user story development. Whatever the approach, it is essential to continuously monitor and pay down technical debt.

REFACTORING

Refactoring is an important technical discipline that serves two very important purposes. First, it is a technique for safely evolving the design or models without breaking previously working features and components. Second, it is a technique for eliminating technical debt without breaking previously working features and components. Note the common elements of these purposes—*without breaking previously working features and components.* An ever-present consideration of iterative development is ensuring that the work we are doing in this iteration does not have an adverse impact on the work we've done in prior iterations. The next chapter introduces the importance of test automation in DW/BI development. Together with testing, refactoring is an essential engineering practice that enables Agile teams to be effective.

The practice of refactoring was first introduced to the software community by Martin Fowler (1999). He defines refactoring as "the process of changing a software system in such a way that it does not alter the external behavior of the code yet improves its internal structure." This practice has had a profound impact on the quality of software application development. It has enabled programmers to improve a design after it has been written. Within a few years after Fowler introduced refactoring, nearly every single interactive development environment (IDE) had support built directly into the tool to help programmers refactor their code.

Scott Ambler and Pramod Sadalage introduced refactoring to the database community in 2006 with a very thorough catalog of database refactorings and transformations (Ambler and Sadalage 2006). They describe a database refactoring as ". . . a simple change to a database schema that improves its design while retaining both its behavioral and informational semantics (in a practical manner)." A database refactoring may affect structural elements of the schema such as tables and views, or functional elements such as stored procedures and triggers. Not only must database refactoring preserve the core database behavior and semantics; it must also preserve all external systems that are coupled to the database schema such as business applications and data extract processes. The database refactoring principles (and most of the refactorings) introduced by Ambler and Sadalage are directly applicable to evolutionary data warehouse development. Therefore, this section of the chapter will provide an overview of the refactoring discipline rather than comprehensive coverage of the topic. Every data warehouse developer should have a copy of *Refactoring Databases* in his or her personal library.

Refactoring is not the same as ad hoc restructuring of code or data models. While restructuring is a good practice, it is important to understand that refactoring means something very specific. In fact, refactoring is *the key* to effective evolutionary database design. Refactoring relies on regression testing to ensure that your changes have not broken anything. Moreover, the regression test suite must be automated to enable you to repeatedly execute your tests quickly and easily in the course of refactoring. The focus of the next chapter is on test automation and test-driven data warehouse development (including regression testing), so we'll defer discussion of those details for now.

Ambler and Sadalage distinguish the six categories of refactoring presented in Table 6.1. Within each category there are several specific refactorings and transformations.

Table 6.1 Database Refactoring Categories

Database Refactoring Category	Description	Example(s)
Structural	A change to the definition of one or more tables or views	Moving a column from one table to another, or splitting a multipurpose column into separate columns
Data quality	A change that improves the quality of information	Making a column non-nullable or applying a common format to a column
Referential integrity	A change that ensures that a referenced row exists within another table and/or that a row that is no longer needed is removed appropriately	Adding a trigger to enable a cascading delete between two entities, code that was formerly implemented outside the database
Architectural	A change that improves the overall manner in which external programs interact with a database	Replacing an existing Java database operation in a code library with a stored procedure in the database to make it available to non-Java applications
Method	A change to a stored procedure, ETL object, stored function, or trigger that improves its quality	Renaming a stored procedure to make it easier to understand
Non-refactoring transformation	A change to a database schema that changes its semantics	Adding a new column to an existing table

What Is Refactoring?

Without rewriting the book on database refactoring, perhaps it would be best to explain the concept of refactoring with an example. Suppose our FlixBuster data warehouse has been in production for some time and the data model includes a conformed product dimension that is keyed on product ID and is used by several fact tables. However, in the current development cycle we are integrating a new syndicated data source that contains rich information about product purchases but is at the *product subcategory* grain rather than the more detailed individual product grain. Because we will be building a new fact table that uses the grain of product subcategory, we decide to split the product dimension into two separate dimensions, Dim_ Product and Dim_ProductSubcategory. The new dimension can be used as a star schema for detailed product facts or linked directly to the more coarse-grained subcategory facts.

Because the data warehouse has been in production for some time, and Dim_Product contains historical data, we'll need to be disciplined in how we split this dimension table to ensure that all existing BI applications continue working properly. That means that we'll need to introduce the new dimension table but establish a transition period during which the original table continues to include subcategory information. This transition period will allow us to carefully refactor the BI applications to use the new subcategory dimension wherever appropriate. We'll use the *Split Table* refactoring for this task (Ambler and Sadalage 2006).

During the transition period we will have some intentional data duplication. To avoid possible inconsistencies between these dimensions we will outfit each table with a trigger to synchronize data across tables in the event of an insertion, deletion, or update. We must create these triggers so that cycles between the two do not occur.

While we don't want the transition period to linger too long, we also don't want to deprecate the old schema too early and risk breaking any BI applications. After careful consideration we've determined that February 1, 2013, is an appropriate date by which to complete the schema transition. To implement this we'll schedule the necessary ALTER TABLE statements to run on that date. This step in the refactoring automates the necessary housekeeping that we might otherwise forget to do. Figure 6.2 depicts the schema before, during, and after our transition period.

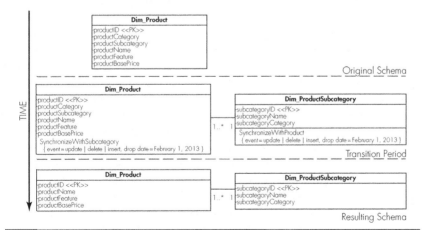

Figure 6.2   Splitting the product dimension table

The code for this refactoring looks like this:

```
CREATE TABLE Dim_ProductSubcategory (
  subcategoryID           VARCHAR(15)NOT NULL,
  subcategoryName         VARCHAR(20)NOT NULL,
  subcategoryCategory     VARCHAR(15)NOT NULL,
  CONSTRAINT PKSubcategoryID
    PRIMARY KEY (subcategoryID)
);

-Trigger to keep all split tables in sync
CREATE OR REPLACE TRIGGER SynchronizeWithSubcategory
BEFORE INSERT OR UPDATE
ON Dim_Product
REFERENCING OLD AS OLD NEW AS NEW
FOR EACH ROW
DECLARE
BEGIN
  IF updating THEN
    FindOrCreateSubcategory;
  END IF;
  IF inserting THEN
    CreateSubcategory;
  END IF;
END;
/

CREATE OR REPLACE TRIGGER SynchronizeWithProduct
BEFORE UPDATE OF productSubcategory
ON Dim_ProductSubcategory
REFERENCING OLD AS OLD NEW AS NEW
FOR EACH ROW
DECLARE
BEGIN
  IF updating THEN
    FindAndUpdateAllProductsForSubcategory
  END IF;
END;
/

-On February 1, 2013
ALTER TABLE Dim_Product DROP COLUMN productCategory;
ALTER TABLE Dim_Product DROP COLUMN productSubcategory;
DROP TRIGGER SynchronizeWithSubcategory
DROP TRIGGER SynchronizeWithProduct
```

But we aren't going to write all that code at one time. Before we even start this refactoring, we'll review the existing test suite to be sure the original schema is well covered by automated tests. We'll take the time to add any new tests we wish we had, and we'll ensure that all the tests are passing.

Then, before we begin writing the code, we'll write new tests to test the code we're about to write.

For example, we'll start by writing some structural tests to verify that the `Dim_ProductSubcategory` table exists and contains the expected columns and constraints. These tests will fail until we write the `CREATE TABLE` query correctly. As we proceed in tiny steps, writing tests along the way, we'll also continue to rerun the old tests to be sure we haven't broken anything. By the time we're finished, we will have a new table, new triggers, and a suite of new tests to validate our work.

Structural database refactorings typically follow a pattern that includes a transition period between the old schema and the new one. These buffers coupled with automated tests are essential ingredients of refactoring safety. Additionally, all of the database code and related artifacts should be managed in a version control system, making it easy to roll back to an earlier version if things go horribly wrong. We'll discuss that in detail in Chapter 8, "Version Control for Data Warehousing."

Many other refactoring situations and corresponding database refactorings are presented in *Refactoring Databases* (Ambler and Sadalage 2006), and future books may introduce even more. However, this example provides a glimpse of what database refactoring looks like and should convey the idea that refactoring is more than simply restructuring or improving database elements.

When to Refactor

Database refactoring applies not only to new warehouse development but also to the ongoing maintenance and revision of existing data warehouses. This means that you may be making improvements to a data warehouse that has been in production for some time and supports multiple business intelligence and analytical applications. For that reason, the refactoring process must be a highly structured and safe one that keeps the supported applications running correctly.

Ambler and Sadalage introduced a set of database smells[1] that suggest the need for a refactoring. These database smells include

---

1. Martin Fowler first introduced the concept of "code smells" to the programming community in *Refactoring: Improving the Design of Existing Code* (Fowler 1999).

- **Fear of change.** Fear of changing the database schema because you're not sure what might break is a sign that the database needs refactoring. Fear of change typically suggests an undesirable level of technical debt in your data warehouse.
- **Multipurpose column.** Columns for which the data semantics vary depending on the context of the row are signs of the need for refactoring, for example, using a date column to store either customer birth date or employee start date, depending on whether the record represents a customer or an employee.
- **Multipurpose table.** Tables that are used to store different types of entities may suggest a design flaw in the data model, for example, storing both consumers and corporations in a Customer table.
- **Redundant data.** Duplicating data introduces the possibility of data inconsistencies, such as customer information that is duplicated in multiple source data systems. Resolving data duplication is one of the roles of a data warehouse.
- **Tables with too many columns.** This smell suggests that the table lacks cohesion (a single well-defined purpose) and is trying to store data from several different entities.
- **Tables with too many rows.** Such tables are indicative of performance problems. Data warehouses often appropriately include fact tables with billions of rows, but this smell may be more applicable to staging databases or system-of-record repositories.
- **"Smart" columns.** These are columns whose values can be decoded to produce additional meaning, such as a customer ID in which the first four digits convey the customer's home branch. Often these are called "smart keys," and they create data management complexities.

In addition to these general database smells I routinely see the following data warehousing smells that may suggest the need for refactoring:

- **Complex ETL objects.** When ETL packages contain too many flow paths and complicated transformation nodes, they can be difficult to troubleshoot and maintain. It is also difficult to write test cases around these multipurpose ETL objects. It is preferable to build a collection of simple, single-purpose ETL objects and link them using a sequencer object.
- **Large SQL modules.** When a SQL script or stored procedure is trying to do too much, it often shows up as a large script containing several multiple SQL statements. Such scripts risk code duplication

and should be divided into a collection of small, separate, highly cohesive and loosely coupled[2] modules.

- **Unconformed dimensions.** Multidimensional data models with two or more dimensions containing overlapping data give rise to data duplication and inconsistencies. Ralph Kimball emphasizes creating singular, multipurpose conformed dimensions to avoid this problem (Kimball and Ross 2002).

- **Indiscriminate use of materialized views.** Indexed, or materialized, views are a powerful feature of modern relational database management systems. Used wisely, they can be an effective buffer between data accessors and the physical implementation of base tables. However, materialized views that call materialized views can severely obfuscate the warehouse design.

- **Underutilization of materialized views.** Data warehouses that rely solely on access to base tables are at risk of fragility. That is, minor changes in the physical implementation of these base tables can have unexpected ripple effects for the various accessors to these base tables. The selection of materialized views should strike an appropriate balance between query performance, cost of view maintenance, and base table flexibility.

- **Overreliance on documentation.** Data warehouse tables, columns, scripts, stored procedures, ETL modules, and other components that are not easily understood without accompanying documentation suggest the possible need for refactoring. Data warehouse components, like software, should be self-documenting and self-explanatory. Cleaner designs lead to a reduced need for documentation.

There may be other smells in your data warehouse design, but smells do not always mean something is bad. As you run across these or other smells in your warehouse, evaluate them, analyze them, and decide if a refactoring makes good sense.

> ### Agile Analytics Practice: Take Small Steps
> Data models evolve toward excellence through many small changes, not big sweeping ones. Agile developers apply refactorings one at a time, making sure that everything is working correctly afterward before applying another one.

---

2. Cohesion is the degree to which a unit performs a single well-defined task; coupling is the degree of interdependence between units (Constantine and Yourdon 1979).

How to Refactor

When you have determined that a database refactoring is appropriate, it is important to carefully follow a series of engineering practices to refactor safely and with confidence. Integral aspects of refactoring are test automation and test-driven database development. Furthermore, refactoring should be conducted in an isolated development sandbox where you can experiment using your own copy of the code and databases. Finally, all development code and artifacts should be kept under version control, enabling you to roll back to a previous version if the refactoring does not go as planned. These practices and concepts are examined in detail in coming chapters.

Ambler and Sadalage advocate the following process for database refactoring:

1. **Verify that refactoring is appropriate.** Does the refactoring opportunity make good sense? Is the change actually needed now, or should it be deferred? Is it worth the effort? These are some of the issues to consider first.
2. **Choose the appropriate refactoring.** Once you've identified the opportunity for a refactoring, be sure to choose the right one. This sometimes requires evaluating other areas in the data model that may affect the refactoring. For example, the FlixBuster team may wish to add `Balance` to the `Account` table using the *Introduce Column* refactoring without realizing that `Balance` already exists in the `Customer` table. Therefore, *Move Column* would be a more appropriate refactoring.
3. **Deprecate the original schema.** When refactoring a data model within a production data warehouse, you will likely need to establish a transition (or deprecation) period to ensure that all BI applications continue to work properly. During this period both the original schema and the refactored schema run in parallel. A BI application uses either the original schema or the new one, but not both. The data in both schemas must be synchronized to ensure that BI applications work properly regardless of which schema is used. During the deprecation period BI applications are modified to move away from the deprecated schema and toward the new one. At the end of this period, the deprecated schema is taken off-line, and final testing commences to ensure that nothing breaks. The deprecation processes should be automated as much as possible to ensure a seamless transition during refactoring.

4. **Test before, during, and after.** The only way to safely change a data model is to surround the area of change with a healthy test suite that can be run and rerun at any time. Before you start making changes, be sure that all of your tests are passing, and evaluate the test suite for completeness, adding any test cases you wish you had. Be sure you test all of the ways BI applications access the database schema. Also, create a test suite to validate the data migration strategy. Test all BI applications to ensure no changes in data or behavior. And, of course, add new tests around the newly introduced schema changes, and remove tests that become obsolete or irrelevant. Test automation is the only practical means of testing and retesting continuously throughout the refactoring (covered in greater detail in Chapter 7, "Test-Driven Data Warehouse Development").

5. **Modify the database schema.** Implement the planned refactoring using small, highly cohesive, scripted changes (not manual). Use a test-driven database development approach to take small tests and build a regression test suite that can be used continuously. As new code is written and new tests pass, check those changes into the version control system. This will enable you to easily back out small changes if necessary.

6. **Migrate the source data.** Many refactorings require migrating data from the old schema to the new one, especially when refactoring a production data warehouse. The *Move Data* refactoring is specifically designed to support this. But sometimes, if data quality improvement is a goal of your refactoring, you may wish to use one or more of the data quality refactorings such as *Apply Standard Type* or *Introduce Common Format*. Data migration should also be scripted, and those scripts should have tests supporting them.

7. **Refactor external access programs.** Typically this involves adapting BI applications to work with the new schema but may involve modifying custom programs that access the data warehouse. Modifying these external access programs should also follow a disciplined refactoring process. See the works by Fowler (1999), Feathers (2004), and Kerievsky (2004) for more on software refactoring.

8. **Run all regression tests.** All those tests that were passing before you started the refactoring, plus all the new tests you've added during refactoring, should still be passing after you finish the refactoring. Ideally you've automated all the tests and have been running and rerunning them continuously during the refactoring process.

9. **Version-control your work.** Be sure to commit all modified files and any new ones into your version control system (see Chapter 8, "Version Control for Data Warehousing"). These include any new

or modified scripts or ETL objects, test data or generated code, test cases, documentation, and models. Now is also a good time to tag the version control mainline with a marker that indicates the completion of your refactoring.

10. **Announce the refactoring.** Publicize the refactoring to everyone on the data warehousing and business intelligence teams, in addition to all parties who may directly access the data warehouse's internal schemas, to ensure that everyone uses the new schema correctly.

Final Words on Refactoring

This section serves only as a summary of database refactoring and aims to accurately convey what refactoring is, what it is not, and how it can be a valuable technique for evolving excellent data warehouse design. As you incorporate database refactoring into your data warehousing technical practices, it is important to continuously balance the structure provided by sound data modeling principles with the flexibility offered by this adaptive approach. That is, underuse of sound up-front design followed by overreliance on refactoring to adapt may cause unnecessary rework. Conversely, an appropriate degree of "rework" can lead to better, and more fitting, design choices and should be tolerated. The mini-book *Recipes for Continuous Database Integration*, by Pramod Sadalage, is a companion book to *Refactoring Databases* that introduces other powerful evolutionary database development techniques (Sadalage 2007). Also, Scott Ambler's Web site, www. agiledata.org, provides a detailed source of information about Agile database practices.

DEPLOYING WAREHOUSE CHANGES

As Agile Analytics teams mature in the evolutionary development of the warehouse, data marts, and BI applications, they strive toward more frequent—nearly continuous—deployment of new features and revisions. Experience has shown that early version deployments involve more data warehouse revisions than later versions. Often these early deployments involve as many warehouse revisions (and refactorings) as the new BI features that those modifications support. Over time the warehouse design tends to stabilize and settle, supporting new BI features with few changes in data models or warehouse components.

However, as time passes, deployments of revisions to a production warehouse and/or data marts have a new set of challenges, namely, the migration of large data sets in structures indexed on surrogate keys and other database optimization elements like partitioning. These are all factors that complicate the ability to frequently deploy improvements in the DW/BI systems and should be balanced against the business benefits of frequent deployment. There is no single right answer to the question of deployment frequency. However, the more frequent your deployments, the smaller they are and the easier they are to back out if needed.

Regardless of deployment frequency, a disciplined and carefully designed deployment process is paramount. Furthermore, the steps in the process, including data migration steps, should be primarily automated rather than manual. Automated deployment scripts and utilities must be thought of as an extension of the production DW/BI system and should be thoroughly tested as such. In fact, Agile Analytics teams think of the production DW/BI system as a combination of warehouse components, BI application components, user and technical documentation, deployment and installation components, and administrative utilities.

If you adopt the recommendations on test automation, version control, and continuous integration that are presented later in this book, you'll find that frequent DW/BI deployment is the logical next step in this set of engineering practices. Conversely, if you envision deploying from development into production relying on final-stage manual testing, and no version control, frequent deployment probably seems like a daunting and risky concept.

Pramod Sadalage and Scott Ambler outline a deployment sequence for general database deployment (Ambler and Sadalage 2006). I have taken some liberties and repurposed their process for data warehouse and business intelligence system deployment:

1. **Back up data.** If the deployment doesn't go as expected, you may need to abort the deployment and restore everything.
2. **Run previous regression tests.** Before doing anything else, be sure that the current production system is running properly and that nothing has become inadvertently corrupted. If any regression tests fail, don't deploy until you've identified and corrected the problem in both the current version and the new version.
3. **Deploy changed BI apps.** Follow existing procedures to deploy new versions of BI applications.
4. **Deploy database changes.** Run all of the newly developed or modified schema change scripts and data migration scripts.
5. **Run new regression tests.** Run the latest version of the regression test suite, including modified and newly added tests. Beware of side

effects from your tests such as leaving test data residue or schema changes (e.g., temporary tables) behind.

6. **Back out if necessary.** If regression testing reveals severe defects, everything must be reverted to the previous version until defects are corrected. In this case back out database refactorings and deployed applications, and abort the deployment.

7. **Publicize the deployment.** When everything is successfully deployed, the project community should be notified immediately. Community members are eager to know how everything went and whether their new BI features are available.

8. **Remove the deprecated schema.** Although this step may occur many months after steps 1 through 7, the deployment is not really complete until deprecated schemas and scaffolding components like triggers and stored procedures are completely removed.

Of course, you'll want to do a dry run of this process first in your preproduction environment to surface as many glitches as possible without affecting the production system. This process should be sufficient for DW/BI systems of small to moderate data volumes. However, if your warehouse contains tens or hundreds of terabytes of data, the data migration alone may take many days, and it is unacceptable to take the production warehouse off-line that long for deployment.

In their book *Continuous Delivery*, David Farley and Jez Humble introduce a comprehensive, well-thought-out set of techniques for simplifying and routinizing frequent software deployments (Farley and Humble 2010). Many of those concepts and practices are directly applicable to DW/BI deployment, and a couple of ideas deserve a brief introduction here.

Blue-Green Deployment

Farley and Humble describe a powerful release technique called *blue-green deployment* that is akin to the hot switch-over strategy long used in the mainframe world. In this approach you have two identical production environments called "blue" and "green." Users access BI applications through a router that points to one or the other of these, whichever is the current production release. Figure 6.3 depicts an example in which the green slice is currently active. The DW/BI deployment occurs in the blue slice and has no effect on the green slice. Before switching the router to the blue slice, we run data migration scripts to populate the blue data warehouse and smoke test to confirm that everything is working properly. When everything is ready, we can switch the router to point to the blue slice with virtually zero

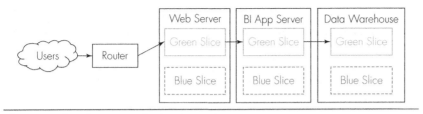

Figure 6.3   Blue-green deployment scheme

downtime. If anything goes wrong with the deployment, we can simply switch back to the green slice and commence debugging the problem in the blue environment. Once a deployment is deemed successful, the green environment becomes available for the next deployment.

Clearly the blue-green deployment scheme requires an investment in additional hardware and software licenses. This cost should be weighed against the person time saved and the value produced by frequent releases. Nonetheless, depending on your DW/BI technologies, the cost can be significant. Virtualization offers one means of reducing this cost depending on performance requirements and data volumes. Another alternative may be to run both the blue and green slices in parallel on the same hardware infrastructure using designated ports, file system partitions, or some other configuration.

Another potential difficulty with the blue-green deployment scheme is the management and migration of high-volume data. No matter what the approach, migrating high-volume databases is a gnarly problem for which there is no simple solution. A recommended data migration strategy in blue-green deployment is to put the green data warehouse in a read-only state while migration scripts are loading data into the blue warehouse. Once data migration is complete, the inflow of new data can be switched back on. This helps avoid inconsistencies but can impact BI users if data migration takes very long to execute, in which case you'll need to clearly communicate with customers and stakeholders so that expectations are managed properly.

Database Versioning

Farley and Humble discuss another powerful technique for managing database releases. This technique involves versioning the database using a single-cell table in the database that contains its version number, a practice first introduced in *Refactoring Databases* (Ambler and Sadalage 2006).

Whenever a change is made to the database schema, two scripts are created. One is a roll-forward script that takes the schema from version x to version $x + 1$, and the other is a roll-back script that reverts the schema from version $x + 1$ back to version x. These include data migration scripts as well as schema change scripts. The deployment scripts need to include a configuration setting that specifies which database version is used in the deployment. Moving from one database version to another involves executing a sequence of one or more roll-forward or roll-back scripts.

This technique should be used for each of the repositories in the data warehouse environment, including the staging and integration schemas, the presentation database, and any data mart schemas. In addition to supporting easier deployments, this technique supports database refactoring very nicely and is generally a good practice.

Agile Analytics Practice: Always Be Ready to Deploy

Agile development teams seek to end every iteration prepared to deploy. Deployment should be driven by business decisions, not technical readiness. By developing an automated and disciplined deployment process, your team can offer deployment as an option to the business at any time. This principle is called "potentially shippable" in Scrum and "potentially consumable" in Disciplined Agile Delivery (DAD).

OTHER REASONS TO TAKE AN EVOLUTIONARY APPROACH

The data warehousing demands of today impose a newer and more challenging set of demands, rendering big requirements and design up front (BRUF/BDUF) even less appropriate. Traditional data warehouse architectures have always been complex and time-consuming to implement. Not only do new pressures add to this complexity, but users are also demanding faster time to availability. These new demands include the following:

- **Broader and more diverse user community.** Historically, the majority of usage of data warehouse implementations has been from a relatively small percentage of users including senior executives and analytical specialists. Executives and their representatives have traditionally used the corporate data warehouse as a tool for strategic planning and forecasting. Analytics professionals have traditionally used the warehouse for more tactical purposes such as customer relationship management and marketing strategies.

Today's business intelligence mantra is "BI for the masses." More and different types of users, with a broader spectrum of usage patterns and needs, are using today's BI systems. Scaling the data warehouse to accommodate a greater number of subject-specific data marts and a higher volume of users is putting strains on data warehousing development groups because doing these things in the traditional way is time-intensive. *Today's data warehousing architectures must accommodate this diversity while still maintaining one consistent and correct version of the truth.*

▪ **New and even more disparate data sources.** Corporate data warehouses have always been challenged by the integration of legacy, ERP, transactional, HR, and other systems. Today legacy systems are even older; many "new" systems aren't so new anymore; and there is a demand for including data from external sources via Web service calls and the like. Moreover, the structure and nature of today's data are more disparate. We now have the need to analyze Web log data, video and image data, unstructured content, and other such data.

Historically, adding a new source system was a matter of analyzing and understanding the structure of the source data, writing the ETL code necessary to extract that data, identifying and rectifying quality problems, and writing the ETL necessary to integrate the new data source into the existing data warehouse schema. This has always been complicated and time-intensive at best, requiring access to knowledgeable domain experts and developing customized ETL code for each new data source. *Handling today's even more disparate data sources places an even heavier tax on the already overburdened data warehousing department.*

▪ **External data sources.** Related to the increasingly disparate nature of source data is the increasing demand to import external data into the data warehouse. For years external data has included customer credit profiles and psycho-demographic data offered by third-party data providers. Importing such third-party data has been relatively limited and has become a routine monthly, quarterly, or semiannual update process. However, today's data warehouses are importing data from corporate partners, customers' systems, and other external sources. This new external data must be updated in the warehouse with the same, or nearly the same, frequency as internal data feeds. *Today's data warehouses must provide the mechanics to frequently retrieve both internal and external data with high reliability.*

▪ **Changing source data is problematic.** Changes in the structure or the semantics of any given data source are problematic for data warehousing. Data extraction jobs break, and data loads fail to finish, causing data in the warehouse to get out of sync. Fortunately this is not a frequent occurrence, but it does happen enough to be of concern. When a new operational system is being deployed, or a new revision is released, it is not uncommon for the data warehousing team to fail to get notified of changes. Other unexpected changes such as database view changes or Web service API changes further compound this problem.

Even more challenging is the possible change in the semantics of source data. This may be a subtle shift such as switching from a corporate-generated smart key for customer ID to an autogenerated surrogate key in the operational system. Nonetheless, these changes can wreak havoc on data warehousing integration and reconciliation processes. *Today's data warehouse architectures must be more immune to the unexpected changes in data source structure or semantics.*

- **New demands for near real-time BI.** One of the latest hot topics in business intelligence is business performance management or BPM. BPM represents an increasing demand for operational BI. Operational business intelligence requires that business users learn about operational situations as quickly as possible so that immediate corrective action can be taken. Nightly data warehouse updates and refreshes are no longer sufficient to support the near real-time demands of operational business intelligence. However, keeping the data warehouse up-to-date with real-time events is a challenging goal that includes pulling new data, cleansing it, integrating it, transforming it, loading it into the warehouse, reprocessing cubes, and so on.

  Imagine the complexities of managing a large airline company. Margins are very slim, so cost control is essential. The airline may have upward of 700 airplanes in its fleet, and at any given time some of these are in the sky, some are on the ground between flights, some are out of service, and some of the in-service planes are nearing their routine maintenance schedules. Pilots must be in compliance with FAA regulations, and flights are expected to be on time. Airlines have significant BPM requirements for keeping airplanes in service, pilots flying safely, fuel costs at a minimum, and passengers happy. Maintenance managers, logistics managers, terminal managers, safety officers, and others need the data as quickly as possible— waiting until tomorrow for the intelligence is too late for intervening in today's problems. *Today's data warehouses must provide near real-time business intelligence.*

- **New demands for proactive push reporting.** Related to this new trend toward BPM and operational BI is a demand for *proactive push reporting.* Users have always wanted exception-based reporting:

"Show me the things that require my attention so I don't have to sort through all the data." This has led to color coding, dashboard presentation, and alerts. Proactive push reporting takes this a step further by sending users a BI notification (possibly to their mobile devices). For example, an airline company's maintenance director may wish to be notified immediately about airplanes whose onboard sensors indicate anomalies, because this may suggest a safety or urgent maintenance problem. *Today's data warehouses must offer users the ability to define push notifications and the events that will trigger a push; and then the system must proactively push that notification as near to real time as is feasible.*

■ **Data loading and reloading are time-intensive.** Most production data warehouses are challenged to complete their nightly data refreshes before the next workday begins. This is especially true when there are BI reports that rely on time-intensive queries. These queries cannot run until all of the data is updated and cubes are reprocessed. Not long ago I consulted for a company that conducts nightly data warehouse updates. One particular BI report was based on a query that took approximately four hours complete. The users of this BI report had to wait until early afternoon to use the report in order to be certain that it contained the most current information. This is not an unfamiliar scenario, and it is an unacceptable one. Business users should be enabled by, not hobbled by, the data warehouse. *Today's data warehouses must provide users with timely data where "timely" is defined as "when the user needs it."*

Each of these constraints and requirements suggests the need for data warehouse architects and data modelers to maintain a minimally sufficient yet highly adaptable warehouse design and data model. Overdesigning the warehouse or the underlying data models inhibits developers' ability to travel light and fast. Underdesigning the warehouse and underlying data models inhibits developers' ability to be well prepared for iterative development. And warehouse designs that evolve without discipline and technical excellence soon become unwieldy and inflexible with increasing technical debt. The aim of Agile DW/BI is to strike the right balance of minimally sufficient, highly adaptive, and technically excellent designs and data models.

CASE STUDY: ADAPTIVE WAREHOUSE ARCHITECTURE

What follows is a summary of a unique Agile data warehousing and BI project that resulted in the evolution of a metadata-driven systems architecture using an adaptive data model for extreme flexibility. A detailed technical description of this architecture is available as a Cutter Consortium Executive Report (Collier and O'Leary 2009). This section is intended to describe the factors that led our team to evolve from a traditional architecture to a surprisingly innovative warehouse architecture.

This architecture evolved out of necessity. In 2004 I was hired as the technical lead and chief architect on an ambitious data warehousing project. The company sought to offer productized business intelligence to its enterprise customers via a hosted software-as-a-service (SaaS) application. The BI product was to be data-warehouse-based and was to enable the integration and analysis of data from a variety of sources, both internal (provider data) and external (customer data). Data could not be easily pulled from across Internet boundaries. This solution required a single warehouse architecture that could adapt to a broad variety of customer types, sizes, and business requirements. The product had to offer a personalized customer experience without being custom-tailored to each enterprise customer or user—creating custom ETL code, custom data models, custom BI applications, and other customized elements was not an option.

Our Agile Analytics team initially applied a typical Kimball-style warehouse architecture on this project, but the complexities of integrating many disparate, and unfamiliar, data sources that varied from customer to customer made it impossible to adapt quickly. Out of necessity ingenuity is born, and we developed what we call the *Message Driven Warehouse*. It turns out that this architecture has many benefits beyond the productization of hosted BI applications. Adapting to new and changing requirements is easier and faster. Adding new data sources is easier. Spinning up new data marts is easier. And the architecture is much less affected by unexpected changes.

The architecture emerged with the continuous customer validation of a maturing, production-quality data warehouse. It evolved in 90-day release cycles divided into three-week sprints. End users were actively involved in the process, reviewing new BI features at the end of each sprint. The message-driven data warehouse has been vetted on real operational data with real customers. This architecture enables warehouse developers to move faster, leaner, and at a lower cost than current data warehouse implementations.

Product Evolution

When the project began in 2004, the stakeholder vision was for an on-premise, productized data warehouse and BI application. After an exploratory 90-day pilot to validate the concept and technology selection, the product vision began to take shape.

Our customers were medium to large companies in the transportation industry—trucking companies. Most modern tractor-trailer vehicles have advanced technology on board that monitors GPS position, speed, fuel consumption, oil pressure, idling and moving states, current gear, as well as driver activity and DOT (Department of Transportation) status, in addition to critical event data such as rapid deceleration. All of this operational data is routinely transmitted wirelessly to corporate transportation hubs, where it is used to support safety initiatives, maintenance optimization, resource utilization, and other purposes.

You can imagine the complexities of managing a fleet of more than 20,000 vehicles, twice as many trailers, and more than 50,000 drivers. Add the fact that these assets are always moving and often in remote locations. Keeping track of scheduled maintenance, driver availability, on-the-road breakdowns, and the goal of on-time deliveries and pickups is an ongoing challenge. Our project involved the effective management and presentation of this data for various analytical and decision support purposes.

Our product's first several releases included on-site installation and configuration. The architecture, built on Microsoft SQL Server technologies, was a fairly typical Kimball architecture consisting of a set of conformed dimensions servicing multiple subject-specific fact tables. However, sometime in early 2007 the stakeholders and product manager concluded that our product would better meet the customer community needs if offered as a hosted product. So, our next release was focused on shifting the implementation to a multitenant, highly available, secure SaaS architecture. Moreover, our product manager, through lots of customer input, determined that the product needed to merge customer-generated data (e.g., HR, ERP, payroll) with the vehicle and driver data on which we had thus far been focused.

Clearly our development team had a new set of technical challenges to embrace. We immediately faced the challenge of how to extract data from customer source systems, across the Internet and through the customers' corporate firewalls. Customer data models and content differed, sometimes significantly, from one customer to the next. That data was to be merged with our company's well-understood vehicle and driver data (previously described). We quickly realized that traditional pull-based data extraction techniques were not appropriate for the new version of the product.

We also quickly discovered that the data model in our integration tier was insufficient to handle the disparate nature of the customer-generated data. That data was to be merged with vehicle and driver data to establish a more holistic view of operations. After we experimented with Web services, data agents, and bulk FTP transfers as techniques for moving data from customer sites to our data center, our systems architecture began evolving toward a message-driven architecture, enabling a shift from data pull to data push. Throughout 2007 and 2008 we continued to develop in 90-day planning cycles. Our systems architecture and underlying data models continued to evolve incrementally, and we incorporated many other innovative elements. By the summer of 2008 our project was winding down and our design was stabilizing. The remainder of this section describes the innovative aspects of our design, and I hope it will serve as a concrete example of how well evolutionary design can work in DW/BI development.

Architectural Overview

The Message Driven Warehouse architecture is a significant overhaul of the data preparation and metadata layers of the generic DW architecture and is aimed at addressing the aforementioned limitations. On the surface the most significant shift in this architecture is that data is pushed into the warehouse via a *message bus* rather than the traditional method of pulling data from operational source systems using ETL processes. Operational source systems publish new and updated data, in a *common message format*, to a corporate message bus. The bus is monitored by the data warehouse *message handler* for applicable incoming messages. As data arrives on the warehouse message queue, the handler deconstructs the messages using a *metadata dictionary* and passes the message payload along to an *adapter* layer. The adapter maps the incoming data into a normalized system of record (SOR) database, which is akin to Inmon's centralized warehouse (Inmon 2005). The SOR is built on a domain-independent *adaptive data model*, enabling developers to rapidly adapt the data model to various industries and business domains. The SOR is the basis for various dimensional data marts, mining marts, and materialized relational databases for presentation of business intelligence to the user community. Figure 6.4 provides a high-level, logical diagram of the Message Driven Warehouse architecture for reference.

Observe that the architecture incorporates elements of both Kimball's Data Warehouse Bus (Kimball and Ross 2002) and Inmon's Corporate Information Factory (Inmon 2007). The real power of this architecture lies in the data preparation layer—getting the data into the warehouse, integrating it, and transforming it prior to loading the various presentation marts.

Central to this architecture is the use of a message bus to push data updates into the warehouse. However, the Message Driven Warehouse is much more than just a push alternative to the traditional pull architectures. The

Data updates are *pushed* to the data warehouse

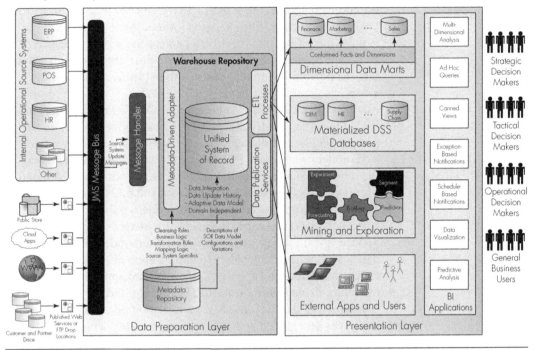

Figure 6.4   Message-driven data warehouse conceptual architecture

following key architectural components and concepts work in concert to make the Message Driven Warehouse faster and easier for practitioners to implement, modify, and maintain:

- **Observation message model.** This highly generalized message format enables source data changes to be conveyed as observations about particular phenomena during specific time frames. Analyzing source data models is significantly minimized, and domain information is codified in the observation metadata. Adding new source systems is a matter of updating the metadata dictionary and instrumenting the source database to publish observation message model (OMM)-formatted messages.
- **Message bus.** The Message Driven Warehouse leverages existing enterprise message bus technologies and concepts to send data to the warehouse. This use of the message bus enables data to trickle into the warehouse as it becomes available, a step toward attaining near real-time business intelligence.

- **Unified system of record database.** Similar to Inmon's centralized warehouse database, the SOR is a 3NF relational database in which the data is integrated and prepared for use. We refer to this as the SOR because it fits into the broader enterprise service-oriented architecture as the single version of historical truth, a purpose that serves a potentially broader purpose than business intelligence alone.
- **Adaptive data modeling.** Although the SOR data model is normalized, it is domain-independent, based on adaptive modeling and meta-modeling techniques. Adaptive modeling is a highly generalized modeling approach that eliminates domain-centricity from the relational data model. It melds very neatly with the OMM and adapts very easily to changes in the data and problem domain.
- **Metadata-driven data adapter.** The adapter is a data-processing layer that converts the data payload from incoming Java Message Service (JMS) messages to the adaptive data model within the SOR database. It relies on metadata to handle anomalies, perform transformations, merge data, purge duplicates, and apply business logic.
- **Metadata-driven configuration.** The Message Driven Warehouse is designed so that ETL and SQL code, data models, and processes remain as generalized and invariant as possible. Elements that are expected to change over time such as business rules and data-cleansing logic are stored in the metadata store. The metadata store is key to the highly adaptive nature of the message-driven data warehouse.

Each of these architectural concepts and components is described in greater detail in the following sections. Once implemented, the message-driven data warehouse can rapidly accommodate the addition of new source systems, making changes to the logical data model, creating new data marts, changing business rules, and so on. Coupled with Agile Analytics development methods, this architecture can place BI applications in the hands of business decision makers within a few short weeks of starting development.

Observation Message Model

A Message Driven Warehouse requires messaging with a payload able to support disparate data sources and data domains. This requires balancing uniformity in representation as well as the ability to augment the representation with new kinds of objects.

The OMM described here draws heavily on the concepts and terminology in the Observations and Measurements model defined by the Open Geospatial

Consortium (OGC) (Cox 2006). This model in turn draws on the Observation and Measurement (OAM) analysis pattern by Martin Fowler (1997).

The OMM uses a set of terms to describe an object in time. These terms form an observation about an object (or feature of interest) that happens at a point in time or over a span of time. As described by the OGC, an observation breaks down into the following components:

- The *time frame* is expressed as a range of time or an instant in time with zero duration.
- The *feature of interest* is the object about which the observation is made, such as a person, product, or other object having attributes that may change over time.
- The *phenomenon* is a reference to the type of aspect of the feature of interest that is observed. This could be any kind of aspect, from a GPS position to an insurance premium payment. This type defines the structure and kinds of data for the aspect. The phenomenon may be an atomic measurement of a single attribute or event, or it may be a collection of measurements of several attributes.
- The *result* is the actual data defined by the phenomenon. It may be a single value or a complex network of nested structures, each containing a set of values.

Essentially, an observation captures a particular kind of result about an object at a given point or period in time. An observation separates information at the *knowledge level* (observation metadata) from the *operational level* (observation data) using XML schemas that define the features of interest and phenomena. These schemas are referenced within the XML file containing the observation collection. Extending the ability to make observations across domains is a matter of defining features of interest and phenomena in an XML schema definition and referring to its URL in the XML file containing the observations.

Let's use a FlixBuster example to understand the mechanics of the model. Using the XML format specified in Cox's *Observations and Measurements* (Cox 2006), our example will present a collection of observations establishing a *studio* that owns the rights to specific *video content* (e.g., the movie *Jerry Maguire*) and a *royalty payment* made to the studio (see Listing 6.1). Two observations are contained in the collection. Both observations refer to a video content object (or feature of interest) that is a movie with an ID equal to '890327762'.

Listing 6.1   Observation Collection about a FlixBuster Royalty Payment

```
01  <?xml version="1.0" encoding="UTF-8"?>
02  <om:ObservationCollection pm:id="coll1"
03    xmlns:om="http://www.opengeospatial.net/om/0.0"
04    xmlns:pm="http://www.flixbuster.com/royalty/1.0"
05    pm:schemaLocation=
        "http://www.flixbuster.com/royalty/1.0 pm.xsd"
06    xmlns:xsi="http://www.w3.org/2001/XMLSchema-instance"
07    xsi:schemaLocation=
        "http://www.opengeospatial.net/om/0.0 ../om.xsd">
08    <om:Observation>
09      <om:time>
10        <pm:TimePeriod>
11          <pm:beginTime>1996-10-11T00:00:00.00</pm:beginTime>
12          <pm:endTime>2100-01-11T17:22:25.00</pm:endTime>
13        </pm:TimePeriod>
14      </om:time>
15      <om:featureOfInterest>
16        <pm:VideoContent>
17          <pm:VideoContentId>890327762</pm:VideoContentId>
18          <pm:VideoContentType>Movie</pm:VideoContentType>
19          <pm:VideoContentName>Jerry Maguire</pm:VideoContentName>
20        </pm:VideoContent>
21      </om:featureOfInterest>
22      <om:observedProperty pm:href=
            "urn:x-ogc:def:phenomenon:OGC:Studio"/>
23      <om:result>
24        <pm:Studio>
25          <pm:StudioId>324223434</pm:StudioId>
26          <pm:StudioName>TriStar Pictures</pm:StudioName>
27        </pm:Studio>
28      </om:result>
29    </om:Observation>
30
31    <om:Observation>
32      <om:time>
33        <pm:TimeInstant>2005-01-19T14:12:41.00</pm:TimeInstant>
34      </om:time>
35      <om:featureOfInterest>
36        <pm:Royalty>
37          <pm:VideoContentId>890327762</pm:VideoContentId>
38          <pm:VideoContentType>Movie</pm:VideoContentType>
39        </pm:Royalty>
40      </om:featureOfInterest>
41      <om:observedProperty pm:href=
                "urn:x-ogc:def:phenomenon:OGC:RoyaltyPayment" />
42      <om:result>
43        <pm:RoyaltyPayment>
44          <pm:StudioId>324223434</pm:StudioId>
45          <pm:payment currency="USD">234.12</pm:payment>
46        </pm:RoyaltyPayment>
47      </om:result>
```

continues

Listing 6.1   Observation Collection about a FlixBuster Royalty Payment
(*Continued*)

```
48    </om:Observation>
49    </om:ObservationCollection>
50
```

The first observation on lines 8–29 establishes studio rights to video content. A studio is paid an agreed-upon royalty percentage each time one of its films is rented by a FlixBuster customer. This observation specifies that the video containing the movie *Jerry Maguire* is owned by TriStar Pictures starting on October 11, 1996, at midnight and extending far into the future.

The second observation on lines 31–49 captures a royalty payment event made to the studio on January 19, 2005, at 2:12 P.M. The studio with the studio ID = '324223434' (TriStar Pictures) was paid a royalty amount of $234.12.

The definitions (or metadata) of the objects in this example are specified by the inclusion of the appropriate namespace and schema references for the pm namespace as indicated in the xmlns:pm and pm:schemaLocation attributes of the ObservationCollection element. The objects defined in the pm.xsd file include VideoContent, Studio, and RoyaltyPayment. The pm schema is separate from the observation collection, which accomplishes Fowler's goal of separating the knowledge level from the operational level.

This OMM specification is sufficient to describe any problem or business domain in terms of the objects, their attributes, their relationships with one another, and all events and activities that occur in the domain. Defining the appropriate OMM metadata is the key to adapting this model to any given domain. It is not necessary that this metadata be complete and comprehensive before using the OMM. The metadata can evolve incrementally and be driven by a prioritized set of user requirements.

Message Bus for Pushing Data

Traditional data extraction is a fragile and trouble-prone approach. Data pulls must be scheduled during off-peak hours; ETL processes must have "insider knowledge" about the structure and form of source data; changes in the structure or format of source data may cause ETL processes to break or fail; and developing this custom ETL is costly and time-consuming.

Our architecture relies on source systems sending data changes using the OMM format previously described. By pushing small messages throughout the day, we also avoid the performance bottleneck of nightly update jobs.

Our message-driven architecture is also a trickle-feed architecture, which has the possibility of approaching a near real-time DW/BI system.

Figure 6.5 shows how upstream source applications funnel their data into the Message Driven Warehouse.

The first time a source application connects to the data warehouse, it may have a lot of data to transmit. In this case, it does a one-time "bulk load" of its data by transmitting a data file to a secure FTP drop box (step 1 in the bulk load path). The drop box then sends a message to the data warehouse's message handler through a message bus to alert the warehouse that there is a data file to load (step 2). The message handler then downloads the file and processes its contents (in the form of an observation collection) to load the application's data into the data warehouse.

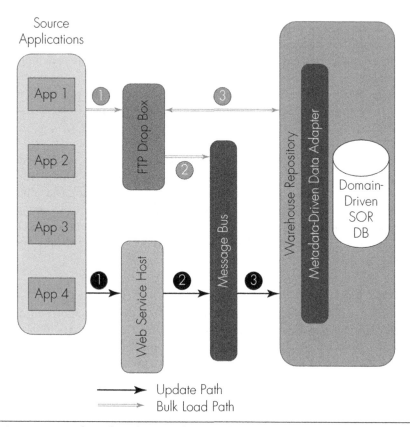

Figure 6.5 Flow of application data into the message-driven data warehouse

After the source application has done an initial bulk load, it can send updates via a Web service (step 1 in the update path) which (as in the bulk load) sends an observation collection as a message (step 2). Once the data adapter receives the JMS message, it processes the observation collection payload, resulting in updates to the data warehouse.

Pushing, rather than pulling, source data has the additional benefit of separating concerns in the warehouse architecture. The warehouse does not have to be concerned with where the source system resides, how to connect to it, or how to interpret its data structures. The source system may reside outside the enterprise as long as it can publish updates as OMM messages onto the enterprise message bus. This separation of concerns may also translate into a separation of responsibilities for developers, thereby increasing parallel development efforts. While warehouse developers are preparing the warehouse to receive new source data, other developers take responsibility for automating the publication of OMM messages from the new source.

Warehouse Repository

The message handler retrieves messages from the bus and passes their payload (OMM observations) to the data warehouse repository for processing and storage. The warehouse repository is the core architectural component of the message-driven data warehouse. It is composed of four key elements: the *data adapter,* the *system of record* database, the *metadata repository,* and the *data access services* tier (see Figure 6.6). This design of the warehouse repository makes it faster and easier to adapt to new requirements. Developers can create a new data mart, add a new data source, or change a business rule in just a few days. Most changes occur in the metadata repository and in the data adapters—minimal database changes are needed.

Data Adapter. The data adapter is a metadata-driven software layer that receives OMM message payloads and uses metadata to validate, interpret, and process payload data and map it into the SOR database through an object relational mapping (ORM) framework. The adapter sequence is shown in Figure 6.7 for a single incoming message.

The message director monitors the message bus for incoming warehouse messages. The payload from incoming messages is passed to an internal data handler that uses the observation globally unique identifier (GUID) to retrieve applicable metadata from the metadata store. This metadata tells the data handler how to process the message payload. Once all atomic processing operations have completed, the resulting data set is loaded into the SOR database via an ORM tier.

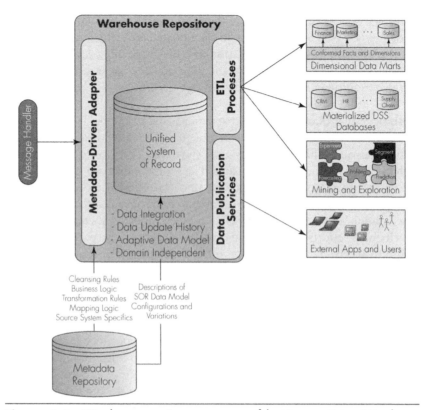

Figure 6.6   Warehouse repository component of the Message-Driven Warehouse

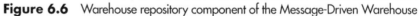

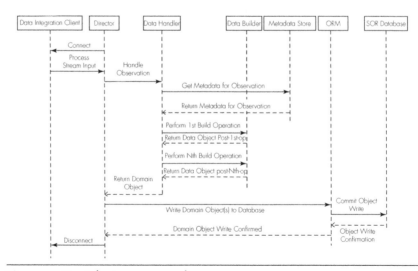

Figure 6.7   Adapter sequence diagram

The adapter is an object-oriented implementation that implements the *Chain of Responsibility*, *Factory*, and *Builder* software design patterns (Gamma et al. 1994) coupled with metadata to process incoming message payloads (see Figure 6.8). When the *message director* retrieves a message, a *factory* instance is autoconfigured based on the observation GUID. This configuration determines the types of *builders* that are needed; the factory organizes the builders into a sequence of operations (or *chain of responsibility*) that is applied to the payload.

For example, when the OMM payload in Listing 6.1 arrives, the director passes this payload to the data handler object. The handler parses this into the respective *video* and *royalty* features of interest plus the collection of phenomena about them and generates instances of the appropriate builders to process each element. As each builder uses the metadata to process its element, it constructs a collection of *prepared data* objects. For instance, the EntityBuilder that is processing the policy feature of interest in the message will create a videoContentEntity prepared data object with the ID of '890327762'.

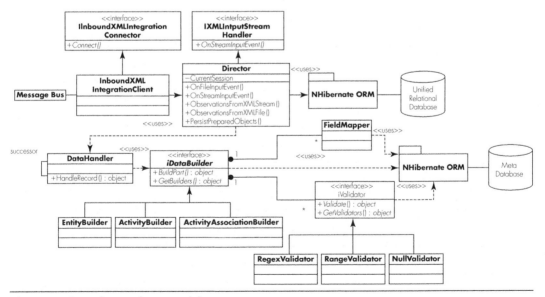

Figure 6.8 Adapter object model

The prepared data object is an ORM object that is handled by a framework like Hibernate.[3] The ORM framework uses a mapping file to map a videoContentEntity object into the SOR data model, minimizing the need for code modifications.

The messages in Listing 6.1 result in a prepared objects collection containing videoContentEntity, studioEntity, and entityAccountability. The director passes each prepared data object to the ORM tier, which issues the appropriate SQL commands to insert or update the data into the SOR database.

The Validator class (also patterns-based) handles data validation and cleansing. For example, suppose the observed property called RoyaltyPayment for an observation is a required field that must be a real number with a value greater than zero. The Validator factory queries the metadata store to find out that a *range validator*, a *null validator*, and a *type validator* are needed. The range validator will query the metadata store to learn that RoyaltyPayment must be greater than zero; the null validator will ensure that the value is not null; and the type validator will assure that the value is a legitimate real number. When data anomalies are detected, the validators look to the metadata store for the data-cleansing rules to apply. As these data-handling rules change, only the metadata is affected.

Because the OMM message format generalizes all data to observations about entities, activities, and associations between entities, the three builder types in the object model are sufficient to handle new data sources with ease. When a new entity type, event type, or association type is discovered, these new types only need to be added into the OMM metadata dictionary. Of course, new business rules or cleansing logic for these new types must be added to the adapter metadata store as well.

System of Record Database. The SOR database is the unifying repository in the architecture. Data processed by the data adapter is loaded into the adaptive schema in the SOR (described in the next section). Like Inmon's centralized data warehouse, the SOR is a normalized relational database. Also like Inmon's model (and Kimball's), this is an atomic, time-variant, and nonmonotonic database—new data and updates arrive over time, and data in the SOR is never deleted or overwritten.

---

3. www.hibernate.org

Unlike Inmon's warehouse, the data model is adaptive and domain-*independent* and is expected to evolve and adapt to new requirements with minimal structural changes and effort. Although the SOR contains the official, single version of the truth, this database is not intended to be accessed directly by outside developers, systems, or users. Instead, it is "wrapped" between the *metadata-driven adapter* and the *data access services* layers. Data entering the SOR is processed through the data adapter, and data is retrieved through the access tier (e.g., materialized views).

This encapsulation of the SOR supports the easy modification of the SOR to accommodate new warehouse requirements. Changes (structural, referential, etc.) can quickly and easily be made in the SOR data model without affecting data producers or consumers because the adapter, access service, and ETL layers isolate external systems. Changes to the SOR schema are further minimized by the use of the metadata base.

Adaptive Data Model. Earlier in this chapter we saw the *adaptive data model* (ADM) as an example of a data model pattern. The power of ADM is that domain model semantics and rules of integrity are stored in a metadata base and are configurable by domain modeling experts without structural database changes. The SOR schema implements a variant of the ADM.

The ADM represents all observed properties related to an entity as attributes. This includes both characteristics (e.g., a studio name) as well as events that occur over time (e.g., a studio royalty payment). This overloading of the Attribute table in the ADM has a tendency to make the data model somewhat more confusing because the semantics of properties and events are different. Also, it adds query complexity in order to separate events from properties. Finally, in a high-volume warehouse the large size of the Attribute table may affect performance.

Our design extends the ADM to separate events and activities from attributes by adding Event and EventType tables to store transactional and operational events (see Figure 6.9). Discrete events like subscription cancellation have zero duration, while activities like a video being checked out have a duration greater than zero. Adapter metadata distinguishes an OMM phenomenon as an event or an attribute. The Extended ADM is expressively equal to the ADM, and implementation choice is situational. Performance concerns remain an issue in the Event table for high transaction volumes. It is important to index this table to address this problem.

The Cutter Report on this subject provides much more technical detail than this summary, including slowly changing dimensions and configuring

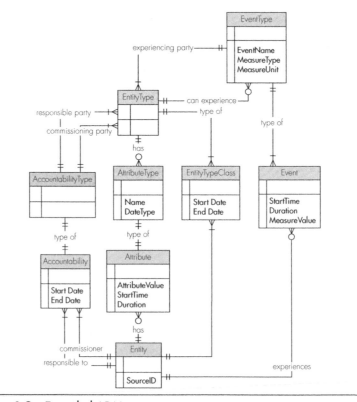

Figure 6.9 Extended ADM

metadata (Collier and O'Leary 2009). Our aim in this design was to drive variability out of the implementation and into the metadata base. Doing so promotes the rapid, inexpensive ability to respond to new and changing business requirements.

This case study demonstrates at least three Agile themes: that agility benefits from adaptive design, that excellent design is not created on the first try but evolves, and that excellent design relies on sound technical practices such as the gentle application of patterns.

WRAP-UP

Agility comes from three sources: an Agile team, an adaptive process, and an evolving design. Agile Analytics relies on a set of practices that enable DW/BI developers to incrementally evolve the system design and underlying data models without a reduction in design quality. Whether you are working on a preexisting data warehouse or are enjoying new "greenfield" development, adaptive design principles are relevant and beneficial, even in the oldest of legacy architectures. As maintenance projects and new development efforts are planned, Agile Analytics practitioners should continuously seek to drive down technical debt and improve quality through the application of evolutionary design techniques like sufficient up-front design, Agile Modeling, gentle application of patterns, managing technical debt, refactoring, and frequent deployment.

Balancing just enough up-front design with ongoing design evolution is part of the art of Agile development. As you practice this art, always seek to do less until you discover that you have done too little; then adjust. Seek to model a little bit and then prove out your ideas by building working features. Learn how to use refactoring to effectively and fearlessly evolve your designs.

Architectural patterns, introduced in the mid-1990s, have proven to be a highly valuable practice in the application development community. Patterns promote reuse and improve quality because they are mature, and proven, solutions to design problems. This chapter described the use of several object-oriented design patterns as well as data modeling patterns. Patterns enable us to leverage the wisdom and experience of those who have gone before us.

The data and data warehousing communities are beginning to embrace design patterns as well. Reusable data models for various industry domains have become more prevalent in recent years. David Hay's 1996 book on the subject, *Data Model Patterns: Conventions of Thought* (Hay 1996), is a good starting point, and his 2006 book extends the concept to metadata and data warehousing (Hay 2006).

For data modeling we can also leverage object-oriented design patterns because objects and their interactions are conceptually the same as entities and relationships. The adaptive data model presented in this chapter has its roots in the object-oriented design pattern *Adaptive Object Modeling* (Yoder and Johnson 2002). In the near future I expect to see *ETL* and *Stored Procedure* patterns to help round out the availability of patterns in our discipline.

Patterns are just one powerful mechanism for creating more adaptive warehouse architectures. Generalization and abstraction, such as the OMM and ADM presented in this chapter, are highly effective methods as well. Driving variation out of implementation and into metadata is a similarly powerful technique for making your warehouse architecture more easily adaptable.

Bill Inmon opened a recent article with these words (Inmon 2008):

> *Data warehouses are a lot of work. Once they are built, they cost money. They need to be monitored. People are constantly requesting changes and additions. The cost of storage quickly adds up. . . . . All in all, data warehouses are quite a mess. They are not easy to build, they are not particularly easy to operate, and they are expensive.*

He is absolutely right! Although some of this complexity is inherent in our BI systems, it is incumbent on us to make our architectures as maintainable, high-quality, and easy to change as possible. And by the way, doing so will help us be more Agile in our development practices.

This page intentionally left blank

Chapter 7

TEST-DRIVEN DATA WAREHOUSE DEVELOPMENT

Remember that our goal in Agile Analytics development is the frequent release of *production-quality*, working software for user feedback and acceptance. At the end of each iteration or sprint, and each release, our working product is expected to be of production quality, even in its most embryonic stages. This objective requires an entirely different approach to our quality assurance methods. Foremost it means integrating testing efforts right into our iterations.

Traditional BI development methods push system and acceptance testing to the end of the project cycle. This back-end testing is typically manually intensive and time-consuming. Under the pressures of on-time delivery, back-end testing often gets shortchanged. We need an entirely different testing discipline for Agile Analytics development.

Foremost, testing must be *integrated* into the development process. Each development iteration must include plans for testing and quality activities. One of the great things about this is that bugs don't get a chance to accumulate over the project lifecycle. Quality feedback is immediate and frequent, and bugs are handled as they arise. Testing specialists become integral members of the development team rather than gatekeepers at the end of the development cycle. Developers become integral to the testing process and learn sound testing practices as an extension of their technical skills. When I first introduce this notion to new Agile teams, I often get pushback from developers who say things like "I don't have time to test" or "Testing is not my job." I generally quell the urge to say something like "If building a high-quality BI system is not your job, then what exactly is your job?" Once developers establish the rhythm of making testing an integral part of development, they usually love it. I've known a number of BI developers who wondered why they didn't learn to integrate testing and development long ago.

Essential to integrated testing is *test automation*. Manual testing is just not practical in a highly iterative and adaptive development environment.

There are two key problems with manual testing. First, it takes too darn long and inhibits the frequent delivery of working software. Teams that rely on manual testing ultimately end up deferring testing until dedicated testing periods, which allows bugs to accumulate. Second, it is not sufficiently repeatable for regression testing. While we seek to embrace and adapt to change, we must always be confident that features that were "Done! Done!" in a previous iteration retain their high quality in the changing system around them. Test automation requires some initial effort and ongoing diligence, but once technical teams get the hang of it, they can't live without it.

The benefits of integrated, automated testing are even further boosted by using *test-driven development* (TDD) for DW/BI (Collier 2005; Ambler 2007). TDD for DW/BI is as much a development practice as it is a testing practice. In this approach test cases are written first, and then the code (or script, or configuration, etc.) is written to pass those test cases. When the system passes all of the test cases, and the BI practitioners can't think of any new test cases, the implementation work is "Done." That is, it works as the developers think it should and is of production quality. It is now ready for user acceptance to consider it "Done! Done!" While test-driven development may not be mandatory like test automation and test integration, it is a technical practice that yields tremendous benefits because testing and development are inextricably linked. The test suite grows alongside the system, and because testing is automated, the suite can be rerun frequently to maintain a high level of confidence in BI product quality.

It is my contention that teams that do not practice integrated, automated testing cannot be Agile. This practice is an Agile Analytics critical success factor (Ambler 2010). It just isn't feasible to create production-quality, working features for user acceptance every one to three weeks without integrated and automated testing. This chapter presents a complete framework for building automated, integrated, test-driven development into your Agile Analytics development. In the spirit of agility, the test-driven database development framework is a collection of principles and practices that are largely derived from the more mature Agile testing practices and tools used in Agile software development.

What Is Agile Analytics Testing?

Not only is Agile Analytics testing integrated and automated, it is more comprehensive than just system testing. I'm always surprised at BI teams that treat final system testing as the only testing that is required in BI development. Agile Analytics developers test every *unit* of code, every *integration* point, every *data structure*, every *user feature*, and ultimately the entire working *system*, no matter how embryonic. Unit testing involves testing the lowest-level components that make up the BI system such as SQL scripts, ETL modules, or stored procedures. Integration testing involves testing all of the data transition points and wherever BI tools are receiving or returning data. As data is pumped from source systems into staging databases, or from staging into multidimensional databases or OLAP engines, each data structure along the data flow path must be tested to ensure that data integrity is preserved or enhanced. Simple mistakes like copying a VARCHAR(50) value into a VARCHAR(30) field in the staging database can wreak havoc on data integrity. Finally, each newly developed feature must be tested for acceptance and accuracy. Does it do what the user wants, needs, and expects; and does it do it correctly? While this is the ultimate acid test, we need confidence that our system is behaving well throughout the process flow.

Test-driven BI development is applied most prominently at the lowest component level, or unit level, which ensures that high quality exists in the building blocks that make up the system. *Storytest-Driven Development* will help ensure that the user acceptance criteria are clearly defined for each user story before development begins. In practice, Agile Analytics testing works like the following example:

Scenario

It's Monday at the start of iteration eight and the FlixBuster BI project team is involved in its iteration-planning activities. Together in the room are the delivery team (including the testers), the project sponsor, and about six end users who participate in story definition and acceptance testing. Arlene, the project manager, is facilitating this planning session, and the group has agreed upon the next four user stories that will be developed during this iteration.

Now the developers are looking forward to understanding in greater detail what they have committed to deliver. It's time to define all of the acceptance criteria for each of the user stories. The team has learned that acceptance criteria are best expressed as actual functional tests to eliminate any ambiguity about feature behavior.

The FlixBuster BI team uses WatiN[1] for acceptance testing. Because WatiN is a tool that tests Web applications through the user interface, this makes it easy for the user group to describe how each feature should work. In fact, Jamal, the user experience designer, loves this part of the planning session because it also helps him refine the UI design.

---

1. http://watin.sourceforge.net/

Arlene facilitates this process by having Jamal display his "scribble frames" for the first user story on the team room projection screen. Last week, Dieter (the product owner), Jamal, and Arlene spent some time together preparing for this iteration-planning session. They groomed the backlog and anticipated which user stories would be tackled during iteration eight. Then Jamal, with input from Dieter, sketched a few low-fidelity prototypes to show how these stories might be implemented. Now, as Jamal and Dieter show-and-tell these for developers and users, they get lots of feedback that will help them refine their ideas.

At the same time, Prakash, the team's technical lead, asks the users to describe a few specific examples showing exactly how user story 54 should work:

> User story 54: As a financial analyst I need the ability to see net profit per customer per transaction over time so that I can identify upward or downward profit trends.

The user group starts out with a series of simple, routine examples by creating a few mock customers and mocking up a series of transactions for each one. This causes them to describe the specifics of the business logic used to calculate net profit per transaction, which involves evaluating the price of each item in the transaction and its corresponding cost-of-goods value. The developers take copious notes about these required data elements.

As the exercise picks up steam, users dream up more mock usage scenarios, and they begin thinking of odd cases and special exceptions to the rules. Arlene has been making sure the group is writing down each of these scenarios on wall charts in a format that corresponds to Jamal's lo-fi prototypes (and ultimately to WatiN).

When the group can't think of any more examples, Henry, the team's testing lead, asks the users and Dieter to confirm that if the new feature handles each of these scenarios correctly, the feature will be done. The users agree, but everyone acknowledges that if the users think of new scenarios, they should share them with Dieter, Henry, and Arlene, and a feature update will be planned and prioritized as needed.

The group goes through the same process for the remaining user stories. It's a tiring but productive exercise that fully clarifies the detailed specifications of each story. The development team is grateful to get the chance to hear directly from end users how the new BI features are supposed to work. At the end of the day everyone is exhausted but has a sense of accomplishment. All the developers know what their job is for the coming iteration.

On Tuesday at 9:00 A.M. the team holds its daily stand-up meeting. Henry commits to setting up all of the WatiN acceptance tests for the first two stories by the end of the day. Each example scenario from Monday will become a WatiN test. Francisco and Bob commit to developing the BI feature for story 54 according to Jamal's revised prototype, using mock data to get Henry's tests passing initially. Prakash and Natasha commit to completing the ETL, data modeling, and database development tasks needed to replace the mock data with actual source data. They plan to connect all these components on Wednesday to have a first working version of story 54.

As Natasha begins creating the ETL packages to pull cost-of-goods detail into the data warehouse, she writes a simple DbFit test to verify that the raw data arrived correctly in the integration tier. Her test fails at first, and then she implements some simple ETL to make that test pass. Then she adds another test to ensure that negative values are trapped and filtered to an audit report, and she modifies her ETL to pass the new test. During each pass through this cycle Natasha looks for ways to improve her design, and she continuously refactors her work as she finds ways to improve it. All of the FlixBuster BI developers use this test-driven approach. They have learned through experience that it results in far fewer defects that they have to fix later, and it results in a suite of tests that can be run over and over again.

With Bob's help Henry adds new data to the test databases to create the acceptance test cases that the group defined during planning. By the second Wednesday of iteration eight the team is able to run all of the new WatiN tests for the four new user stories. It can also run all of the new unit tests for each of the new modules and components that were developed. Moreover, the team can run all of the tests that were previously created in the first seven iterations to make sure those still pass.

Henry reviews the test suites and tries to think of any other ways to "break" the evolving BI system. He adds a few more tests that he thinks of and is pleased to find that all of the tests still pass. The team will spend Thursday updating documentation, running performance tests, and getting ready for Friday's feature showcase. It has been a good iteration and it doesn't look as if the team will have to pull any late nights to finish their commitments.

Integrated automated testing in database development presents a unique set of challenges. Current automated testing tools designed for software development are not easily adaptable to database development, and large data volumes can make automated testing a daunting task. Data warehouse architectures further complicate these challenges because they involve multiple databases (staging, presentation, and sometimes even pre-staging); special code for data extraction, transformation, and loading (ETL); data-cleansing code; and reporting engines and applications.

AGILE TESTING FRAMEWORK

There are four key perspectives against which software and systems must be tested for overall acceptability. According to Brian Marick, leading Agile testing expert and author of *The Craft of Software Testing* (Marick 1994), these are

- **Business acceptability.** This testing dimension is end-user-centered. It focuses on the capability of the system to deliver the expected features and value. That is, does the system do correctly what the end users need and expect it to do?

- **Product validation.** This dimension is focused on critiquing the product. It addresses whether the system produces accurate results and performs as expected. That is, does the system work correctly?
- **Technical acceptability.** This dimension is developer-centered. It is focused on the capability of the system to meet the technical product requirements. That is, does the system do what the developers think it should do?
- **System validation.** This dimension focuses on supporting the programmer. It reassures programmers that their code behaves as intended under a wide variety of conditions.

These testing dimensions are the basis for the testing matrix depicted in Figure 7.1. The first two dimensions are business- and user-centric and are aimed at critiquing the product. These dimensions ensure that we are building the right product. The last two dimensions are technology- and programmer-centric and are aimed at reassuring developers that they are building the product the right way.

We can complete the matrix by adding the following testing strategies:

- **Unit testing.** At the junction of system validation and technical acceptability lies unit testing. This is developer-driven testing at the

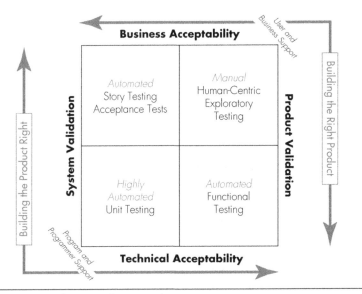

Figure 7.1   Agile testing framework

system component level. This level of testing is highly automatable using tools like Quest Code Tester,[2] SQLUnit,[3] DbUnit,[4] and even DbFit.[5]

- **Story or capability testing.** At the junction of system validation and business acceptability is story testing or capability testing. This level of testing is akin to integration testing in traditional testing methodologies. However, the focus is on validating user stories. Fit[6] (Framework for Integrated Testing) and FitNesse[7] are powerful tools for automating story testing. DbFit is an extension of FitNesse for database testing.

- **Functional or acceptance testing.** To test product validation for technical acceptability we conduct functional testing. While unit and story testing test system functionality beneath the GUI, functional testing involves the user interface. Testing tools like Selenium,[8] Watir,[9] WebTest,[10] and others are well suited to the automation of usability tests.

- **Exploratory testing.** There is no substitute for having real users take the system out for a test drive. Exploratory testing occurs at the end of each sprint or iteration, and sometimes more frequently. This level of testing is manual and human-centered. It highlights ways that real users might interact with the software that we may not have considered for our automated tests. Periodically my team conducts a "bug bash." At a bug bash everyone in the project community (developers, testers, project manager, product owner, users, sponsors) puts aside regular work to pound on the system, trying to find new ways to break it. The testers log the defects or undesirable characteristics they find and then we review the findings. Awards might be given to the person who finds the most bugs or the worst bugs. The goal is to find problems in the system. This focused approach to exploratory testing generally provides much more concentrated feedback than simply asking users to use the system during their daily routines and provide feedback.

2. www.quest.com/code-tester-for-oracle/
3. http://sqlunit.sourceforge.net/
4. www.dbunit.org
5. www.fitnesse.info/dbfit
6. http://fit.c2.com
7. www.fitnesse.org
8. www.openqa.org/selenium/
9. http://wtr.rubyforge.org
10. http://webtest.canoo.com/webtest/manual/WebTestHome.html

The Agile Analytics testing imperative is to employ all of these testing strategies during each development iteration. Developers should be in the habit of using unit testing throughout their daily development activities. I prefer to have the testing specialists on the team review the unit test cases that developers create as part of their development. Story testing occurs periodically during the iteration and is driven more by the product owner/sponsor in partnership with testing specialists. The entire project team should be involved in defining the acceptance criteria for each user story (more on this later). Usability and UI testing typically occurs throughout the iteration but tends to become more important later in the iteration. It is driven by the testing specialists with assistance from technical team members as needed. Finally, exploratory testing is done primarily by the customer community with guidance and assistance from business analysts, project manager, product owner, and others. Ideally exploratory testing is always in progress. By releasing new features to users as soon as they are done, we give users the continuous ability to provide feedback about their exploratory use of the system. Alternatively it may be necessary to schedule specific exploratory testing sessions with the user community.

What about Performance, Load, and Stress Testing?

Okay, so functional testing isn't the only thing we must consider in BI development. Keeping in mind that user acceptance includes the BI application's response time, availability, reliability, and other intrinsic characteristics that are important to users, we must still be concerned about the pressures of high data volumes and concurrent users. So, Agile Analytics augments the user acceptance testing framework with additional system-level performance, load, and stress testing. Each of these testing strategies involves a preproduction sandbox that mimics the production environment. As with acceptance testing, these tests are all automated and can be run frequently against the latest build of the BI system.

Performance testing in the BI systems context is focused on evaluating the ability of the BI system to effectively handle large data volumes during initial load, during periodic update periods (e.g., nightly refresh), and during periodic archival processes and maintenance efforts.

Data warehouse performance testing involves contriving a high-volume test bed (a static representation of the production data sources that feed your BI system). As a guideline I recommend extrapolating the largest data volume that the system is expected to handle during its life span and tripling it to create the contrived test bed. For example, if you expect to have 80,000 customers who conduct 12,000 transactions per day on average, you should contrive a test bed of 240,000 customers who conduct 36,000 transactions per day for performance testing.

Performance testing should also examine potential bottlenecks in the application, operating system, and network layers of the architecture, as they relate to the movement of large data volumes. Of course, there are also traditional application performance testing issues to consider, but we'll focus here on performance as it relates to data volume and complexity.

Load testing focuses on the performance of the system when a large number of concurrent users or HTTP connections put pressure on the system. Automating load testing requires specialized load-testing tools such as Open-STA.[11] Similar to performance testing, load testing should be conducted in a preproduction environment that mimics the configuration of the production environment. Each new release (at least one per iteration) should be exposed to load testing.

Stress testing overloads the system resources to the point of failure to determine how gracefully the system fails, and how well it recovers from that failure. Like performance and load testing, stress testing is conducted in a preproduction environment that closely replicates the production deployment environment.

Stress testing involves introducing chaos and unexpected events into the running system to see how it behaves. In a BI application this may mean randomly disconnecting the database from other system components, failing or partially completing a nightly data refresh, disconnecting user applications from the network, or other interference. Agile teams think of all the things that might disrupt the normal flow of data through the BI system and mimic them during stress testing. You can automate stress testing by scripting these events and forcing them to occur at random intervals or in random combinations.

BI Test Automation

BI system testing presents a unique set of challenges that aren't inherent in software testing. It takes a bit of creative thinking to avoid being stymied by

---

11. www.opensta.org

the effort required to automate your BI testing processes. Here are a few of the issues that we face:

- **Data volumes.** Unlike application software, our systems must handle potentially large volumes of data. While it is easy to think about writing a test case for the conversion of Swiss francs into U.S. dollars, it is more difficult to imagine writing a test case for a system that merges 10 terabytes of data from three separate operational databases into a data mart.
- **Non-object-oriented code.** We don't typically write object-oriented software to manipulate the data in BI systems. We develop stored procedures, ETL scripts, and other declarative and procedural code to process the data. Software testing tools are best suited to object-oriented software whose "units" are well defined with high cohesion and low coupling. It's hard to think in terms of units in a BI system.
- **Systems integration.** A lot of what we do in database development and data warehousing involves the integration of commercial software into a complete system. While we do write custom code, we don't generally build our systems completely from scratch. This means we are testing a heterogeneous collection of components rather than a homogeneous code base.
- **Proprietary components.** OLAP cubes and other proprietary analytical engines in BI architectures are black boxes that include materialized tables, summary tables, optimized physical data structures, and more. These components are often complex data structures that are difficult to test.
- **Mixed code base.** The code we write in BI systems includes a variety of languages such as SQL, T-SQL, PL/SQL, MDX, XMLA, and even VBScript or JavaScript, not to mention the variety of end-user BI application coding languages. It's hard to think about automated testing for each of these disparate programming languages and paradigms.

You may be able to think of other challenges, but these were my initial reactions when I first began thinking about adapting Agile software testing practices to Agile Analytics development. In fact, in the creation of the Agile Analytics development style one of the most significant hurdles my teams faced was integrated, automated testing. We had to rethink our development practices, and we had to adapt the testing tools to work for database testing. Since then testing tools have evolved and matured to be more suitable for database testing.

In fact, there's nothing special about databases that prevents us from using the same testing approaches that we use for application code. The principles of Marick, Beck, Cunningham, and Kerievsky apply to BI systems quite nicely. It's the mechanics of automation that we need to adjust to fit these unique challenges. The biggest problem is that open-source testing tools for database and data warehouse development have lagged behind those for application development.

BI Testing Process

Before we worry about test automation, let's tackle the testing procedure. Once your team has established an effective testing method, automation becomes quite simple. Fundamentally BI testing involves the following steps:

1. Load a fixed set of test data.
2. Run the process that is under test.
3. Verify that the resulting data is what you expected.
4. Return everything to the way you found it.

Let's dissect each step in turn.

Test Data Set

The test data set should be as small as possible while still containing a representative sample of the actual production data. For example, if we are testing the process that calculates the net profit per transaction using item price, quantity, and cost of goods (CoG), we want the test set to represent the variety of possible values for these data elements. At the same time we want the test set to be as small as possible.

To contrive this set we might select records from production data containing the maximum price, maximum quantity, and maximum CoG, as well as the minimums for these values. We might also choose a few test records that represent average or normal values. Additionally, we'll want to test the boundaries, so we might create some records with negative and zero values for these elements as well as other unexpected or unusual values. Over time we may add new test data to this data set as we discover areas of insufficiency. Otherwise, the test data set remains fixed and reusable for the duration of the project.

The testing environment must mimic the production environment, but with test data in the place of production or development data. We must be able to quickly load or reload the test data as a precursor to running the process under test. Moreover, it is important to avoid mixing test data with development or production data in the testing environment. Also, consider replacing sensitive data in your test databases with artificial replicas that accurately reflect actual data.

Process under Test

For unit testing, the process under test should be as small and cohesive as possible. In other words, it should perform exactly one well-defined task. How many times have you seen (or maybe created) a large, monolithic SQL script or ETL package that performs a sequence of tasks because they are related? Not only is it difficult to test these multipurpose components, but it's also hard to debug them when something goes wrong. Agile Analytics developers learn to create small, highly cohesive components and then link them together through sequencer processes. For example, the calculation of net profit per transaction is a well-defined and simple process that can be easily tested.

For story or acceptance testing the process under test is not so atomic. However, if we have done a good job of unit testing each of the components that make up a user story, the story-testing procedure can focus entirely on the integration of those components. In other words, we can test the proper execution of business scenarios rather than the verification of lower-level computations.

Verify the Results

Corresponding to your test data set is an "expected results set." You should know precisely what the resulting data will include and what it will exclude. Every time a new test record is added to the test data set, a result record should be added to the expected result set. It is insufficient to simply spot-check a few of the resulting values to determine if your tests are passing. It is necessary to confirm that *every* expected result is actually present, and that there are no unexpected results present after running the process under test. Because the test data was carefully constructed to include a minimally sufficient set of test records, it is critical that we check the result of every single test record. It's nearly impossible to do this reliably using a manual testing procedure.

Clean Up

After the testing is completed, everything should be returned to its original state and made ready for the next test suite to run. Doing this ensures that the results of one testing procedure don't influence the behavior of another testing procedure. We want each test process to be as isolated as possible so that the results are accurate and repeatable, and so that problems can easily be analyzed and fixed.

Database Testing Tools

There are two main approaches to automated BI testing. The first focuses on testing the structure, content, and state of a resulting data table after an action has been applied. The second focuses directly on the procedural or declarative code component (e.g., stored procedure, SQL script, PL/SQL) used to perform actions on the data. Several open-source and commercial tools are aimed at database testing using one or the other of these approaches. Test automation tools have tended to evolve from the JUnit framework developed by Kent Beck or the Fit framework developed by Ward Cunningham. There is an additional class of testing tools that simulate users interacting with a system through the application's user interface.

The xUnit family of open-source testing tools has grown to include tools designed for nearly every popular programming language available, and new variants continue to emerge. For software development these are really class libraries rather than stand-alone tools. These unit-testing tools isolate smaller units of code (such as function, procedure, method, class) and create the scaffolding necessary to call the code module and then make an assertion about the result. If the assertion is correct, the test passes. Otherwise, the test fails. Each module ends up with a suite of many such assertions designed to test it extensively.

Like the xUnit tools for software, there are a few database unit-testing tools that follow this testing model. In fact, SQLUnit is a database unit-testing tool implemented as a JUnit test that simply reads a SQLUnit test file to execute database tests. The SQLUnit test file is in XML format and a test case might look something like this:

```
<test name="Checking net profit from transaction">
  <sql>
    <stmt>select NetProfit from transaction where tranId=?</stmt>
    <param id="1" type="INTEGER" inout="in" is-null="false">
      1
    </param>
  </sql>
  <result>
    <resultset id="1">
      <row id="1">
        <col id="1" type="FLOAT">44.32</col>
      </row>
```

```
    </resultset>
  </result>
</test>
```

Although this test may look a little cryptic at first, it is a simple test, following the net profit per transaction calculation, that checks to see if the first transaction has the expected net profit amount of $44.32. This single test would be just one of many such tests in the same SQLUnit test suite. Fortunately there are graphical tools that enable testers and developers to create these test cases more simply. This unit-testing tool targets the resulting data table (e.g., Transaction). Other database unit-testing tools such as TSQLUnit[12] and utPLSQL[13] are aimed at testing stored procedures written in T-SQL and PL/SQL respectively.

Another class of database testing tools can be used at the unit- or micro-testing level as well as the integration- or macro-testing level. Software developers have been using Fit for years, as well as a more recent variant developed by Robert C. Martin called FitNesse. These frameworks use a browser-based wiki for specifying the test cases, describing the expected results, and executing the tests. The Fit/FitNesse frameworks are easily extensible by creating fixtures, which are small source code modules typically written in a programming language like Java or C#. The fixture tells the framework how to "talk to" the system under test.

Gojko Adzic was kind enough to develop a set of fixtures for database testing called DbFit.[14] DbFit makes it easy to issue SQL queries directly against the database and compare the results against an expected result set. Figure 7.2 shows a series of simple DbFit tests of a Microsoft SQL Server Integration Services (SSIS) package for merging data from a collection of source tables into a single invoice table in the integration tier of the FlixBuster data warehouse.

In this example the setup section (collapsed) runs a series of test preparation scripts that create the source tables and populate them with test data. Then the SSIS package under test, Load.Invoice.Stage.dtsx, is executed. Following this is a series of simple tests to check that the table got created and has the expected number of records and the correct column names. Not shown in this example are the additional tests needed to test the actual data values against the expected ones.

---

12. http://TSQLunit.sourceforge.net

13. http://utplsql.sourceforge.net

14. http://gojko.net/fitnesse/dbfit/

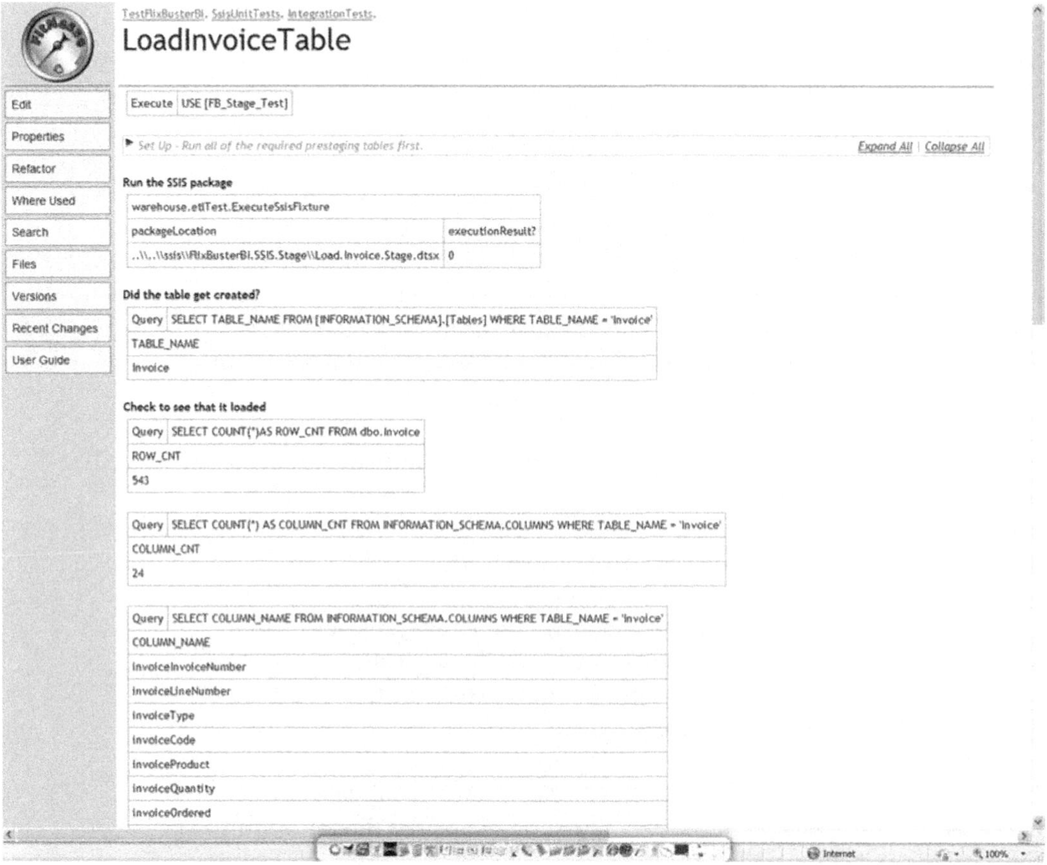

Figure 7.2 DbFit/FitNesse test example

Notice that each test table has, as its first row, a SQL query followed by a row containing one or more result set column headers. These column headers are followed by the expected values contained in the result set. When the test is executed, the cells in these tables are colored green if the actual result matches the expected result, or red if they do not match.

Also notice that the execution of the SSIS package is included in a table in which the first row describes the fixture `warehouse.etlTest.ExecuteSsis-Fixture`. Because DbFit does not inherently know how to run SSIS packages, I needed to create a fixture to tell DbFit/FitNesse how to do so. Following is the code for that fixture, written in C#.NET. While this chapter is not intended as a fixture tutorial, it should be apparent that fixtures are not overly complicated. Once they are working, they can be used repeatedly.

```csharp
using System;
using System.Collections.Generic;
using System.Text;
using Microsoft.SqlServer.Dts.Runtime;

namespace warehouse.etlTest
{
  public class ExecuteSsisFixture: fit.ColumnFixture
  {
    public string packageLocation = null;//Path to .dtsx file
    public int executionResult    //0 = "Success"
    {                             //1 = "Failed"
      get                         //3 = "Cancelled by user"
      {                           //4 = "Unable to locate file"
        return runThePackage(); //5 = "Unable to load file"
      }                           //6 = "Internal error occurred"
    }

    public int runThePackage()
    {
      Package pkg;
      Application app;

      app = new Application();
      pkg = app.LoadPackage(packageLocation, null);

      return(Convert.ToInt32(pkg.Execute()));
    }
  }
}
```

Yet another class of testing tools is aimed at system testing through the user interface. Tools such as Selenium, Watir, WatiN, and WebTest are designed to test Web-based applications, and tools such as Mercury QTP, SilkTest, and TestComplete are better suited to stand-alone or client-server applications. These tools create scripts that simulate users interacting with the application and then testing to see if what appears on screen is what is expected. These are easily adaptable to BI applications. However, these tests can be rather fragile because they do not accommodate UI changes particularly well.

As quickly as new testing tools emerge, this section cannot possibly include a complete list of them, and I'm certain that I have failed to list someone's favorite testing tool. By the time this book hits the shelves there are likely to be new testing tools and tool advancements. The field of test automation has been evolving and maturing rapidly and is a mainstream practice for software development. The BI community can only stand to benefit from those advancements, and as Agile Analytics grows deeper roots, we will benefit from the great ideas of people in our own community.

What to Test?

Now let's examine the test-driven database development methodology as it applies to classical data warehouse architectures. Figure 7.3 highlights the key testing points in the classical warehouse architecture.

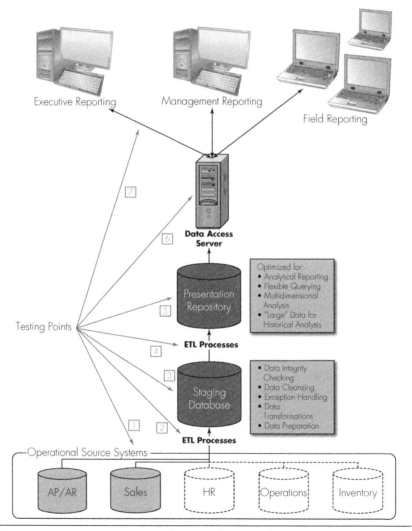

Figure 7.3 Testing points in a data warehouse architecture

In this architecture data flows from one or more operational systems on the left to one or more end-user applications on the right of the diagram. There are multiple points in this architecture where testing is needed to ensure data consistency and correctness. These include

1. **Operational databases.** Generally the operational systems are running in production by the time data warehouse development begins. However, these systems should also undergo test-driven development during their development cycles. For systems already in production I encourage the use of test-driven development for new revisions and bug fixes.
2. **Data update code.** The ETL scripts that extract data from operational systems into the staging database must be validated. These scripts typically run on a nightly basis and include slowly changing dimension type 1 and type 2 updates.
3. **Data preparation code.** The code used for data merge/purge, cleansing, preparation, and processing in the staging database.
4. **Data transformation code.** The ETL scripts used to extract data from the staging database and transform it into the multidimensional database schema of the presentation database (e.g., star schema).
5. **Data derivation code.** The code or scripts used within the multidimensional presentation database for further data transformations and derivations (e.g., data mining scoring).
6. **Data access layer code.** Any customized server-side applications that are responsible for providing user access to the data in the warehouse. This includes OLAP cube specification code, deployed analytical models, and others.
7. **BI application code.** The customized client-side applications that present data to end users and enable end users to query the data warehouse.
8. **Administrative application code.** There may additionally be a warehouse administrator interface application (not in the diagram) that must be tested as well.

In general, we seek to write automated tests anywhere and anytime the data is manipulated within the BI system. Although Figure 7.3 depicts a classical data warehousing architecture, you should adapt this principle to the specifics of your BI system's technical architecture.

Testing "Black Box" BI Technologies

Many commercial BI tools promote pulling data directly from operational data stores. These tools generally provide some built-in capabilities for data cleansing and merging. This use of BI tools creates a sort of "black box" effect, making it difficult to test the discrete units of data manipulation. In general, I don't advocate pumping raw, untreated data into these tools. I've experienced better performance and higher-quality BI results by conforming to architectural patterns and best practices for preparing data. Nonetheless, this use of BI tools deserves a word about testing. It is not necessary to test commercial third-party code. We can generally rely on the vendors to have done their own testing. But it is important to test whatever configurations, OLAP cube specifications, calculated measures, and so on you may have established in your use of the tool. The testing practices remain the same. Each new tweak in software parameters, each new alteration in the cube specs, each new calculated measure, and any other data manipulation that is specified through the BI tool deserves test cases against the resulting data set.

SANDBOX DEVELOPMENT

Typical BI systems are built using a shared *development* environment, a *test* or *preproduction* environment, and a *production* environment as a means of separating work under construction from work being validated from the system available to users in production. Developers commonly share the development environment, making it difficult for individual developers to experiment with new ideas. I've been on several projects where developers run the risk of treading on each other's work because one developer's modification conflicts with the work of another. Furthermore, promoting the system from the development to the testing environment can be a complex ordeal involving lots of manual setup, configuration, and tweaks to get everything working. This is normally deferred until late in the development cycle in preparation for system testing. The promotion to production is a similarly complicated affair.

Because Agile Analytics calls for the frequent release of new features to the user community, this traditional infrastructure is not sufficient. We require a development, test, and production environment that

- Provides a separate, experimental development environment for each developer
- Supports frequent execution of the entire test suite (unit tests, story tests, acceptance tests, etc.)
- Supports rapid and simple deployment of new features into preproduction and production

- Provides a way for users and stakeholders to work with new features, features under construction, and other changes in the system
- Supports frequent, automated build and deployment of the BI system into the test environment
- Supports the ability to easily revert to any earlier version of the system at any time

These requirements are met by using development *sandboxes* (Ambler and Sadalage 2006). A sandbox is a fully functional replica of the production environment in which the system is expected to be deployed. A sandbox might be a dedicated server, a partition on a shared server, a virtual server, or simply a dedicated directory on a shared server. The complete development infrastructure includes a multitude of these sandboxes—one for each developer, one for integrating everyone's work, one for demonstration purposes, one for preproduction testing, and possibly others. Such a development infrastructure requires plenty of hardware and software. Fortunately these are cheap relative to people time, and the benefits of this investment are quickly realized and readily apparent. Figure 7.4 shows a logical depiction of this sandbox development model.[15]

Foremost it must be easy and fast to deploy the current version of the BI system on any of these sandboxes as well as to remove it. This requires that all "code" be held in a code management (CM) repository using a tool like CVS or Subversion. The CM system should include all ETL scripts, stored procedure code, DDL scripts, batch data load scripts, application code, OLAP cube definitions, data mining scripts—everything that is needed to build the BI system once the technology stack has been installed on the server. Code management is covered in greater detail in Chapter 8, "Version Control for Data Warehousing."

It is also beneficial to use a build automation tool to automate code checkout, BI system build, and execution of test suites. Chapter 9, "Project Automation," covers BI project automation in greater detail. Build automation and continuous integration are essential for the integration sandbox and allow the BI system to be quickly built and tested multiple times per day with no manual intervention required (unless the build breaks or tests fail). Build automation is also used within developer sandboxes to expedite the checkout and installation of the most current version of the system.

---

15. Thanks to Scott Ambler and Pramodkumar Sadalage for first framing this concept in *Refactoring Databases* (Ambler and Sadalage 2006).

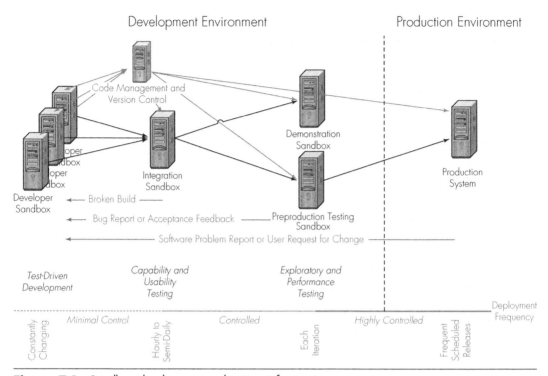

Figure 7.4   Sandbox development and testing infrastructure
Scott W. Ambler and Pramodkumar J. Sadalage, Refactoring Databases: Evolutionary Database Design, 1st Edition, ©2006. Reprinted by permission of Pearson Education, Inc., Upper Saddle River, NJ.

Each team member must have his or her own sandbox to experiment with ideas, to complete development tasks, and to create and run unit tests. Ideally each developer's sandbox should include a separate instance of the database schemas populated with development data. Since development data is typically a smaller, more manageable replica of actual production data, it is often possible for all developers to work on the same physical hardware using shared software. Virtual servers on a single physical server can be useful to ensure that each developer sandbox is isolated from the others. However, it is generally sufficient for each developer to have his or her own instance of the database and a sandbox directory in which to work. Developers must frequently check working and tested code into the CM repository, and they should frequently update the code in their sandbox to make sure they are working with the latest revisions. This activity should occur every 15 minutes to one hour. Developers write unit tests as they create new code. *All test cases are checked into the CM system alongside the code.*

When a developer checks new code or code changes into the CM repository, the build automation software detects that a change has occurred. This triggers a new build of the system in the integration sandbox. Once the system has been built successfully, the entire test suite is run to ensure that the changes did not break anything, and to ensure that new tests are passing. It is this automated process that gives the team members constant confirmation that they are *building the product right*. All of this should occur multiple times throughout a development day, or at the very least once per day.

Whenever a new user story or capability is complete, tested, and confirmed by the team, it is deployed into the demo sandbox to be shared with the user community for exploratory testing and feedback. At least once per iteration new features are showcased to the user community. These user showcases offer the opportunity for a first round of feedback. Additionally, it is important for users to continue using new features so they can provide continuous and deeper feedback. For this reason it is important that the demo sandbox contain live or nearly live data. Perhaps the fastest way to turn off your users is to show them development data or mock data. Users need to see how the new features address their current business problems. And what could be a better way to score points with your users than to give them a feature that helps them solve current problems? This doesn't mean that the new features are deployed to the production system yet, and the user community must understand that the new features are still being validated to confirm that you are *building the right product.*

As new features are reviewed and accepted by users, they are deployed to the preproduction sandbox for performance, load, and stress testing and any other system testing that is required. It is critical that the preproduction sandbox accurately represent the configuration of the production environment. Although I use the term *system testing*, I want to emphasize that I don't mean back-end testing as in traditional serial development styles. Because we are building production-quality features in each iteration, the line between integration testing and system testing is blurred. We are constantly evolving the BI system by adding new features, maturing existing features, and adapting features based on user feedback. Therefore, system testing begins early in the development cycle and continues throughout the process.

Since we are conducting performance, load, and stress tests in the preproduction sandbox, we'll be using much larger data sets and computationally intensive test cases. Sometimes running the full battery of tests can take several hours, so this system testing may occur less frequently. Nonetheless, system testing must occur routinely to reassure the project community that the evolving BI system remains robust, reliable, efficient, and scalable.

This sandbox development and testing infrastructure ensures that new features and capabilities can be deployed into production at any time rather than having to wait until some predefined release date. Whenever the stakeholder community or project sponsor feels that the business can benefit from new capabilities, a release to production can be executed as described in Chapter 6, "Evolving Excellent Design." Of course, there may be additional IT governance considerations impacting frequent releases into production. An objective of Agile Analytics is that frequent production deployment is always an option, and the choice about when it is appropriate to deploy is business-driven rather than technically bound.

TEST-FIRST BI DEVELOPMENT

Test automation is an essential set of quality assurance practices for Agile DW/BI development. However, a more advanced and powerful practice involves writing tests before you begin implementing a solution. Test-first or test-driven development makes testing integral to the development process. In this way testing becomes more than purely a quality assurance activity; it becomes the specification process for what is to be constructed, and it establishes a very crisp definition of "Done!" Test-first development is a powerful practice at the story level as well as the unit level of development. The following sections outline how test-first DW/BI development works. As Agile Analytics continues to mature, we can expect an increasing number of tools to help support these practices.

Unit-Test-Driven Development

Test-driven development (TDD) was developed by Kent Beck, a founding father of eXtreme Programming (XP). Kent is also the inventor of the xUnit family of automated unit-testing utilities and author of *Test-Driven Development: By Example* (Beck 2003), which highlights both TDD and JUnit.

TDD is really a development method rather than a testing method. It just so happens that testing occurs as part of the development process. The principal idea behind TDD is that you think of a little test, and then write just enough code to pass the test. This cycle continues until you can't think of any more tests. Moreover, you write only the tests you need based on the user requirements rather than possible but unspecified future requirements.

The TDD methodology is relatively simple in concept. Developers work in small steps. First, they write a little test that fails. Then they write the code necessary to make the test pass. Finally, they refactor the code to make it better. Beck describes the TDD rhythm as "test tiny/build tiny" (Beck 2003):

1. Quickly add a little test.
2. Run *all* the tests and see the new one fail.
3. Make a little change in the code.
4. Run all the tests and see them succeed.
5. Refactor to make the code better.

In other words: *Write a test, make it run, make it right!*

Although TDD was designed for object-oriented programming, adapting this development method to BI is relatively easy. As an example, let's examine the TDD steps as they apply to building the ETL object that calculates net profit for a single item in a transaction. We'll use DbFit for test automation:

1. **Quickly add a test.** We might start by adding a single test item into the test data set. Let's start simply by adding a normal "happy path" transaction containing an item with an average price, an average CoG, and a quantity of one.

    Additionally we'll create a DbFit test page for our ETL module. Like the prior DbFit example, this DbFit page will

    a. Set up the test by creating the necessary source tables and loading test data into those tables
    b. Execute our ETL module (which doesn't exist yet)
    c. Test the result to see if the net profit for our single test case is correct

2. **Run *all* tests.** When we first run the new test it will fail, because the ETL object doesn't exist yet.

3. **Make a little change.** We'll create the smallest, simplest ETL package possible. In fact, for starters we might even hard-code it with the expected result rather than doing the actual net profit calculation. In the next pass, we'll replace the hard-coded result with a simple calculation. On successive passes we will incrementally improve the calculation to handle odd cases and bad data.

    While that approach may seem silly, the aim is to move in very tiny steps, making lots of small improvements. Learning to work like this is a powerful way to build quality into your code organically. Once you are comfortable working in tiny steps, you may choose to take slightly bigger steps.

4. **Watch the test pass.** Now we'll run our DbFit test again. This time it passes because the package exists, and it creates the expected result. Watching tests pass is very satisfying!

5. **Refactor.** Step 3 is focused on making the test pass rather than the best approach. However, we want good design, so this step is focused on improving the code we implemented. During this step we want to remove duplication, eliminate inefficiencies, simplify the implementation details, and so on. While we're improving the design, we must keep running our test(s) to be sure that they still pass.

6. **Repeat from step 1.** Now we'll add another test, make another little change to make it work, and then make it right. We will repeat this cycle many times every hour during the development day. In fact, we keep repeating this cycle until we can't think of any new tests to add to the ever-increasing test suite.

The beauty of test-driven database development is that as you evolve toward the right solution, you are also growing a suite of valuable tests that are run and rerun many times. This test suite not only serves to confirm that the unit under test is done; it also serves as a set of regression tests to confirm that future changes haven't broken the previous ones. When you work like this, you don't have to allow for time at the end to add all the tests you wish you had; nor do you have to allow time at the end to rework your design. These steps are integrated into the development process.

Some tests are as simple as verifying that a table was successfully dropped or created; field names are correct; foreign key constraints are enforced; field types, lengths, and precision are correct. It is important to conduct other validity checks in your unit tests such as verifying row counts, distinct value checks, minimum and maximum value checks, and so forth. Agile Analytics teams adhere to the agreement that *no new code gets created without first having a test case.*

There are a few things you should expect from TDD. As with any practice change, TDD will feel awkward in the beginning, and you may feel less productive for a while. Keep in mind that you are now doing detailed design, development, and testing combined in the same cycle. You may produce less, but it will be production-ready when finished. Expect that the volume of test cases will approximately equal the volume of production "code." This is actually a good thing but can be surprising. Also expect that you will be tempted to make bigger development "steps" in each TDD cycle. Sometimes those tiny steps feel overly simplistic. Bigger steps aren't necessarily bad, but they can be expensive to undo if necessary. It's better to err on the side of too tiny rather than too large.

Agile Analytics Practice: First Write a Little Test

Team working agreement: No line of code gets written without having a test case first.

Storytest-Driven DW/BI Development

As discussed in Chapter 4, "User Stories for BI Systems," data warehouse stories translate into user-demonstrable features presented to the user via BI applications. These features include reports, charts, graphs, multidimensional (OLAP) reports, data mining scores, and data visualization, as well as features enabling users to change settings, adjust parameters, modify their view, and so on. Story testing is focused on these types of end-user features.

TDD is extremely effective at reducing defects at the unit development level, and Josh Kerievsky has adapted this method to user story development with storytest-driven development (STDD). Storytests are specific *examples* of user stories. While unit tests are typically written by the programmer to test low-level components or units, storytests can be written by users or business analysts because they describe examples of business stories. The STDD methodology embeds TDD into the development rhythm:

1. Write a storytest that fails.
2. Make the storytest pass by using TDD to develop component parts (units).
3. Run *all* storytests and watch the new storytest pass.
4. Refactor to make the implementation better.
5. Repeat from step 1 until all storytests are passing.

Like unit-test-driven development, storytest-driven development is more a development process with testing built in than a quality assurance process. STDD is the precursor to unit-test-driven development. In fact, Agile Analytics teams follow the agreement that *no work begins on a story until that story's tests have been written.*

Agile Analytics Practice: Lead with a Storytest

No work begins on a user story until at least some storytests have been written for that story. Customers, product owners, and testers can continue adding storytests, but there must be at least one before developers can start building.

Generating Storytests

In practice the project team may write as many storytests as the team members can think of during iteration planning, as in the example scenario at the beginning of this chapter. In this case, the STDD cycle proceeds by taking one storytest at a time and making it pass through TDD, then taking another storytest and making it pass, and so on.

Imagine the user story "As VP of sales I need the ability to analyze gross margins over the past year by account manager, by dates of purchase, by product, and by customer location." This is a classic OLAP-style requirement for which we must ensure that the data presented in our system is accurate down to the finest-grained detail and up to the highest levels of aggregation.

Working with the VP of sales, you might discuss several concrete examples of the behavior of this user story. For example:

> *VP sales*: "Gross margin at our company is calculated by subtracting the *item cost* and the *cost of sale* from the *sales amount*, then dividing that by the *sales amount*."

> *Agile team member*: "Okay, we know that *item cost*, *cost of sale*, and *sales amount* are available for each item in the transaction file, so we can calculate gross margin. Can you give me an example of one way you'd like to analyze that information?"

> *VP sales*: "I want to list the gross margin for all sales by each account manager in the southeast region for December 2008 and compare those margins with the ones from December 2007."

This information provides the basis for the storytest cases presented in Table 7.1.

The team would validate with the sales VP that the calculations in these test cases are correct, and that the VP wants to see two digits of precision in the gross margin field. This is a start, but there's more.

> *Agile team member*: "We noticed that Becky Thatcher was reassigned to the Northeast region in early December 2008. How would you like the system to display that change?"

> *VP sales*: "That's a good observation. I think I would like to see Becky's gross margin for the whole month of December 2008 regardless of region. But I also want to see her margin for the period of December when she was assigned to the Southeast."

Table 7.1 Basis for the Storytest Cases

Year	Month	Region	Account Manager	Item Cost (Total)	Cost of Sale	Sales Amount	Gross Margin
2007	Dec.	Southeast	Huck Finn	$20,000	$3,000	$30,000	23.33%
			Tom Sawyer	$35,000	$6,000	$50,000	18.00%
			Becky Thatcher	$27,000	$4,000	$45,000	31.11%
			Joe Harper	$19,000	$2,500	$37,000	41.89%
2008	Dec.	Southeast	Huck Finn	$22,500	$2,000	$35,000	30.00%
			Tom Sawyer	$15,000	$2,000	$25,000	32.00%
			Becky Thatcher	$4,000	$400	$5,500	20.00%
			Joe Harper	$25,000	$7,000	$43,000	20.93%

This would generate an additional set of test cases that shows Becky in both regions and combined. After a continuation of this discussion, this user story will receive a complete set of acceptance tests, including examples that are drilled down to individual products per day as well as other regions. The goal is to ensure that there is at least one storytest for every possible variation of this user story, including edge cases such as when there are gross margins of around 0 percent and above 100 percent.

Storytest writing involves a high degree of collaboration with your user community to ensure that you develop a realistic and complete set of storytests. In fact, you may think of storytests as detailed requirements specifications. The Agile technical team collaborates with users to write a complete set of storytests. When the team agrees that the storytests are complete, it is very clear what needs to be developed and when that feature is done. It's done when it passes all the storytests, and if the team can think of another storytest, the feature can quickly be adapted to pass the new storytest as well as the old ones.

BI TESTING GUIDELINES

Now that we've looked at the Agile testing framework, an Agile Analytics testing process, tools for automating BI testing, and the test-driven and storytest-driven development methods, there are some guidelines to consider when designing a testing strategy. These include

- **One test set per "unit."** Create one test file per system component (e.g., script or stored procedure). One file will contain all of the test cases for its corresponding unit.
- **Keep test cases under version control.** Check your test case files into your code management repository just as you check in code. Use these test cases for all regression testing whenever you must modify your scripts or create new scripts.
- **Build tiny/test tiny.** Add one simple test case to the test suite, then write a little bit of code to make the test pass. Repeat this until the script is complete.
- **Low coupling/high cohesion.** By designing your scripts and procedures as small, independent, single-purpose modules, you make them much easier to test, debug, and maintain.
- **Don't retest commercial software.** We only need to test our own code. Since data warehousing generally involves systems integration, our focus is on the glue code that we write to stitch these systems together.
- **Do test all new code.** Temporary tables, working tables, and views should be tested just like the persistent tables that make up your system.
- **Keep your test database small.** The larger the database gets, the harder your testing becomes. Ensure that it contains a complete set of example cases, but it should be barely sufficient to exercise every test you have thought of. If you discover new cases, add them to the test database as part of new test-driven development.

Application development and other traditional programming within a data warehouse environment should follow the test-driven development methodology described by Kent Beck. An increasing number of xUnit frameworks are available on the open-source domain, including NUnit (.NET), CPPUnit (C++), HTMLUnit (HTML), and JsUnit (JavaScript). There is an xUnit framework for almost any of today's popular programming languages. These frameworks are in various states of maturity, JUnit being the most mature. However, it is valuable to integrate automated testing into as many aspects of custom coding as possible.

SETUP TIME

The primary reasons that most developers resist the adoption of automated testing are the setup time and learning curve associated with using these testing tools and frameworks. This is a legitimate concern. First-time adoption of these practices, establishing the testing infrastructure, and learning a new testing tool can be time-consuming.

In my experience it takes two to three days for a single developer to learn to use test automation and TDD. This includes time to learn the testing tool's "language," time to integrate the tool into the development environment, time to learn how to extend the tool, and time to become comfortable with the TDD development method.

Finally, it typically takes one to two days to integrate and configure a test automation tool for your development infrastructure. I prefer to allocate one complete team week to focus on getting all developers familiar and comfortable with Agile database testing tools and methods.

Jim Highsmith promotes the concept of "iteration zero" on any Agile project. Iteration zero serves the purpose of ensuring that your development infrastructure is established among other project initiation activities such as initial requirements and architectural modeling. This iteration is not expected to produce any new features. Iteration zero is the ideal time to adopt and integrate these Agile database testing tools and methods.

FUNCTIONAL BI TESTING

Most of this chapter is devoted to unit testing and story testing. These methods test underneath the user interface. If you do a good job in these testing approaches, you've likely addressed the majority of quality issues. However, functional testing through the UI is required to complete the picture.

Functional testing is a diverse topic subject to the BI application approaches and technologies in your system. Are BI applications homegrown or commercial? Are they browser-based or stand-alone? Are they thin client, fat client, or "chubby" client applications? Are there multiple BI application technologies or a single one? Does the app involve customization of a commercial product? And the list goes on.

The answers to these questions determine which functional testing tools and approaches you employ. There are two aspects to functional BI testing:

- **Controls.** Test the user controls and interaction to ensure that they behave correctly and produce the correct results. This testing focuses on ensuring that application components exhibit the

correct behavior, the application handles invalid inputs and actions elegantly, and the application recovers from errors gracefully.
- **Content.** Test to ensure that the data presented is accurate relative to the back-end data architecture. This includes ensuring that OLAP drill-down, roll-up, drill-through, and other actions produce the expected results; predictive modeling scores are properly presented; and ad hoc queries produce the correct results (and avoid big outer joins or other resource-intensive queries).

How you conduct each of these depends largely on your choice of portal and BI presentation technologies. For example, I once worked on a project for which the back-end database and OLAP engine were based on Microsoft's SQL Server Analysis Services (SSAS). The front end was a custom-built ASP.NET application with embedded Microsoft Office Web Components (OWC) for the delivery of data using Microsoft Excel's pivot table and pivot chart functionality. On a prior project we developed on the SAS Institute's BI technology stack for back-end data management and delivered the end-user application via a homegrown J2EE-based Web application using HTML tables and custom components for data presentation. The functional testing approaches were quite different for each of these scenarios.

An increasing number of script-based functional testing tools simulate user interaction with the application through the UI. These were described previously and are expected to continue evolving and maturing. BI application content testing may require some creativity to automate. Many functional testing tools are limited in their ability to isolate values in reports or tables.

Wrap-Up

Manual database testing involves building the data structures, writing some code to access the database, running the code, then writing some queries to verify that the data got into the database correctly. Even the most rigorous database testers generally verify a database by running several queries and visually inspecting the results for validity. The problem with this is that as changes are made to the database, we don't generally rerun all the old test queries to revalidate that everything is still fine. Even if we do rerun the old queries, the task of visually inspecting the results quickly becomes overwhelming.

Rerunning automated tests is painless and transparent (as long as the tests keep passing). It provides continuous assurance that new changes don't adversely impact already working code. Test cases provide documentation and make it easier to understand other people's code and intentions.

Automated test-driven database and data warehouse development has a unique set of challenges. However, with a little effort the Agile software testing concepts, principles, and practices can generalize to provide a powerful framework that significantly exceeds traditional database testing practices. If you adopt test-driven database development practices:

- Expect test code volume to be roughly equivalent to new code volume. However, the test code does not contain the complex logic that is in the new code.
- Don't expect a large reduction in initial productivity. It will take some time and practice with these tools and techniques to improve productivity. However, you will spend much less time tracking down and fixing bugs later in the project.
- Don't expect a large reduction in script size. Your stored procedures won't necessarily get smaller. They will get better.
- Do expect large improvements in software reliability.
- Do expect a large reduction in defect rates.
- Do expect clean code that works.

Chapter 8

VERSION CONTROL FOR DATA WAREHOUSING

If your data warehouse server(s) failed catastrophically, how long would it take to redeploy the system into production?

If you discovered a critical defect in your production DW/BI system, how long would it take to revert to a previous version while you resolve the problem?

If you had to prove that what you had in production was the same as what you think is in production, how long would that take?

As with other mission-critical systems, it should take no more than a few days to rebuild your DW/BI system from scratch—including reconfiguring new servers and reloading data. The actual redeployment of your warehouse implementation (database schemas, ETL scripts, BI applications, etc.) should range from minutes to hours, not days or weeks.

Rapid deployment not only is essential because of the mission-critical nature of today's DW/BI systems; it is also a critical aspect of agility. Remember that our highest priority is to satisfy the user community through early and continuous delivery of BI features. This means releasing new BI features into production every iteration or every few iterations. Doing so requires a highly optimized deployment process.

Optimizing data warehouse deployment time requires a combination of several good engineering and IT practices. Central to this goal are proper code management and version control, concepts with which many seasoned DW/BI professionals remain unfamiliar. Proper code management requires that *all* project artifacts be stored and managed in the same version control system. DW/BI systems are built using a disparate set of technologies and tools, each with its own coding language or configuration. These tools often store system artifacts in proprietary data stores or in encoded binary files. Furthermore, ETL developers often manage their code separately from database developers, separately from BI application developers, and so forth. These and other factors have a tendency to steer teams away from, rather than toward, effective version control. Fortunately, our colleagues in the software development community have been managing code for decades and have paved the way with effective tools and techniques that we can use.

This chapter is devoted to the adaptation of those effective version control and code management methods to the nuances of DW/BI systems. Scott Ambler addresses this topic for general database development in *Agile Database Techniques* (Ambler 2003). This chapter is intended to be general to all (or most) version control software and as such is not a tutorial on how to use any one specific tool. There are very good books available to teach you how to use the more popular version control tools. Instead, this chapter is intended to guide you toward effective practices and habits for managing your DW/BI system code much as good software developers manage their source code.

Also, this chapter does not provide comprehensive coverage of the topics of release management or configuration management. These topics are related to version control but are not synonymous, and each one is worthy of its own book. Version control is about tracing the history of events and changes in project code and artifacts; release management refers to the processes and procedures needed to ensure a successful system deployment; and configuration management is about the collection of activities (technical and nontechnical) that are required to reproduce the successful deployment of any version of the system at any time. This chapter specifically focuses on the topic of version control—how a DW/BI team manages its system code and artifacts to support other Agile practices such as frequent releases, test automation, and build automation.

WHAT IS VERSION CONTROL?

Traditionally, data warehouse developers have worked in a shared development environment, on a shared server, using shared database instances. Development work progresses in this environment day after day, and there is no clear means of rolling back to a previous state. Data model changes must be carefully orchestrated so that developers don't trip one another up. When mistakes are made in this environment, the team must either carefully unravel its work or apply patches and fixes to overcome the mistakes. Many teams working in this way establish a series of rigid "change management" policies to help prevent a developer from making changes that adversely impact the work of other developers. This effectively slows the team down and may create an environment of fear within the team—fear of costly mistakes, fear of experimentation, and fear of unexpected side effects.

Version control is mandatory on all Agile Analytics projects. Not only is it central to the goal of rapid deployment, but it offers the following advantages to the team and to the developers:

- **Rewind.** Version control offers the ability to undo any changes made during development to a previous point in time or a previous version. It's like a rewind button on the development process.
- **Controlled sharing.** Version control enables developers to work on the same system at the same time without inadvertently changing or overwriting the work of other developers on the team.
- **Audit trail.** Version control systems maintain a record of changes that developers make over time. When a change in a data model or ETL script is puzzling, it is easy to see who made the change and any notations entered about the change.
- **Release control.** Version control eliminates the need for a "code freeze" prior to each release. Developers can continue working on the mainline without affecting the release candidate code. Additionally, it affords the ability to keep track of which releases were in production at which point in time.
- **Fearlessness.** Version control enables developers to experiment with different solution alternatives, explore new ideas, and make changes without fear of adversely impacting the rest of the team or the project. Only when this experimentation and exploration evolve into production-ready solutions does the developer check the changes into version control, making them official.

Recall the sandbox development concepts presented in Chapter 7, "Test-Driven Data Warehouse Development." The use of separate development, integration, preproduction, demonstration, and production sandboxes is made possible by version control. As changes are checked into the version control system, the sandboxes are updated to include these changes so that they remain synchronized with one another. Here is an example of what working with version control is like:

Scenario

Prakash, a database developer, is working late one night on some improvements in the dimensional data model of the FlixBuster data warehouse. His improvements include a new `territory` dimension and a new fact table containing `order shipment` measures. The rest of the team members have gone home, but Prakash wants to be sure they can work with the new fact and dimension tables first thing tomorrow.

Prakash updates his local copy of the data warehouse code[1] and writes a set of DbFit tests that should pass once the new data model changes are in place. Next he implements his physical data model changes in the DDL scripts that are used to automatically build the dimensional database schema. He runs all of his new tests to make sure they pass and reruns the existing tests to be sure he didn't break anything with his changes. When he is satisfied that his changes are production-ready, he checks the new and modified DDL scripts and his new DbFit test cases into the central version control tool.

The next morning, when the team arrives, each team member updates his or her local copy of the data warehouse code. Natasha looks at the change log produced by her update and sees Prakash's changes. She is a little concerned that the new `F_OrderShipment` fact table may affect the ETL code that she's been working on to populate the `F_Sales` fact table, which had previously contained some shipment information.

Since Prakash worked late last night he hasn't yet arrived this morning, so Natasha can't ask him about the changes directly. So, she reviews the change comments that he entered when he checked in his revisions and she sees this comment:

Extracted `quantity_shipped` from `F_Sales` into new `F_Shipment` table.

This confirms that Natasha's ETL script for populating the `F_Sales` fact table will break when looking for the `quantity_shipped` field. Fortunately she hasn't checked in her ETL changes yet, so she can make the necessary changes to ensure that her code will play nicely with Prakash's changes. She rebuilds her local copy of the data warehouse to include Prakash's changes and then modifies her test cases so that they will not test for `quantity_shipped` in the `F_Sales` fact table. Then she modifies the ETL code that populates the `F_Sales` fact table to remove this reference. Next she runs her newest tests to be sure they all pass, and she reruns the existing tests (including Prakash's new tests) to be sure she didn't break anything with her changes. Finally, she checks her new ETL code and tests into the central version control system for other team members to retrieve.

It's now 10:00 A.M. and time for the daily stand-up meeting. Both Natasha and Prakash are able to tell the team about the changes they have successfully completed since yesterday. Since the team practices frequent check-ins of changes, and frequent updates of their local development sandboxes, everyone takes these changes in stride. This enables other team members to proceed with their tasks in order to be prepared to showcase the new BI features for the user community on this coming Friday.

The feature showcase on Friday is a success, with the user community accepting three new BI features. However, on Monday morning the forecasting analyst in the CFO's office reports an apparent bug in the current production version (release 3.1) of the BI system. It appears that some of the data in the forecasting tool is

---

1. In this context the term *code* refers to any SQL queries, data definition (DDL) scripts, stored procedures, ETL packages, operating system scripts, and database scripts.

inaccurate, and the business is currently in the budgeting process, so this problem is critical and high-priority.

The bug is entered in the bug-tracking system, and Henry agrees to take the lead on researching and resolving the problem. He quickly creates a new virtual development sandbox, checks out the release 3.1 branch from the version control system, and runs the build script to re-create the production version in his sandbox.

Using development data, Henry is able to replicate the problem and identify the root cause. One of the ETL packages has a mistake in the logic for deriving a new measure used in forecasting. The logic applies only in certain situations. Henry reviews the unit tests for this code and discovers that there aren't any tests to cover these situations. So, he writes a few new test cases, runs the tests, and sure enough, the new tests fail.

Henry creates a new tag in the version control system on the release 3.1 branch to mark the point in time before the bug was fixed. He makes the necessary changes in the ETL code to get his new tests passing and then reruns the entire suite of unit tests for that ETL package to be sure they all pass. When Henry is confident that his changes have fixed the defect, he checks his changes (as well as the new tests) into the version control system and creates a new tag on the release 3.1 branch as a post-bug-fix marker.

The continuous integration server detects the changes in the version control system and automatically rebuilds the system and runs all of the integration and functional tests. At 3:15 P.M. Henry notifies the team that the defect is fixed and all tests are passing. The team reviews his changes and everyone agrees that the system is ready to deploy into the preproduction testing sandbox for final validation. Since the team is doing its new feature development using the mainline of the code repository, Henry merges his changes and new tests from the 3.1 release branch into the mainline to fix the problem there as well.

Francisco is the acting release manager during this iteration, so he runs a version control update to retrieve the latest release 3.1 code changes and initiates a build on the test servers. He coordinates this update with the testers and users who are evaluating this preproduction environment. He also asks the forecasting analyst in the CFO's office to review the changes and verify that they have fixed the problem she reported.

By 5:30 P.M. Bob has received confirmation that the bug has been fixed, and he has coordinated with the user community to update the production system after hours. He agrees to stay late to redeploy version 3.1 into production during off-hours so that when users arrive tomorrow, they will have the latest updates.

This correct use of version control enabled everyone on the team to work fluidly and efficiently. It minimized the need for manual coordination of changes to the system under development and allowed the developers to experiment freely without impacting their teammates. You can see from this scenario that version control is most effective when coupled with test automation, sandbox development and test environments, and continuous integration. All of these are discussed elsewhere in this book.

THE REPOSITORY

At the heart of version control is the central repository that contains all of the files that make up the DW/BI system and the history of changes made to those files. Depending on the version control tool, the repository may be a database management system, a file system, or some combination of the two. The repository contains everything necessary to reconstruct the DW/BI system at any point in time since the start of the project.

The repository is the official container for the most up-to-the-minute state of the system under development. As such, it must reside on a secure, safe, and reliable server that is routinely backed up. Development and testing environments can easily be scrapped and rebuilt, but the loss of the repository is catastrophic.

The repository must always be available and accessible to all developers. Therefore, a dedicated, networked version control server is recommended for DW/BI projects. Ideally the repository is securely accessible to developers from any location whether inside or outside the organization's firewalls. This enables developers to work asynchronously from remote locations without the risk of working with out-of-date code, test data, lookup tables, and other elements.

What to Store?

Every digital artifact in your project is a candidate for version control. In general, it is better to keep too many things under version control than too few. However, there is a balance between completeness and complexity. Here is a list of the artifacts that should be under version control:

- Code and scripts
- Configuration files
- ETL object files
- Analytical models
- OLAP cube configuration files
- XML and XML for Analysis (XMLA) files
- Metadata
- Test data

- Test suites
- Documentation files
- Project wiki or similar files
- Release notes
- Deployment scripts
- Lookup table data
- Other relevant data (not production business data)

You may wish to add items to this list based on the specifics of your DW/BI technologies and situation.

The code that makes up your DW/BI system is the most essential collection of items to store in the repository. Obviously this includes SQL queries and scripts, ETL packages, DDL code, configuration files, and operating system scripts. All of these items must be stored in the same version control system so that the team always has a complete snapshot of each version of the DW/BI system.

Unlike application source code, many of the "code" artifacts in a DW/BI system are contained within the technology used to create them. For example, Microsoft's SSIS packages are contained in Visual Studio projects, and Informatica objects are contained within the PowerCenter repository. In these situations you may need to export the objects to external files or identify where the technology stores these as external files. The external files should be stored in the repository.

Similarly, much DW/BI system development involves configuring settings through an application's user interface. For example, Microsoft's SSAS involves visual cube configuration via the Visual Studio interface. In these situations you may need to learn how these configurations can be exported to external files for version control and reimported into the technology during the build and deployment process. For example, SSAS cube configurations can be extracted to XMLA files, and there are command-line utilities that can be invoked to build the cube from scratch using the corresponding XMLA file. In this case the XMLA files should be stored in the version control repository.

DW/BI systems also typically involve metadata that drives their configuration. This metadata should be kept under version control as well as any static data used to populate lookup tables or other static tables in the data warehouse.

Test suites and test cases should also be stored in the repository. Teams that effectively use automated testing in DW/BI development discover that the test suites grow large very quickly. These test suites should exist side by side with the system under test and should be readily available to any person or process that might build and test the system.

Project documentation should be kept under version control. Although Agile Analytics seeks to hold formal documentation to a minimum, there are likely to be some important documents that evolve as the system evolves. Keeping this documentation in the repository will assist the development team in accessing it and updating it as system changes occur. Many teams use a wiki to collaborate and document project discussions and decisions. These artifacts are also candidates for version control and should be considered.

All release and deployment scripts should be stored in the repository. In fact, you should seek to fully automate the deployment process (see Chapter 9, "Project Automation"), which may involve a series of scripted steps. Each of these scripts should be in the repository.

In general, the repository should contain everything that is necessary to build and deploy the fully working DW/BI system and anything that is needed to make sense of the implementation later on. However, this does not include storing the commercial and third-party technologies that form the base stack on which your DW/BI system is built.

What Not to Store?

If you aren't careful, the version control repository can become bloated with unnecessary or even harmful items. Artifacts that are automatically generated by the tools in your DW/BI stack should generally not be stored in the repository. For example, when Microsoft's SSAS processes a cube, it produces a file with a .cub extension. These files should not be stored in the repository because they can be reconstituted using the cube configuration files that are already in the repository. Similarly, temporary files and working files are not typically stored in the repository.

In general, you should seek to avoid duplication within the repository. If the repository contains automatically generated artifacts as well as the code or configurations used to generate them, there is a possibility that they may become inconsistent with one another. However, in some cases there are practical reasons to store generated artifacts in the repository. For instance, if the generated artifact is particularly difficult or time-consuming to regenerate, it may make sense to store it in the repository. I once worked on a DW/BI project that used InstallShield to automate the deployment of the system. InstallShield is designed to orchestrate a sequence of complex installation steps such as verifying that the DBMS is configured properly and running the DDL scripts to build the correct database schemas. Our version control repository contained a `Deployment` folder that held the InstallShield script as well as all of the utilities and scripts used by it. Some of those utilities and scripts were compiled programs whose source code was stored elsewhere in the repository. In this case it made sense to store the generated files in the repository. However, the development team had to take extra precautions to avoid letting the source files become out of sync with the generated files.

WORKING WITH FILES

Although the repository is the heart of the version control system, it isn't where you actually work with the files to make changes. Instead, you retrieve working copies of the desired files from the repository into a workspace on your local development sandbox. This local *workspace* is typically a file folder or subdirectory on your local workstation. You can think of the workspace as a collection of unofficial copies of repository files. You can modify or delete those files, and you can create new files, without directly affecting the official files that are in the repository. Recall from Chapter 7, "Test-Driven Data Warehouse Development," that your development sandbox is an unofficial replica of the data warehouse server that allows you to experiment with and test your development ideas. The workspace is the directory on this sandbox where this experimental code resides. Only when you are satisfied with your changes are they made official by being checked into the repository. The good thing about the workspace is that you can explore, experiment, and make mistakes without fear of accidentally messing up the official code base. The bad thing about the workspace is that if you delete the files in your workspace before storing the changes in the repository, your changes are lost for good. This means that it is a good practice to make small changes, test your changes, and frequently check them into the repository so they aren't lost. It is also a good practice to frequently update your workspace with any changes that your teammates may have checked into the repository so that your workspace stays up-to-date.

All version control tools provide a set of commands to interact with the central repository. Many of these commands support the administration and management of the central repository. However, three essential commands are used frequently by developers: `checkout`, `update`, and `commit`. Each tool uses its own command syntax or client application for executing these commands. For example, in the Subversion command-line interface the command is

```
$ svn checkout http://repos.flixbuster.com/dw/trunk
```

In this example the $ represents the command-line prompt, and the URL is an example of the address where the project repository resides.

The checkout command enables you to populate your workspace with any or all of the files in the project repository. For smaller projects it is often convenient to check out the entire project into your workspace. For larger projects it is more manageable to check out just the subdirectories containing the files you need to work with. The update command enables you to retrieve the latest repository changes into your workspace, including new files that have been added as well as file modifications that have been checked in by other team members. The commit command enables you to check your local workspace changes into the repository, making them official within the central repository.

Agile Analytics Practice: Frequent Updates

Frequently updating your workspace will help the development team stay synchronized. Updating your workspace frequently will help you avoid spending too much time working on an outdated file.

Agile Analytics Practice: Frequent Commits

Local workspace changes that haven't been checked in for many days will cause problems for other team members and during merge attempts. Check in your work many times a day.

Various version control utilities implement these command concepts slightly differently. For example, adding a new file into a Subversion repository is a two-step process, first using the add command to flag the new file as ready to add, then using the commit command to insert it into the repository.

Agile Analytics Practice: Take Small Steps

Work in small increments, and whenever you have a little something working and tested, check it into the repository.

Frequent workspace updates and check-ins are essential to effective collaborative DW/BI development. Agile Analytics developers work in small steps, solving one little problem at a time and testing as they go. As soon as a small problem is solved, the developer checks in his or her changes and test cases, then verbally notifies teammates of the changes so that they can keep their workspaces up-to-date. Problems often occur when developers allow many changes to accumulate in their local workspace and then check them in all at once.

Agile Analytics Practice: Check in Finished Work
Check in only completed chunks of working and tested code. Avoid checking in unfinished work.

What Are Versions?

Now that we've seen what it looks like to work on a DW/BI project that is under version control, it is useful to understand what is happening within the central repository as all these changes are made. The real power of every version control system lies in the central repository. For any single file that is under version control the repository doesn't just store the file. It stores every single version of that file since it was first checked into the system.

For example, imagine creating a simple ETL package that derives a `netProfit` measure using `revenue` and `costOfGoods`. We develop it, test it, and check it into the version control system. Then we modify this logic by further subtracting `shippingCost` from `revenue`. After committing these changes, there are two versions of the file in the repository, and we can retrieve either one. Each new version of the file receives a unique version identifier, so our ETL file may have version numbers 1.0 and 1.1 to reflect the sequence of changes. In actuality most version control systems store only the differences from one version to the next rather than entire copies of each one.

A complete DW/BI system is made up of hundreds or even thousands of files, each one with its own version history. Because each of these files has a unique change history, the version identifiers are not the same for all of them. Therefore, a specific version of the entire DW/BI system is really just a snapshot of all of the file versions at a particular point in time. In Agile Analytics, every iteration results in a new version of the system, which includes the newest features that have been built, tested, and accepted by users. Each new version is a release candidate, which may be deployed into production.

Tags, Branches, and Merging

So far we've been talking about the version control repository as a collection of files, each one with its own revision history. Obviously it isn't feasible to describe a version of the DW/BI system as a collection of file version identifiers. Instead, we need a way to insert labels, such as "Release Candidate 3," into the repository at critical points in time, as placeholders for system versions.

There is another problem with the repository concept presented so far. Imagine that release 1.3 of the FlixBuster BI system is currently in production and has been for five weeks. During that time the development team has been developing new features, checking in the changes frequently. Suddenly members of the user community discover a defect in the system. If the developers fix the bug and check in their changes, how can they deploy the new version of release 1.3 without including the new features, which will be in release 1.4? We need a means of separating one set of changes in the repository from another set of changes. But we also want to make sure that the bug fix is applied in both places.

Version control systems give us tagging, branching, and merging capabilities to address these challenges. Tags enable us to label a group of files in the repository at a particular point in time. This group can be the entire file collection or a subset of the files in the repository. A tag is simply a label, such as `Release_1_3`, that we can use to refer to the group of file versions at a particular time. Agile Analytics teams make frequent use of tags to mark significant events in the evolution of the DW/BI system and to keep track of historical changes. Once the tag is assigned, you can use it to check out this set of file versions. However, you cannot check in new changes at a tag point because a tag is simply a label associated with a point in time.

> **Agile Analytics Practice: Tag Each Iteration Result**
>
> Inserting a tag in the version control system at the end of every iteration enables the team to reproduce the DW/BI system as it existed at any of those important milestones. The tags can be used for incremental release roll-backs if needed.

As developers check changes into the version control system, they are typically making those changes on the *code mainline* or *trunk*. The mainline represents the evolution of the project over time. Figure 8.1 depicts this concept. The *head* of the mainline is a virtual tag that is always assigned to the

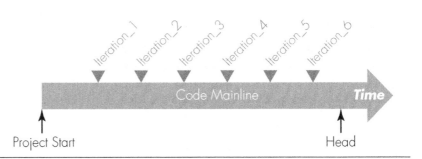

Figure 8.1   Mainline tagging at every iteration

latest version of each file. Executing a `checkout` typically means retrieving the head of the mainline. Similarly, executing an `update` typically means synchronizing your workspace with the head of the mainline. Figure 8.1 also shows the concept of tagging the mainline at each iteration.

Branching enables us to create a code path that runs parallel to the mainline. This is especially useful for managing production releases separately from new feature development. Figure 8.2 depicts the repository history from the FlixBuster scenario. As the team members were preparing for release 3.1, they created a release branch from the mainline. This branch replicates the mainline at a point in time and provides a path for final stabilization and deployment. The branch also enables the team to continue with new feature development along the mainline without disrupting release preparations. Notice that the actual release version of the system is tagged as release 3.1.0. When the defect was reported by the users, the branch provided the developers with a place to research and fix the bug separately from new development. Once the bug fix was complete, the branch was tagged as release 3.1.1 to denote a minor revision. Like the mainline, each branch has a head.

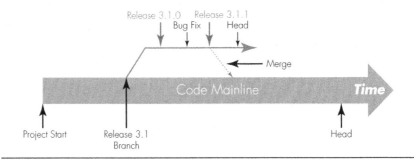

Figure 8.2   Branching from the mainline

When developers check out the branch code, they are typically checking out the head of that branch. Changes checked into the branch are checked in at the head of the branch.

Merging is also depicted in Figure 8.2. As developers identify and fix the bug in release 3.1, they recognize that this bug still exists in the mainline code. They could check out the mainline and duplicate the changes they made on the release branch, but doing this is time-consuming and error-prone. It would be better to ask the version control system to compare the files that have been fixed with their counterparts in the mainline and merge the changes into those files. Version control systems are very good at comparing the differences between files. Merging takes advantage of this power and enables developers to quickly migrate the bug fix into the mainline.

Resolving Conflicts

An issue version control systems must address is how to resolve file change conflicts. What happens when two developers change their copies of the same file and then try to commit those changes? Suppose Prakash has modified the ETL code contained in the `CalcNetProfit.dtsx` file and committed his changes to the repository. Sometime later Natasha, who has also modified this file, attempts to commit her changes. Clearly, it is unacceptable for the system to allow Natasha's changes to replace Prakash's changes because his important work will be lost. Version control systems typically use a type of locking scheme to handle such conflicts. The most common schemes are *strict locking* and *optimistic locking*.

In a strict locking model a file is available for modification by only one person at a time. Others may check the file out for read-only access. So, assuming Prakash is the first to check out the file, Natasha would not be allowed to modify her copy. Instead, she would have to wait until Prakash committed his revisions and released the lock on the file. Then Natasha would have been able to check out the file for editing and insert her changes alongside the ones Prakash already made.

In this way strict locking preemptively prevents file change conflicts. However, this scheme also inhibits productivity because only one person at a time can work with a file. This downside can be further compounded if the person with the lock fails to release it as soon as possible. Many strict locking systems automatically change the local file permissions from read/write to read-only following a commit to prevent this problem.

Agile Analytics Practice: Collaboration Avoids Conflicts
A high degree of face-to-face collaboration within the DW/BI development team will help team members avoid file change conflicts because
each member is aware of what others are working on.

Optimistic locking handles file change conflicts only if they occur rather
than by preemptive prevention. In this scheme all developers may check
out copies of the same file for editing. However, when multiple developers
make changes to the file, the system attempts to merge these changes in the
repository. When a merge is infeasible, the system requires the developers to
resolve the file conflicts before committing.

So, in our example, both Prakash and Natasha may edit their copies of
CalcNetProfit.dtsx. When Prakash commits his changes, a newer version
of the file is added to the repository. Then, when Natasha attempts to commit her changes, the system will notify her that there is a newer version of
the file and will ask her to update her local copy to the latest version. In
this situation, there are several possible scenarios. Suppose that Prakash
revised lines 6–12 of the file and Natasha's revisions affected lines 23–30. In
this case, when the changes do not appear to conflict with one another, the
system invites Natasha to merge the newer version of the file into her local
copy. Because his changes don't affect hers, and vice versa, Natasha accepts
the merge and the system updates her local copy without losing her changes.
After rerunning all the tests for this code module, Natasha can now commit
her changes into the version control system.

However, suppose that Prakash revised lines 6–12 and Natasha revised lines
8–17. In this case, the system detects a conflict and requests that Natasha
resolve this collision before she is allowed to commit her revisions. Natasha
talks to Prakash about why they were both working on the same section of
code at the same time, and about how best to resolve the current conflict.
Together they add Natasha's changes to a copy of the latest version of the
file, test it, and commit these newest changes.

Agile Analytics Practice: Small Cohesive Files
Keeping DW/BI source code files (stored procedures, ETL packages,
SQL scripts, etc.) highly cohesive and modular will help avoid file
change conflicts because changes are more isolated from one another.

It may seem that optimistic locking is highly prone to these conflicts and that it will frequently disrupt the development process. Yet in practice, especially in highly collaborative teams, these types of collisions are extremely infrequent. Typically when work is divided among developers, each developer is working on separate parts of the system. But conflicts can occur when developers' working directories are not updated frequently. Developers who frequently update their working directory minimize the likelihood of these conflicts by ensuring that they are working with the latest version of the code before making changes. Additionally, the occurrence of these conflicts is increased by large, multipurpose code units. For example, one file with multiple stored procedure definitions, or one ETL package that performs a sequence of complex tasks, tends to cause more conflicts. Isolating small, highly cohesive units of functionality into separate modules (and files) helps reduce the occurrence of conflicts.

While it may seem that a version control system with a strict locking protocol would be preferable to one using optimistic locking, it turns out that strict locking causes an undue set of complications for the development team. Most modern version control systems use some form of optimistic locking with the option of enforcing strict locking through some administrative commands.

ORGANIZING THE REPOSITORY

How you organize the project repository is an important aspect of effective version control. The project repository is typically organized into a directory or folder hierarchy. This enables the team to store files of the same type side by side. For example, DDL scripts may be stored in a separate folder from stored procedure definitions. Although the repository structure can be changed later, it is much easier if you plan ahead for all of the future artifacts that will be developed and stored in the repository.

While there is no single right way to organize the repository, here is a recommended structure that has worked well on projects in which I've been involved. This directory structure is much like many software application development repository structures but has been adapted to the uniqueness of DW/BI systems. These suggestions are based on the wisdom presented in the Pragmatic Programmer Version Control series of books (Thomas and Hunt 2004; Mason, 2006).

Explanatory Files

Future developers are one customer community that we haven't talked about yet. We need to leave sufficient information for them to pick up where we left off. Moreover, a few years from now we may not even recall the details of the project we're working on today. So, it's beneficial to create a set of simple explanatory files in the root directory of the project's repository. These may include the following:

- **README.** This is a short and simple overview of the project, the business domain and problem scope, the last deployment date, and any contact information for management sponsors and key stake-holders. The document is purely a memory prompter and should be correspondingly brief.
- **BUILDING.** This file contains a set of prerequisites for building the system and instructions for performing a clean build. The document should outline the technology stack on which the DW/BI system is built, including tested versions of all third-party software. Ideally the build itself is automated (covered in detail in Chapter 9, "Project Automation"), so this document is a brief set of initial instructions on the build steps.
- **GLOSSARY.** Include any project-specific terminology in this file to help familiarize future teams with any jargon that they may encounter.

Directories

It's generally a good idea to keep the directory structure relatively flat. Any more than two or three levels deep can become confusing and hard to navigate. The following top-level directories will help with this organization:

- `build/`. This directory contains all of the files and components needed for the automated build and deployment processes. Chapter 9, "Project Automation," will provide more detail on the files that are stored in this directory. All scripts and utilities used to automate the deployment of your DW/BI system are stored here. It is often useful to store deployment instructions and release notes either in this directory or in the top-level directory.
- `doc/`. Check in all formal and semiformal project documentation here. This includes project wiki content, e-mails documenting decisions made, digital photos of important whiteboard discussions, and other artifacts. It typically makes sense to organize the `doc/`

directory into a collection of meaningful subdirectories by document purpose or project phase.

- data/. Use this directory for any non-source data that is loaded into the system, such as data for lookup tables or data used by key business rules. Keeping this type of data under version control is often helpful.

- db/. This directory holds all of the database schema definition SQL scripts. By keeping schema definitions scripted and under version control, you will have a history of the database changes from one release to the next, which can help with migration of one database version to the next. It is useful to divide this directory into subdirectories for the different data tiers in the architecture, such as ddl/stage, ddl/integration, ddl/warehouse, ddl/financeMart.

- etl/. All ETL modules should be stored in this directory. Depending on the ETL application being used, this may require exporting the modules into stand-alone files. For example, Informatica objects are stored in the Informatica Server repository but can be exported to XML-formatted files to be kept under version control.[2] Conversely, Microsoft's SSIS maintains its objects as Visual Studio project files in the file system. All of the Visual Studio project directory structures (including subdirectories) can be placed directly under the etl/ directory.

- mdx/. If your DW/BI system includes the use of multidimensional queries using the Multidimensional Expressions (MDX) language, these queries should be scripted and stored in this directory. Alternatively, if your DW/BI system uses a proprietary language for issuing multidimensional queries, use a different name for this directory and store the queries in that directory.

- svcs/. If your DW/BI system includes a Web service API or other services, they should be stored in this directory. For example, suppose the DW/BI system's authentication process uses services that communicate with the organizational Active Directory system. These interface services may be stored in this directory.

- sp/. Use this directory to store all procedure definition scripts. Additionally, create a build script that automatically executes these definition scripts to load them into the DBMS during the DW/BI system build process. Depending on how your DW/BI system uses

---

2. Readers may be aware that the Informatica suite includes a version control system. However, at the time of this writing, it is too rudimentary for real version control because it is incapable of storing non-Informatica objects in the same repository.

stored procedures, it may be useful to split them into a series of subdirectories based on the data tier in your architecture to which they apply.

- sql/. Use this directory to store all scripted SQL queries that are used in your DW/BI system, including any queries used to populate static reports, preprogrammed queries that are available to users, and so on.

- test/. This directory houses all of the unit, integration, functional, acceptance, performance, and stress test suites that are created during the iterative development of the system. It should be organized into subdirectories that coincide with the tiers in your DW/BI systems architecture. For example, all of the tests for the data integration tier may reside in a test/int/ directory. Those directories may be further divided into testing tool subgroups such as dbfit/ or sqlunit/. Alternatively, you may wish to divide these into test type subgroups such as unit/ or functional/. This alternative enables you to run smaller test suites more easily. Finally, many developers prefer to store test cases alongside the code that they are designed to test. This can be very beneficial, especially for unit tests, but makes it more difficult to separate production system code from test code.

- util/. This directory is used to store various utility scripts and programs that support the DW/BI project but are not part of the production system. These may include deployment scripts or utilities to import files into their corresponding applications.

- vendor/. Use this directory to store any third-party vendor libraries or customizations. For example, many BI dashboard products offer a highly customizable user interface look and feel. All of this customization should be kept under version control. Microsoft's ProClarity product (now integrated into Office PerformancePoint) supports the customization of elements such as on-screen logos, screen layouts, and button and tab labels. This is done by modifying files that are part of the ProClarity server installation. These modified files should be checked into version control as part of the BI system build that uses them.

- vendorsrc/. Sometimes third-party DW/BI applications involve development and configuration within the tool, using a visual development environment or wizard-driven process. These tools often produce a binary file in a proprietary format. You should keep these binary files under version control in this folder and, whenever possible, the exported configuration sources used to produce the binaries.

- views/. Use this folder to store any SQL view definition scripts that are part of the DW/BI system. Alternatively, you may wish to make this a subdirectory under the sql/ directory previously described.
- xmla/. If your DW/BI system uses XMLA, use this directory to store those files.

There are no absolutes in how you choose to organize the version control repository. Instead, carefully evaluate the tools and languages that are used in your DW/BI system development, and identify all of the files and artifacts that should be kept under version control. Then design your file organization around these file types. Figure 8.3 depicts one effective way to organize a project repository.

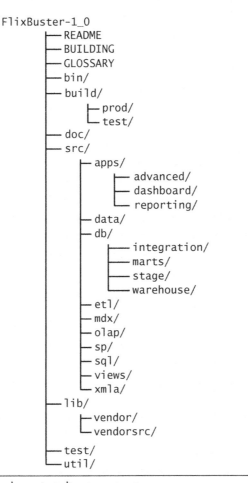

Figure 8.3 Example project directory structure

For those file types that require extra steps, such as exporting and importing, it pays to develop utilities to automate them. Doing so will streamline your build process and make it much easier to quickly deploy the system in any of the sandboxes or into production.

TAGGING AND BRANCHING

The mechanics of tags and branches were described earlier in this chapter, but it is useful to establish a set of development standards for tagging and branching in your repository. These standards should cover everything from experimental development work, to ending each iteration, to managing new production releases, to fixing defects found in production. Such standards should include

- When to assign tags and when to create branches
- Naming conventions for tags and branches
- How to avoid complex and problematic branching

As for the repository directory structure, the standards recommended here are based on a set of fairly widely accepted practices in the software development community. After using version control on many DW/BI projects, I have found these standards to be very effective in our domain as well. These standards are presented in greater detail in the Pragmatic Programmer book series on version control (Thomas and Hunt 2004).

Each version control utility handles branching and tagging differently. This chapter is not specific to any particular version control tool. However, all fully functional version control tools will support tagging and branching. For example, the Subversion tool uses a separate copy[3] of the repository as a branch; the CVS tool uses a special variant of the release tag command (rtag) and handles the actual branch internal to the repository. In practice it is possible to make things unnecessarily messy when branching if you aren't careful. Therefore, it is important to clearly and accurately understand how the system you are using handles these concepts.

When to Tag and Branch

Tagging is easier to manage since a tag is just a symbolic name assigned to a particular point in time within your version control repository. In fact,

---

3. In actuality, Subversion uses a "cheap copy" strategy to avoid actually copying all of the data in the repository, thereby optimizing repository storage space.

you can think of HEAD as a system-generated tag that is continuously being reassigned to the most current version of all the files in the repository. Version control systems also allow you to execute checkouts by specifying a date and time. These date/time combinations behave like system-generated tags as well. The trouble with relying on date/time tags is that they require us to remember specifically when the repository was in a particular state of interest. So, version control systems allow us to assign meaningful tag names at key milestones in the repository.

Tags come in two flavors: regular tags and branch tags. Depending on your version control system, the differences may only be conceptual. For example, in Subversion there is no material difference between a branch tag and a regular tag other than the context in which each is used. Tags can be used for a variety of purposes, but too many tags can make it difficult and confusing to review the code history. Agile Analytics teams routinely use tags to mark the following important events in the code base:

- **End of iterations.** The goal of every iteration in an Agile project is to have a potentially deployable DW/BI system. While actual deployment every two weeks may be too ambitious for some teams, it is a healthy objective. Tagging the code mainline at the end of each iteration helps the team establish a pattern of asking the question "What is keeping us from deploying this version right now?" Reviewing the changes between these tags also conveys the team's progress in terms of new features delivered.
- **Branches.** Anytime a branch is created from the code mainline, it should be tagged with a label that conveys the purpose of the branch. Different reasons for branching will be discussed shortly.
- **Releases.** A tag should be added at every point when the code is tested, stable, and deemed ready for release. This helps prevent the need for a "code freeze" in order to deploy the latest release and enables developers to continue making refinements. As we will discuss, each release candidate should be managed on a release branch.
- **Defects.** After a release has been deployed into production, end users may report defects and issues. Since fixing bugs carries the possibility of introducing other problems, it is useful to insert a tag just prior to the bug fix in case you need to roll back to the pre-fix state of things. Additionally, it is useful to insert a tag just after a bug fix in order to isolate the fix from other changes in the release code.

Branching was previously introduced as a means of establishing a code path that parallels the mainline. Figure 8.2 depicts how you might think of a code branch. Branches are more complicated than tags because a branch is a physical replica of the path it branches from rather than just a symbolic marker pointing to a certain event. You can check out and modify a branch in the same way you can check out the mainline, whereas you can only check out (not modify) the code at a tag. If you aren't careful, too many branches can easily complicate your version control repository, making code management difficult and confusing. For this reason, branches should be planned and used carefully and with express purpose. Experience has shown that there are two good reasons to branch:

- **Experimental branches.** Every DW/BI project has a degree of uncertainty, whether it is an uncertain technology decision, a fundamental design decision with significant ramifications, or just some technical question that remains unanswered. Agile Analytics teams occasionally find it useful to conduct small and simple experiments for the express purpose of resolving uncertainty or finalizing a decision. Since these experiments may result in throwaway code, it is beneficial to create an experimental branch where developers can try out different ideas without corrupting the production code mainline. Experimental branches should be tagged to denote their purpose. If the experiments result in working/tested code that is worth keeping, that code can be merged back into the mainline. In this way the development team can continue working on the mainline while the experimental developers work on their branch.
- **Release branches.** Each planned release of the DW/BI system should be managed on its own branch off of the mainline. These branches should be tagged to denote the point at which a release candidate begins being prepared for the actual release. Release branches are typically considered to be "feature complete" for that release. In other words, developers should avoid doing any new feature development along a release branch. The release branch is for any final testing, documentation, and refinement of the DW/BI system before it is released into production. As my friend Luke Hohmann says, "We need to let the bits settle prior to launch." Of course, any of these final refinements that are appropriate should be merged back into the mainline so that they are naturally propagated into future releases as well.

As previously described, any bugs that are found after the system is deployed should be tagged and fixed along the corresponding release branch. It may be useful to insert tags along the release branch to denote key events prior to the release. However, it is not necessary to tag bug fixes prior to release unless they are significant code revisions. This helps separate formally reported defects from those found during routine testing and release preparation.

Naming Tags and Branches

Each team should adopt a tag-naming convention. As with many of the recommendations in this chapter, I favor the naming conventions introduced by Thomas and Hunt (2004) with some slight modifications. These include the following:

- **Release branch.** The tag convention is RB_*releaseID*. For example, RB_3_1 denotes a release branch for version 3.1, RB_3_1_2 for version 3.1.2, and so on.
- **Experimental branch.** The tag convention is TRY_*codename*. For example, TRY_abinitio may denote an experimental branch using Ab Initio tools for data integration; TRY_adaptivemodel may denote an experiment using an adaptive data model design alternative. Another convention for these branches is TRY_*initials_date*, which includes the initials of the developer conducting the experiment and the date the branch was created. For example, TRY_kwc_20100301 reflects a branch created by Ken W. Collier on 3/1/2010.
- **Iteration end.** The tag convention is IT_*iterationID*. For example, IT_2_5 might refer to the fifth iteration during the second release cycle, or IT_8 might refer to iteration number eight, or IT_20100326 might refer to the iteration ending on March 26, 2010. Ideally, each iteration results in the real production release of new features. When this is your routine, there is no need to use separate tags to mark the end of each iteration. The release branches and tags will serve that purpose. If your team uses Scrum terminology, you may wish to use the convention SPR_*sprintID* instead.
- **Release.** The tag convention is REL_*releaseID*. For example, REL_3_1 tags the point on the release branch RB_3_1 when the code was actually deployed.
- **Pre–bug fixes.** The tag convention is PRE_*trackingID*. For example, PRE_158009 marks the code just prior to applying the fix for defect ID 158009. The ID corresponds to the ID assigned by the bug-tracking system.
- **Post–bug fixes.** The tag convention is POST_*trackingID*. For example, POST_158009 marks the code just after applying the fix for defect ID 158009.

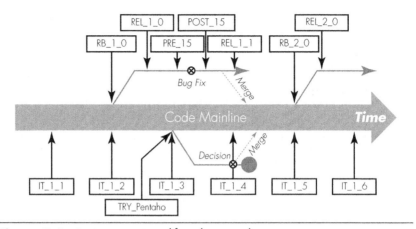

Figure 8.4   Project repository lifecycle example

Figure 8.4 offers an example of how one might visualize a project repository over time using this scheme.

Scenario

At the end of iteration two the FlixBuster Analytics project community decides to deploy the finished features into production as version 1.0. The development team tags the code mainline and creates a release branch to prepare for the deployment. David has volunteered to act as release manager for this release, allowing the rest of the development team to continue with iteration three's development of new features. David runs a complete rebuild of release candidate 1.0 in the pre-production testing environment; reruns the entire suite of functional tests; and then runs the load, stress, and performance tests to validate the behavior of the DW/BI system in a production-like setting.

After a week of final preparation, David reviews the test results with the product owner and the team, and they decide that the release candidate is ready for production deployment. David subsequently executes the DW/BI system build script on the production servers while the product owner coordinates with the user community to launch the system using live data.

After the initial data load is complete, the system is made available to the user community. Within the first week after launch, the users begin to notice a data anomaly in the customer profitability features. A problem report is entered into the defect-tracking system, and the team agrees that this issue has high priority. Adriana volunteers to tackle the bug during iteration four.

Luckily, Adriana discovers the root cause quickly in one of the ETL modules. Natasha agrees to pair program with her to fix the problem. They quickly add a pre-bug-fix tag along the release branch and begin working. First they write the test cases that should have detected the problem. They run the tests, and sure enough, the new tests fail. They apply the bug fix in the ETL module and rerun their tests to make sure they all pass, and then they add a post-bug-fix tag to surround the fix. They evaluate whether any other problems might be related to this one and agree that the new bug fix is sufficient.

After Adriana and Natasha review the problem's root cause and their fix with the rest of the team, everyone agrees that the problem is solved. Adriana and Natasha agree to merge their bug fix into the mainline. However, the team decides to wait a few days to deploy the bug fix because it is so close to the end of iteration four and the team may deploy new features as well as the bug fix. As it turns out, the project community decides that the new features aren't ready for deployment, so David releases version 1.1 so that the users will benefit immediately from the bug fix.

Later, during iteration four, the team has decided to explore the use of the Pentaho open-source DW/BI platform as an alternative to the commercial tools they have been using. Lead developers Johannes and Bert create an experimental branch to evaluate the Pentaho tools, while the other developers continue building new features on the mainline.

The expected outcome of this experiment is a simple prototype DW/BI system with a small set of features using FlixBuster development data. The project community will review this prototype at the end of iteration four and decide as a group whether or not to switch to the new platform. The experiment is very successful, and the project community agrees to switch technologies. They agree upon a cutover plan, which begins immediately during iteration five. They also discover that Johannes and Bert did some experimental work that is worth keeping, so this work is merged into the mainline.

The technology switch goes surprisingly smoothly, and the team is able to reproduce all of the DW/BI features from version 1.1 in Pentaho, at production quality, by the end of iteration five. After reviewing these features, the community agrees to rerelease the Pentaho version of the system into production. The team creates a new release branch and continues preparing for the release of version 2.0.

As you can see, the version control system coupled with a set of good engineering practices enables the FlixBuster Analytics team to work efficiently and effectively. The team maintains its feature-driven goals despite the disruptions caused by defects and technology changes. Team members worked closely with the product owner and user community to review new features, and because they focus on production quality in all development, they are able to release frequently into production.

Keeping Things Simple

Effective code management relies on careful management of your version control repository and judicious use of branching and tagging. I once worked with a client whose DW/BI team was using the CVS version control tool to manage project artifacts. Unfortunately, over time, the repository had devolved into convoluted branching structures that were multiple layers deep. The tags didn't follow any common convention, and the team members were so confused by the version control system that they avoided committing new changes or updating their sandboxes. The version control system wasn't helping them, it was hurting them.

Like your house, your project's repository must be kept tidy. The following is a set of habits, practices, and good ideas for ensuring that your team benefits from version control rather than suffering because of it:

- **Develop on the mainline.** The vast majority of your team's development work should be committed along the mainline and checked out from there as well. Working on code branches should be the exception, not the norm. The mainline represents the primary historical timeline in the evolution of your system. The bulk of activity should be collected and tagged along this path. This practice will help ensure that everyone is working with the same code base and evolving the system collaboratively.
- **Avoid branching a branch.** Suppose you're working on an experimental branch and decide to conduct a small side experiment. You may be tempted to branch off of your experimental branch so that you don't corrupt your primary experiment. This practice should be avoided. It is preferable to use a tag to mark the point to which you may wish to roll back if the secondary experiment goes awry. When this temptation arises, think carefully about the purpose, and look for alternative ways to accomplish the same goal without multilevel branching. This habit encourages continuous convergence toward, rather than divergence away from, the mainline.
- **Keep branches single-purposed.** Avoid using a branch to achieve multiple objectives. For example, a release branch should not include any new feature development, only refinements, new tests, and bug fixes. This habit helps minimize the merges back to the mainline and simplifies code management.
- **Shorten branch life span.** The longer a code branch remains an active path of development, the more likely it is to become out of sync with the code mainline. As soon as a branch has served its

purpose, all appropriate changes should be merged to the mainline, and development activity should halt along the branch.

▪ **Merge early and often.** Merging from a branch to the mainline is least difficult when the change is a single, small, simple one. Larger collections of changes are often more challenging to merge correctly. Additionally, as time passes, the ongoing development along the mainline causes the code to increasingly deviate from that along the branch, and the version control system may have a difficult time merging properly. While a branch remains active, team members working on the branch should frequently make small merges whenever applicable.

▪ **One question per experimental branch.** Experimental branches are for experimentation, exploration, and evaluation. Their purpose is to give you a place to answer a question you have. Always seek to keep these branches focused on a single question, and do the smallest, simplest amount of work necessary to answer that question. This habit will help keep the life span of an experimental branch as short as possible so that you can get back to the business of building a production-quality, working DW/BI system.

▪ **Truncate experimental branches early.** This practice relates to the previous one. It is often tempting to take an experiment or exploration much farther than is necessary. Bear in mind that experimental branches hold throwaway work. This habit will help prevent you from expending unnecessary effort along these branches. Once the question is answered, move back to the mainline.

▪ **Assign pre-bug-fix tags as late as possible.** Wait until you've identified the root cause of a defect, have a plan of attack, and are ready to implement the changes before you tag the release branch with the pre-fix tag. This will help isolate your bug fix changes from other refinements along the branch.

▪ **Assign post-bug-fix tags as early as possible.** Similar to the prior recommendation, tag the release branch with the post-fix tag as soon as you are confident that the issue is resolved. This will help isolate your bug fix changes from unrelated changes along the same branch.

CHOOSING AN EFFECTIVE TOOL

Because version control is essential in the support of Agile Analytics development practices, selecting the right version control system is important. It's also important to select a tool that you expect to live with for some time, since it can be difficult to migrate a project repository from one version control system to another. There are several criteria to consider when selecting the right version control tool, including the following:

- **Storage for everything.** The tool you select must be capable of storing all of your DW/BI project artifacts in the same repository. These include digital images, written documents, e-mails and text messages, text files, binary files, and any other file types that are generated by your DW/BI technologies. Evaluate your DW/BI project and consider all of the items that you expect to house in your version control system, then be sure to select a tool that will accommodate them. Some version control systems cannot.

- **Support for Agile habits.** The tool you select must support frequent workspace updates, frequent commits, and other routine version control interactions. Be sure that the tool you select supports a client application that makes these frequent interactions easy. Almost all version control tools support a command-line interface; many also support clients that are integrated into the development tools (as plug-ins) or are integrated into the operating system (as OS command extensions). If it is clunky for developers to exercise frequent version control functions, they will avoid doing so.

- **Free or commercial.** Many enterprise-capable open-source software (OSS) products provide version control. However, there is some solace in the confidence that commercial vendors will provide the necessary support and maintenance for their products. OSS version control systems tend to evolve to address flaws and shortcomings in earlier systems, while commercial systems tend to focus on market opportunities by offering greater functionality or ease of use. Balancing cost of ownership against richness of function is an important consideration when choosing a version control system.

- **Hosted or installed.** With the advent of software as a service (SaaS), many vendors have emerged that offer hosted project management solutions, including version control. Such hosting options relieve the DW/BI development organization of version control administration tasks such as frequent repository backups, repository configuration, user access, and other responsibilities. Conversely, an internally managed version control system ensures that project artifacts are contained within the corporate firewall and are not subject to the long-term viability of a hosting provider.

- **Existing standards.** Of course, if your organization already has an established version control infrastructure to support other projects, it is probably best to use that corporate standard. Unfortunately, sometimes the corporate version control standard was established long ago and does not benefit from new advances in version control technologies. When this is the case, evaluate the standard against the Agile Analytics team's need for seamless integration of version control in the work environment. On the other hand, organizations with an established standard also have internal expertise in the maintenance and usage of the adopted tool. This can greatly benefit a DW/BI team that has little or no experience with such tools.

■ **Integration with build automation.** Build automation is introduced in the next chapter but relies heavily on a version control system to monitor and detect the code changes that will trigger a build. Not all version control systems are easy to integrate with all build automation tools. It is best to select a version control tool that integrates easily with your build tool (or vice versa). This enables the development team to focus on building the DW/BI system rather than administering the development infrastructure.

Consider other factors that will be impacted by your selection of a version control technology. This chapter is intended to be tool-agnostic, although under full disclosure I have managed several successful DW/BI projects (as well as the elements of this book) in Subversion[4] using the TortoiseSVN[5] client, so these remain favorites of mine. As of this writing, there is a very comprehensive Wikipedia entry that compares and contrasts version control tools, both OSS and commercial.[6] It will serve your project well to carefully consider which technology will best support the values and principles of Agile Analytics.

WRAP-UP

Agile Analytics is all about the early and frequent delivery of value to users. Achieving this goal using old-fashioned manual methods is nearly impossible. To be successful we need the support of development tools and infrastructure. Version control is a core component of this infrastructure. It is at the heart of release management and build automation.

This chapter introduced version control as an essential part of every Agile Analytics project. We examined how effective version control benefits the development team by providing an "undo button" to back up to a previous stable situation. We examined how version control enables developers

---

4. http://subversion.tigris.org/
5. http://tortoisesvn.tigris.org/
6. http://en.wikipedia.org/wiki/Comparison_of_revision_control_software

to work together on the same system without tripping over one another. We saw how version control provides a bread-crumb trail of changes made in the system over time. And we saw how version control enables the team to execute a production deployment without having to manage a "code freeze."

Agile Analytics developers are in the habit of keeping their local workspace in sync with the central code repository. Many times every hour, developers check out the changes their teammates have made and check in their own tested changes. The Agile team makes judicious use of tags and branches to create a history of important events and milestones during the project. Each release gets its own code branch where the team can handle all of the release preparation activities and can resolve any issues that arise after the release. Teams can use branching for exploratory and experimental work, giving developers a way to test ideas without messing things up in the mainline of code.

In this chapter we looked at the storage of more than just code. Teams should also keep their documentation and other project artifacts under version control. By keeping everything in the version control system, the team can retrieve a snapshot of the entire project at any given point in time during the project lifecycle. We also acknowledged that there are some things that don't belong in the version control system. Items that are generated from other items, by compiling or processing them, are typically not kept under version control. This helps prevent duplication within the version control system.

This chapter also highlights the importance of developer collaboration to minimize file change conflicts. But it is helpful to understand how version control systems behave when file conflicts do occur. Teams that have a high degree of developer collaboration benefit from the flexibility of optimistic locking, which allows multiple developers to edit copies of the same file at the same time. Strict locking lets only one developer edit a file at a time, which ensures that no conflicts will occur, but it is much more restrictive.

Effective use of version control is simply a better way to work. It helps developers become more organized. It reduces the burden on developers to manage their own code locally. It establishes a single, official location for project items. And it frees developers to focus on creating new features rather than managing project artifacts.

Agile Analytics requires being fearless. We can't be effective if we are afraid of quality problems in the system, how changes will affect existing features, or a disruptive deployment. The knowledge that we can quickly revert to an earlier version if needed encourages us to deploy more frequently. The simplicity with which we can spin up a testing environment gives us confidence that the system is of high quality. The ability to experiment with new ideas without corrupting the project makes us more likely to arrive at the best solution. Good code management is just one of many practices that enable fearlessness.

Chapter 9

PROJECT AUTOMATION

The general goal of DW/BI systems development is to automate and optimize data-based decision support for our customers. In fact, automation of routine processes is a primary goal of most systems and application development. Such automation makes end users' jobs easier, more reliable, more repeatable, and faster. Unfortunately, like the fabled cobbler's children, we often don't automate our own work to gain the same benefits. DW/BI developers don't typically make the time or have the wherewithal to automate the routine processes that make up a large percentage of their work.

The previous two chapters introduced test automation and version control for DW/BI systems development. I occasionally work with DW/BI teams that stall out on those crucial technical practices. Such teams cannot really be Agile, because their manually intensive efforts quickly become impediments to the goal of frequently delivering new high-value BI features. However, with those foundational practices in place, DW/BI teams are poised for fully automated continuous integration, deployment, and monitoring. These are the practices exhibited by a finely tuned and highly effective DW/BI team.

Software product development teams have been using automated installation for many years. Most of us have experienced either push-button or wizard-driven software installations on our own workstations, if not on the installation of server software. Not only are today's software products designed for automated deployment that minimizes manual intervention; these products are routinely and automatically updated with upgrades, bug fixes, and improvements.

But, with some exceptions, today's DW/BI system deployment is a highly manual effort. More advanced DW/BI teams have a sequenced checklist of steps to complete during an installation, while less advanced teams perform an ad hoc series of actions until everything seems to be working. Either case is error-prone and time-consuming. Imagine the possibilities if we took a bit of time to automate all of those steps the way our software development colleagues do. We would have a reliable, repeatable, efficient means of installing the latest version of our DW/BI system—and that means that we could deploy new features more frequently.

But wait, that's not all! If we can automate DW/BI system deployment, then without too much extra effort we can create automated builds within those development sandboxes introduced in Chapter 7, "Test-Driven Data Warehouse Development." Then we might as well combine those automated builds with our automated tests to quickly, easily, and frequently rebuild and retest the system. What a great way to maintain high confidence in the quality of our DW/BI system!

Our software development colleagues have been practicing continuous integration for a while now, and the results are exciting. Developers spend much more time working on software and less time chasing down bugs. They can make fearless changes and quickly get confirmation of whether or not their changes have broken the system.

This chapter draws on that experience and introduces approaches for DW/BI system build automation, continuous integration, and automated deployment. Fortunately, there are lots of open-source software tools to help with this automation. Unfortunately, most of these tools are designed for building compiled software systems. We will examine techniques for adapting these tools to the nuances of technology integration and customization. Gone are the days of wondering if you're building a fragile DW/BI system that will break under the pressure of use.

WHAT IS PROJECT AUTOMATION?

If we expect to do something more than once, we should consider automating it. After all, isn't that what our customers are asking for help with? The steps required to build and test the DW/BI system are candidates for automation, as are the steps necessary to deploy the system into production. The procedure for generating a release bundle from the version control system should be automated. Automating the build, monitoring, release, and deployment of the business intelligence systems under development is core to Agile Analytics. In practice it looks something like the following:

Scenario

Bob arrives early this morning to finish some project work before the daily stand-up. He wants to be sure that Natasha and Henry aren't blocked waiting for him to finish the code that imports syndicated third-party customer demographic data into the integration tier of the data warehouse. Bob realizes it's been a while since he has fully rebuilt the system in his local sandbox, and he wants to be sure that he does his final testing on the most up-to-date version of the system. So, he initiates an update to his local workspace, executes the uninstall script to remove the older version from his sandbox, and then executes the build script to install the latest version of the DW/BI system on his sandbox environment. Finally, he runs the data load scripts to populate the new installation with development data. All of this takes a little less than 30 minutes, including time for Bob to get his fresh coffee while the uninstaller script was running. Now Bob is ready to get his work done using the latest system version.

As Bob works on his new code, he notices the small green icon in the lower corner of his screen. It represents the utility that is monitoring the continuous integration sandbox. The green icon tells Bob that the last integration/test sequence (sometime overnight) completed successfully. If something had gone wrong, the icon would be red. Bob is happy to see that everything is working as expected, allowing him to add his new code into the system.

Francisco also arrives early and decides to pair program with Bob so that he can learn more about the syndicated data import process. They finish up the third-party import code about 45 minutes before the stand-up and check in the new code along with the new test cases. This check-in is detected by the continuous integration server, which automatically executes the build/test sequence. As Bob and Francisco anticipated, everything works fine and all of the tests (including the new ones) pass. The team will be happy to hear about this progress during the daily stand-up.

During the stand-up Natasha also reports her latest ETL modifications, which were checked into the version management system along with her new test cases late yesterday. These include the deployment of the latest customer profitability segmentation model from the data mining that Prakash completed last week. The scheduled nightly build included Natasha's latest changes, and the team is very happy that the recent builds are successful.

During the daily stand-up Henry commits to finishing up the BI features that will enable users to see the customer profitability segments. He anticipates having something that can be demonstrated to users by tonight's scheduled system build.

Francisco commits to modifying the customer dimensions in the warehouse to include the new customer demographic data, and Natasha commits to finishing the ETL modifications that will merge this syndicated data with the FlixBuster data. They anticipate that these modifications will be ready for the scheduled nightly build as well.

As the end of the current iteration approaches, the team continues to make this sort of progress. Dieter, the product owner, is delighted. The automated continuous integration system gives him confidence that new changes aren't breaking previously working capabilities. On Wednesday before Friday's feature showcase, Dieter tells the team that he would like to deploy the latest version into production if the users accept these latest features and improvements. The team agrees to finish its last few tasks and begin preparing for a deployment.

In preparation for Friday's feature showcase Henry, the acting release manager for this iteration, creates a new release branch in the version control system, tags it as `RB_2_0`, and checks it out into his workspace. He runs the release bundler script that the team has developed for automatic deployments, which creates a self-contained package that can be copied to any properly configured server. Unpacking and executing this release bundle will automatically check for the proper server configuration and then, if everything checks out, will automatically install the latest DW/BI system version on the server.

After running the uninstaller script to clean up the preproduction demo server, Henry copies the release bundle onto the demo server, unpacks it, and executes the installer. He runs the data loader scripts to populate the system and runs the diagnostic scripts to verify that the installation completed successfully. This dry run installation gives Henry (and the team) confidence that the deployment is self-contained and does not require a connection to the version control system for successful completion. By 4:00 on Thursday Henry has reviewed the demo deployment results with the team, and Dieter leads a walk-through of the new features that will be showcased tomorrow.

By 10:00 A.M. on Friday the feature showcase is successfully finished. The user community is excited about the new improvements and has identified only a few minor refinements needed before version 2.0 is deployed into production. The team spends the rest of Friday making these final changes on the release 2.0 branch, and by 4:00 P.M. Henry has re-created the release bundle and will run one final test of this installation on the test server. By 4:30 P.M. the team is satisfied that the release bundle is stable, and by 5:15 version 2.0 has been installed on the production servers and the data migration scripts are running. Since tonight is the team's "Extreme Bowling" night, everyone is ready to turn the lights out and head to the bowling alley by 6:00 P.M. The team members worked a little longer than normal today, but their sense of accomplishment is high and their spirits are good.

This example shows how test automation, version control, and project automation all coincide to give an Agile Analytics team continued confidence that their system is always ready for production. This triad of practices enables the Agile Analytics team to react quickly and smoothly to address problems with the build or to respond to the wishes of customers for production deployments.

In this latest FlixBuster scenario we saw examples of the following types of automation:

- **One-step builds:** automating the build process so that the entire system build is triggered by one execution step. This step may trigger a multistage "wizard" but is still initiated in one step.

- **Triggered builds:** system builds that are automatically triggered by some event, such as a change in the version control repository.
- **Scheduled builds:** system builds that are executed at a prescheduled time, such as late at night while developers are asleep.
- **Push-button release:** the automated creation of a stand-alone release package that omits non-production items such as test suites and utility files.
- **Installation and deployment:** the automation of the installation procedure for rapid deployment.
- **Monitoring:** the automatic monitoring of triggered and scheduled builds to notify developers of build success or failure.

This chapter outlines an adaptation of the principles and practices presented in detail by Mike Clark in *Pragmatic Project Automation* (Clark 2004). This book is an excellent treatise on complete project automation for Java software development projects using the Apache Ant[1] and CruiseControl[2] open-source build automation tools. In this chapter we will explore the adaptation of these and other tools to the unique differences in DW/BI systems automation.

GETTING STARTED

There are a few things that must be in place and working before project automation makes sense. These include

- **Version control.** As discussed in Chapter 8, "Version Control for Data Warehousing," all of the project files must be stored in a central version control repository. This code management system provides the automation processes with a single source from which to get the files needed to build the project. The version control system also enables the development team to create automated build scripts for different versions of the DW/BI system.
- **Automated tests.** As discussed in Chapter 7, "Test-Driven Data Warehouse Development," automated tests are tests that run and check their own results automatically. They enable the team to incrementally build quality into the DW/BI system. These automated tests are an integral part of project automation. They are run automatically during continuous integration to confirm that

---

1. http://ant.apache.org/
2. http://cruisecontrol.sourceforge.net/

the system builds are successful. Without these automated tests we would have confirmation that the DW/BI system components are successfully installed and configured, but not whether they function as expected.

■ **Utility scripts.** Scripts are the building blocks of project automation. They may be operating system command scripts, database scripts, or other small scripts that automatically perform simple and singular tasks in the build process. In the FlixBuster scenario, Bob uses an uninstaller script that the development team had built to simplify the removal of the DW/BI system components from the server(s). Scripts should be small and simple to debug and should not require their own separate build processes. These are most commonly shell scripts using command-line statements.

■ **Monitoring devices.** In the FlixBuster example there is a small green icon on Bob's workstation desktop that tells him that the most recent build was successful. A red icon would have signaled a problem with the build that Bob would need to look into. Some teams configure their automation systems to send SMS messages to team members' mobile devices, others to send e-mail or Twitter messages; and some monitor build success using visual controls like the red/green icon on developers' desktops. Whatever the communication technique, the entire development team must be notified immediately when a build fails. We will look at some tools and techniques to assist with this monitoring requirement later in this chapter.

BUILD AUTOMATION

A one-step automated build is the point of departure for more comprehensive project automation. This commanded build is used routinely by developers within their sandboxes during the develop-test cycle. Once established, the one-step build is the basis for scheduled and triggered builds.

A one-step build process changes the nature of your project documentation. How many projects have you worked on that included a written sequence of installation instructions for installing and configuring the DW/BI system? The one-step automated build replaces the need for step-by-step instructions, with guidelines on how to change the build configuration.

Project automation expert Mike Clark describes the ideal automated build as being CRISP—Complete, Repeatable, Informative, Schedulable, Portable (Clark 2004). Here is what that means for DW/BI system builds:

- **Complete.** A complete build is one that builds the system entirely from scratch on a properly configured baseline platform. The build should complete as many of the installation steps itself with minimal manual intervention. While some build utilities may require certain prerequisites, such as properly installed DBMS and BI software, other tools have the ability to install these prerequisite technologies as part of the build.

- **Repeatable.** The build should be consistently repeatable with the same outcome every time as long as the prerequisite configuration is present. Each new release candidate of the DW/BI system should include a fully tested build file. When this build file is maintained in the version control system alongside the other system components, anyone can check out any version of the system and quickly build it with minimal additional effort.

- **Informative.** An informative build broadcasts the details of build success or failure to developers. At the most basic level, the build must report whether or not all build steps were completed successfully. But more important, the build should take advantage of all those automated tests that we talked about in Chapter 7, "Test-Driven Data Warehouse Development." The build should run a test suite to confirm that everything is functioning properly.

- **Schedulable.** With relative ease, a complete, repeatable build can be run on a schedule like the scheduled nightly build in our FlixBuster example. Scheduling your builds is the next aspect of completely hands-off project automation. The scheduled build can be set to run on a time interval such as every hour or at prescheduled times. Since the version control system holds everything needed to build the system, the computer can simply do a fresh checkout of the system and run the build file. Moreover, the build can be triggered by certain events, such as when new or modified files are checked into version control.

- **Portable.** The build should run on any platform with the proper prerequisites. In a DW/BI system this means that we must take extra care not to hard-code server names, database names, IP addresses, and similar elements. These specific references and settings must reside in configuration files, the system registry, or some other location that is independent of the DW/BI system components. This characteristic can be particularly challenging in complex DW/BI environments, but it is well worth the investment of effort to separate machine- or database-specific references from DW/BI system code.

Rudimentary Automated Build

Let's take a look at what a CRISP build process for a DW/BI system looks like in action. Depending on your choice of technologies and architecture, your build process might include the following high-level workflow:

Precondition: servers configured and all prerequisite software installed/configured

1. Check out all of the files for the build from the version control system.
2. Create all database instances and/or schemas.
3. Create physical data models for the integration and presentation database tiers.
4. Install all required stored procedure definitions.
5. Install the ETL modules for extracting source data into the integration schemas.
6. Install the ETL modules for manipulating data in the integration tier.
7. Install the ETL modules for moving data from the integration into the presentation tier.
8. Configure the OLAP cubes (if applicable).
9. Install the analysis tier modules (dashboard code, report definitions, analytical models, BI apps, etc.).
10. Configure the source database connections.
11. Configure the BI system database connections.
12. Run the initial data load sequence.
13. Process the OLAP cubes (if applicable).
14. Run the complete suite of automated functional tests for verification.

Post-condition: analytical applications working and displaying expected data

It is this workflow that we need to automate. Unlike the homogeneous nature of building a complete Java application using a Java compiler, a tricky challenge in automating DW/BI projects is in the multiple heterogeneous steps that must be completed. That is, there are several steps and each requires a different "compilation" technique ranging from operating system shell scripts, to special command-line interfaces provided by BI tools, to importing XML configuration data. So, the first order of business is to figure out how best to perform each of these workflow steps with a single command.

We should start by building the necessary script or utility to verify that the preconditions are present before executing the first step. We want to execute the first step only if the preconditions are met. This might be a shell script that issues OS commands to confirm that the server meets the minimum hardware requirements and that the required software is installed and configured properly.

The steps for creating database instances and creating the physical data models and stored procedure definitions are typically done with SQL data definition language (DDL) commands. We will place these DDL commands into SQL files that can be executed using the command-line utility provided by most DBMS software. We'll take advantage of the SQL IF EXISTS (...) DROP <item> command prior to our CREATE <item> ... commands to ensure a clean installation on servers on which our DW/BI system has been previously installed.

The steps for installing ETL modules or packages vary depending on the ETL tool. SSIS packages are conveniently stored in separate files and organized in Visual Studio project directories on the file system. Informatica modules can be exported into XML files and stored on the file system. Other ETL tools can store code in other file formats. Regardless, these files must be managed in the version control system where they can be automatically checked out, loaded into, and executed by the automated build. For example, SSIS modules can be executed from the operating system command line using the SQL Server utility dtexec.exe. So, our build step for SSIS ETL will involve checking out the Visual Studio project files from version control and installing them in an appropriate location on the server where they can be executed by other build steps using the dtexec.exe utility.

Similarly, configuring and processing OLAP cubes (if your architecture includes these) will vary depending on the technologies involved. Microsoft's SSAS enables the export of cube creation scripts into XMLA files. So, our build process for this technology can use the SQL Server command-line utility ascmd.exe to execute those XMLA scripts. Later on the build process will use this utility to process the cubes.

Likewise, our build process must automate the installation and configuration of end-user BI applications. This step ranges from automating the installation of custom applications to loading report templates and analytic configurations into commercial BI presentation tools. Finally, we'll need to automatically configure the database connections needed to hook everything together and run the initial data load sequence.

Most of the technologies we use in business intelligence provide some type of API or command-line utility that can be used by the automated build process. It sometimes takes some creative thinking, or a bit of extra programming, to automate the setup and execution of these steps. However, this up-front investment will more than pay for itself over time.

The final step in the build process is to kick off the automated testing tools to run the entire suite of integration and functional tests. This is the step that will satisfy the Informative aspect of the CRISP characteristics. Seeing our tests passing after running the build process gives us confidence that our system is of production quality.

With each of these steps automated it is now pretty simple to create a master script or batch process that will execute the steps in the proper sequence (see Listing 9.1). With that script, we have a simple and rudimentary automated build that has all of the CRISP properties. Using the Subversion version control software and Microsoft's SQL Server technologies as an example might result in a simple build script like the one in Listing 9.1. Note that this example uses the `dtexec.exe` utility for most of the steps. This approach takes advantage of SSIS packages to execute the steps and enables database connections to reside in a configuration file on the server, thereby making the build script portable to other servers, provided the configuration file is present on those servers.

Listing 9.1   SimpleBuildScript.bat Listing

```
01   :: Verify that preconditions are present before starting build.
02   CALL verifyPreconditions.bat
03   ECHO Server Preconditions Verified
04
05   :: Check out mainline source files for build
06   MKDIR C:\BuildWorkspace
07   CD C:\Buildworkspace
08   svn checkout http://repos.flixbuster.com/dw/trunk ^
     C:\BuildWorkspace --username builder --password h0ping4Succ3ss
09
10   :: Create database instances
11   dtexec /f ^
     "c:\Buildworkspace\db\staging\createStagingInstance.dtsx"
12   dtexec /f ^
     "c:\Buildworkspace\db\integration\createIntegInstance.dtsx"
13   dtexec /f ^
     "c:\Buildworkspace\db\warehouse\createWarehouseInstance.dtsx"
14   dtexec /f ^
     "c:\Buildworkspace\db\marts\createFinanceMartInstance.dtsx"
15
16   :: Create physical data models
17   dtexec /f ^
```

```
        "c:\Buildworkspace\db\staging\createStagingModel.dtsx"
18   dtexec /f ^
        "c:\Buildworkspace\db\integration\createIntegrationModel.dtsx"
19   dtexec /f ^
        "c:\Buildworkspace\db\warehouse\createWarehouseModel.dtsx"
20   dtexec /f ^
        "c:\Buildworkspace\db\marts\createFinanceMartModel.dtsx"
21
22   :: Install stored procedures
23   dtexec /f "c:\Buildworkspace\sp\staging\createStagingSPs.dtsx"
24   dtexec /f ^
        "c:\Buildworkspace\sp\integration\createIntegrationSPs.dtsx"
25   dtexec /f ^
        "c:\Buildworkspace\sp\warehouse\createWarehouseSPs.dtsx"
26   dtexec /f "c:\Buildworkspace\sp\mart\createFinanceMartSPs.dtsx"
27
28   :: Configure OLAP cubes
29   dtexec /f "c:\Buildworkspace\olap\createFinanceCube.dtsx"
30   dtexec /f "c:\Buildworkspace\olap\createCustomerBuysCube.dtsx"
31   dtexec /f "c:\Buildworkspace\olap\createInventoryCube.dtsx"
32   dtexec /f "c:\Buildworkspace\olap\createProfitabilityCube.dtsx"
33
34   :: Install analytical applications
35   CALL c:\Buildworkspace\apps\dashboard\install.bat
36   CALL c:\Buildworkspace\apps\reporting\install.bat
37   CALL c:\Buildworkspace\apps\advanced\install.bat
38
39   :: Run Initial Load Sequence
40   dtexec /f ^
         "c:\Buildworkspace\etl\masterInitialLoadSequencer.dtsx"
41   dtexec /f ^
        "c:\Buildworkspace\olap\masterCubeProcessingSequencer.dtsx"
42
43   :: Run DbFit Functional Test Suite
44   CD C:\Buildworkspace\test\fitnesse
45   java -cp fitnesse.jar fitnesse.runner.TestRunner ^
        localhost 8085 FrontPage -html TestResults.html
```

More Advanced Automated Build

Although the batch script in Listing 9.1 is functional, it isn't an ideal solution. One problem is the absolute path references to the various build files. This script isn't very portable. Also, for this simple script to really be useful it needs some conditional expressions to verify that each step has completed successfully; and we should echo those results to the screen to make it more informative. Suddenly our simple script is not so simple anymore. It's quickly becoming a procedural program that is error-prone and not particularly adaptable to changes. It reflects additional code that must be maintained, debugged, tested, and updated. Furthermore, it is only informative inasmuch as there is a human watching the output while the build executes. We need a better approach.

Once again we can benefit from the prior advancements made in the application development realm using build automation tools such as Ant, Maven,[3] NAnt,[4] MSBuild,[5] and others. Although these build tools were initially tailored for use on software projects implemented with Java, .NET, and other languages and frameworks, they can easily be adapted to automate our DW/BI system builds.

Build tools operate using a build specification file, typically an XML data file containing predefined elements that the tool knows how to interpret and act upon. It isn't possible to include a full tutorial on build tools in this chapter, and many such tutorials are available online. However, a simple example should help show how they work, so let's re-create the prior SQL Server example using NAnt. It would also be appropriate to choose MSBuild for a SQL Server–based data warehouse. NAnt and MSBuild are intended for Windows and .NET platforms and provide predefined tasks that are designed for Microsoft technologies. Conversely, Ant and Maven provide predefined tasks that are better suited for UNIX and Java/J2EE platforms and tend to be more suitable for Oracle-, IBM UDB–, or MySQL-based data warehouse architectures.

Here are the essential steps that we need our automated build to perform:

1. Delete and clean up all traces of any prior builds if there are any.
2. Execute the build workflow steps as previously outlined.
3. Execute the automated test suite.

Define the Project

The first step in creating our NAnt build is to create the NAnt project specification file that will contain the required build tasks and dependencies. To do this simply open a text editor and add the following lines, then save the file as FlixBusterBI.build:

```xml
<?xml version="1.0"?>
<project name="FlixBusterBI" default="all" basedir=".">
  <target name="all"/>

</project>
```

---

3. http://maven.apache.org/
4. Ant for .NET environments: http://nant.sourceforge.net/
5. http://msdn.microsoft.com/en-us/library/wea2sca5(VS.90).aspx

If we turn NAnt loose on this skeleton build file, we will see the following
output:

```
>NAnt -buildfile:FlixBusterBI.build
NAnt 0.90 (Build 0.90.3780.0; release; 5/8/2010)
Copyright (C) 2001-2010 Gerry Shaw
http://nant.sourceforge.net

Buildfile: file:///C:/FlixBusterSandbox/FlixBusterBI.build
Target framework: Microsoft .NET Framework 2.0
Target(s) specified: all

all:

BUILD SUCCEEDED

Total time: 0 seconds.
```

The first line of this skeleton build file tells us that the file is an XML 1.0
file. The `project` element surrounds the entire body (currently empty) of
the build file. It identifies the project name as `FlixBusterBI`. The `default`
attribute is the most important attribute in this line. It tells NAnt which
default *target* to execute. In this case, the target named `all` does nothing
because it does not specify a task to perform. A target is an action step with
a name that can be referenced elsewhere. We'll look at targets in more detail
shortly. The `basedir` attribute tells NAnt that the base directory, from which
other files are referenced, is the same as the build file.

Define the Directory Structure

Now we need to tell NAnt about our project directory structure. This will
make it easier later when we need to tell NAnt where to find various files.
We'll do this with *properties*. Properties are like variables. Once they are
defined, they can be referenced in the build file using the syntax ${prop-
erty.name}. Properties are a great way to avoid repeating actual values
throughout the build file. If we decide to rename the `etl` directory to `ssis`,
we only need to change the property definition in the build file. The following listing adds some of these properties to `FlixBusterBI.build`:

```
<?xml version="1.0"?>
<project name="FlixBusterBI" default="all" basedir=".">
  <property name="build.dir"        value="build"/>
  <property name="build.prod.dir"   value="${build.dir}/prod" />
  <property name="build.test.dir"   value="${build.dir}/test" />
  <property name="db.dir"           value="db" />
  <property name="db.stage.dir"     value="${db.dir}/stage" />
  <property name="doc.dir"          value="doc" />
  <property name="etl.dir"          value="etl" />
```

```
<property name="olap.dir"          value="olap" />
<property name="test.dir"          value="test" />

<target name="all" />
```

```
</project>
```

> ### Agile Analytics Practice: Use Properties Files
>
> Storing volatile or machine-specific configuration settings, file paths, and connection strings in a local properties file and referencing these settings in the build script will make your build highly portable from sandbox to sandbox. Keep a local properties file template under version control, and create instances on each build platform.

Define the Build Tasks

Now that NAnt knows about our project's directory structure, it's time to tell it about the build tasks that need to be executed. Tasks are actions that are specified by the target elements within build.xml. For example, we can use the following target to specify the task that creates our staging database instance:

```
<?xml version="1.0"?>
<project name="FlixBusterBI" default="all" basedir=".">
  ...
  <property name="db.dir"           value="db" />
  <property name="db.stage.dir"     value="${db.dir}/stage" />
  ...

  <target name="all" depends="createStaging" />

  <target name="createStaging">
    <exec program="dtexec">
      <arg value="/f" />
      <arg path="${db.stage.dir}/createStagingInstance.dtsx" />
    </exec>
  </target>
</project>
```

The new target element executes the SQL Server utility dtexec.exe to execute the SSIS package createStagingInstance.dtsx. Also, notice the new depends attribute that has been added to the original target named all. This attribute specifies that the all target depends on the successful completion of the createStaging target before it can execute.

Like SQL, NAnt is declarative rather than procedural. NAnt executes its target tasks according to a set of dependencies specified in the build file. This enables us to be concerned with tasks and their prerequisites rather than the order in which they appear in the build file. The script in Listing 9.1 must execute commands in sequence. If the initial load sequence is executed before the databases are created, the process will fail. NAnt doesn't care about the order of the tasks in the build file since it follows the specified dependencies. This declarative approach can be very powerful, allowing you to run just part of a build by specifying an intermediate target. For example, if we wanted to install only the databases and OLAP cubes, we might run this command:

```
> NAnt –buildfile:FlixBusterBI.build configureOLAP
```

The configureOLAP option tells NAnt to execute the target element of that name and everything it depends upon (i.e., all of the prerequisite database targets). Most build automation tools use some form of declarative paradigm coupled with dependency specification to determine the execution order, simplifying management and support of your build script.

It is important to perform a clean installation every time we run the build script. This will ensure that the build is neither corrupted by nor utilizes any residual elements from a prior installation. You could use NAnt to create an uninstaller that is invoked from within your build script, or you may have an uninstaller script that is executed in the build script using dependencies like this:

```
...
<target name="uninstallFlixBusterBI">
  <exec executable="cmd">
    <arg value="/c"/>
    <arg value="masterUninstaller.bat"/>
  </exec>
</target>

<target name="createStaging" depends="masterUninstaller.bat">
  <exec program="dtexec">
    <arg value="/f" />
    <arg path="${db.stage.dir}/createStagingInstance.dtsx" />
  </exec>
</target>
...
```

Define the Testing Tasks

Now, after adding the necessary exec tasks to run our remaining installation steps, the only thing from our original batch script that is missing is the automatic execution of tests to verify that the build is working correctly. We need to create a target element in our NAnt build script called test that will run the automated test suite. In fact, this is the culminating target in the script and probably should be the default target named in the script header. For this example we will assume that our functional test suite is in DbFit, an extension of the FitNesse testing framework designed for database test automation. One way to do this is to use the exec task to run the FitNesse test runner like this:

```
<property name="fitnesse.dir"       value="${test.dir}/dbfit" />
<property name="fitnesse.server"    value="localhost" />
<property name="fitnesse.port"      value="8085" />

<target name="test" depends="processOLAPCubes">
  <exec program="${fitnesse.dir}\dotnet2\TestRunner.exe">
    <arg value="-r" />
    <arg value="fitnesse.fitserver.TestRunner,dotnet2\fit.dll" />
    <arg value="${fitnesse.server}" />
    <arg value="${fitnesse.port}" />
    <arg value="${fitnesse.test}" />
  </exec>
</target>
```

At the time of this writing there is an open-source project called Fitnesse. NAntTasks[6] that is in the alpha stage of readiness. This extension of NAnt includes a set of predefined tasks that streamline the execution of test suites. For example, the following NAnt sequence starts an instance of FitNesse, runs the tests on fitnesse.tests, converts the format to XML for reporting purposes, and then stops the FitNesse instance:

```
<fitnesse-start workingdir "${fitnesse.dir}" port="8085" />
<fitnesse-testrunner-dotnet outputfile="fitnesse.results"
      testpage="fitnesse.tests" />
<fitnesse-formatoutput inputfile="fitnesse.results"
      outputfile="fitnesse.results.xml" testpage="fitnesse.tests" />
<fitnesse-stop />
```

NAnt as well as other build automation tools is highly extensible. New tasks like the ones in the code just listed can be developed and easily added to the task library. Unfortunately, at this time the extensions (plug-ins) available for mainstream DW/BI technologies are limited. As the previous examples have shown, automating DW/BI builds commonly involves executing command-line utilities. While this is a feasible approach, it would be better to interface with the tools' APIs, and to capture the resulting output and format it for effective reporting. Well-designed plug-ins can provide this

---

6. http://sourceforge.net/projects/fnessenanttasks/

capability. Today's DW/BI teams must be prepared to exercise some creativity to achieve the goal of one-step automated builds. Ideally, in the not-too-distant future there will be an increasing number of extensions to these build tools from which we can benefit.

Agile Analytics Practice: Store Test Frameworks

Testing frameworks such as FitNesse that are kept in the version control repository are available on any build platform as soon as the DW/BI system is checked out on that platform. No additional setup is required.[7]

Another SQL Server Approach

So far I've been showing examples using **dtexec.exe** to run SSIS packages inside NAnt exec targets. Another alternative uses the SQL Server utility **osql.exe**, which executes a SQL script contained in a file with a .sql extension. Here is an example of how this can be implemented within NAnt. First, create an **exec** target that generalizes the command-line call to **osql.exe** like this:

```
<target name="exec.sql">
  <exec program="${osql.exe}">
    <arg value="${osql.conn}" />
    <arg value="-n" />
    <arg value="-b" />
    <arg value="-i" />
    <arg value="${target}" />
  </exec>
</target>
```

Next, you can bundle a sequence of SQL script executions with explicit calls to the **exec.sql** target like this:

```
<target name="buildIntegrationDB">
  <property name="target" value="${db.int.dir}/createDB.sql" />
  <call target="exec.sql" />

  <property name="target" value="${db.int.dir}/createModel.sql" />
  <call target="exec.sql" />

  <property name="target" value="${db.int.dir}/createSPs.sql" />
  <call target="exec.sql" />
</target>
```

---

7. Build tools such as Maven support plug-ins to ease the integration of other utilities such as test automation libraries. This eliminates the need to store those utilities in the version control system.

While this approach is more procedural than the earlier examples, it has the benefit of being more self-documenting within the sequencing target. In the earlier example, one must look at the SSIS package to see these lower-level execution steps. Conversely, the approach presented earlier makes it simpler to store local settings in a local properties file that is used by the SSIS packages to ensure build portability.

When to Get Started

There is no time like the present to get started automating your DW/BI build. Even if your team is in the midst of a development cycle, it is well worth the allocation of some effort to begin automating your build. However, the preferable time to set up a one-step build is at the start of the project—during iteration zero. If you're lucky enough to be starting the first version of your DW/BI system from scratch, you have the luxury of creating a simple one-step build script and evolving it incrementally alongside your DW/BI system.

Unfortunately, most of us aren't so lucky. Instead, we are working on the maintenance, refinement, or advancement of an existing DW/BI system. In this case, it is ideal to allocate time at the start of the next project cycle (or between development efforts) to establish your automated build. Investing time and effort into doing so will yield high returns during the next development cycle.

Finally, if your team is in the throes of a development project, and it's likely to be a while before there will be a break between projects, the team should treat build automation as a series of user stories. These stories should be given high priority alongside the BI feature stories and should be scheduled into the iterative development routine. The team may not achieve fully automated one-step builds in a single iteration but will quickly reap the benefits of incremental automation. And in just a few short iterations, the one-step build will become a reality.

CONTINUOUS INTEGRATION

Once your team has a CRISP build, it has established the strong foundation for more comprehensive project automation. The next question is when to execute the build and how often. Agile Analytics teams continuously integrate newly completed code into the build/test cycle, and they monitor the results of this continuous integration.

The primary benefit of build automation is increased confidence in the quality of the DW/BI system under development. Every time the build completes successfully, the team gets confirmation that it is not introducing defects. In the early days of your Agile Analytics project the build can run all test suites in a reasonable time frame. However, those test suites will quickly grow to a point where the build/test time is unacceptably long. When that happens, the team becomes disinclined to run the build, thereby reducing the build frequency, and ultimately diminishing the team's confidence—a negative feedback loop.

To mitigate this tendency it is best to create multiple build variants, one that executes the unit test suite, another that executes the acceptance (functional) test suite, and so on. This can be done by simply using a single build file with multiple testing task blocks that are run selectively depending on the build purpose. Alternatively, multiple build files, each performing a distinct and well-defined task, can be coordinated through a build sequencer that selectively invokes the correct build files. If you take the latter approach, be sure to avoid task duplication across these build files. Yet other build tools like Maven enable you to create reusable build modules and build profiles that use just the modules needed for their purpose.

Build Frequency

A key benefit of the one-step automated build is the ability to quickly spin up developer sandboxes. You may have experienced situations where the developers' sandboxes have gotten out of sync over time. Even with the judicious use of version control as described in Chapter 8, "Version Control for Data Warehousing," developer sandboxes tend to accumulate residue over time that isn't necessarily included in the production artifacts under version control. It's a healthy practice for each developer to periodically tear down his or her sandbox and rebuild it from scratch to eliminate this residue. Each developer should do this at the start of each new iteration. Virtualization can greatly help with the management of various sandboxes in the development infrastructure.

Agile Analytics Practice: Use Virtual Machines

With the use of virtualization with tools like VMware, Xen, and others, a sandbox can be rolled back to a baseline instance in seconds. An added benefit is that developers can mimic distributed systems on a single workstation using virtualization.

You should expect to run your unit test build every 5 to 15 minutes as incremental code changes are checked into the version control system. The more comprehensive acceptance test build should be run every couple of hours, or three or four times per day. The performance testing build should run once every day. Since the performance build probably involves higher data volumes and a more time-intensive setup and execution, it is best to run this at night.

Recall the discussion in Chapter 7, "Test-Driven Data Warehouse Development," about development and testing sandboxes (refer to Figure 7.4). The integration server is where the functional testing builds are executed, and the preproduction testing server is where performance testing builds are executed. The benefit of this infrastructure is that developers can continue working unfettered while a build is executing on another computer. Therefore, the only constraint on build frequency is ensuring that one build has completely finished executing before another one starts. For large, complex, and high-volume DW/BI systems, build times can become quite lengthy. So, depending on the size, scope, and complexity of your DW/BI system, you will need to find a build frequency that balances frequent feedback against build times.

Scheduled Builds

At this point you have a commanded build, one that runs whenever you execute it, saving precious time and effort. The next step is to run this build automatically without having to do anything yourself. Scheduled builds run at regular intervals while developers are doing other things (including sleeping) and alerts them only if there is a problem. Not only does this recurring build test the newly completed code, but it also serves as a regression test to ensure that new changes haven't broken formerly working components.

One approach might be to use scheduling utilities built into most operating systems, such as cron or at, to run the build script. With a bit of extra effort we could easily create a script or batch file that will check out the current files from version control, run the build file to build and test the system, redirect the build output to a log file, and use the scheduling utility to run the master script at predetermined intervals. We might even develop an easy method for broadcasting the log file containing the build results to the team.

Good news: This approach is rather anachronistic. Today's automation tools support the scheduled execution of build scripts, so there is no need to use separate scheduling utilities.

Triggered Builds

Sometimes you want the build to run when a particular event occurs. For example, you may want the build to run as soon as a team member commits changes into version control. Although these changes will be picked up in the next scheduled build, if a lot of changes accumulate between builds, it can be hard to fix a broken build. A build triggered by a single version control update is much simpler to diagnose if it breaks.

Unfortunately, scheduling utilities aren't designed to detect events, and creating such a utility is not trivial. The good news is that there are free and commercial tools available that automate scheduled and triggered builds, as well as many other beneficial features. These tools are called continuous integration (CI) utilities; some examples include AnthillPro, CruiseControl, CruiseControl.NET, Hudson,[8] Team Foundation Server, and TeamCity.

CI software is installed on the integration and preproduction testing servers. It runs in the background and follows the directions in a configuration file to execute the build process. For example, if the configuration file specifies a NAnt build to execute whenever a change is made to files under version control, the CI software will periodically poll the version control system. When it detects a change, it will run the specified NAnt build file and publish the results to the team.

Setting Up Continuous Integration

Setting up the CI build generally involves the following steps:

- **Configure the build server.** Install all prerequisite DW/BI software on a dedicated build server. This server is either a physical or, preferably, a virtual server and should be sufficiently powerful to run the entire DW/BI system using a small test data set.
- **Install the build software.** Install the build software on the build server (e.g., NAnt) that will be used to run your build files.
- **Install the CI software.** Install and configure the continuous integration software on the build server (e.g., CruiseControl.NET) that will be used to execute the scheduled or triggered builds automatically.
- **Create the build workspace.** Create a directory on the build server that will act as a container where the files involved in the build

---

8. http://hudson-ci.org/

process are managed. This directory will be used by the CI software to check out the project, generate log files, and produce the informative results that are published to the team.

▪ **Create the log directory.** Make a directory within the build workspace where the CI software can create and manage the log files generated during the build.

▪ **Check out the project.** Check out all of the project files into a project directory within the build workspace. If everything goes well, this will be the only time you'll need to manually check out the project on the build server. Once everything is working, the CI software will do that automatically. Some continuous integration tools, like Hudson, may perform this step for you automatically.

▪ **Configure the CI process.** Ensure that the continuous integration process includes the following steps:

1. Deletes all traces of the last build
2. Checks out the current version of the project from version control
3. Runs the build

Mike Clark (Clark 2004) calls this a "scorch-the-Earth" build—one that starts everything from scratch to avoid the odd side effects that can happen when detritus is left hanging around from previous builds. The master build file is written for execution by your build software, so an example NAnt CI build file for a project stored in Subversion might look like this:

```xml
<?xml version="1.0"?>
<project name="ci-build" default="build" basedir="checkout">

  <property name="project.dir"  value="project"/>
  <property name="build.file"    value="FlixBusterBI.build"/>

  <target name="build">
    <delete dir="${project.dir}" />
    <exec executable="cmd">
      <arg value="/c"/>
      <arg value="masterUninstaller.bat"/>
    </exec>
    <svn command="checkout"
     destination="c:\builds\checkout\project"
     svnroot="http://repos.flixbuster.com/dw/trunk"
     username="builder"
     password="hOping4Succ3ss" />
    <nant buildfile="${project.dir}/${build.file}" />
  </target>

</project>
```

This file is called CIBuild.build and is stored in the top level of the build workspace where it can orchestrate the build process. The syntax should look familiar since it is just another NAnt specification, although it contains a few new tasks that we haven't seen before. The CI build file will eventually be executed by the CI software but should be tested manually to make sure everything works as expected.

- **Check in the CI build file.** CIBuild.build should be checked into version control, which might seem confusing because it contains the checkout command. In fact, this file is unlikely to change much, so we will keep the active copy of it on the build server. But it should also be kept in version control so we don't lose it, plus we can use it to easily set up other build servers if necessary.
- **Configure the CI process.** Just as the build software relies on a build file for its instructions, so does the CI software. In fact, most CI tools use XML specification files like build tools. However, a new generation of CI tools is emerging that enable developers to configure the CI build through a graphical interface and keep the XML build file under the covers. Hudson is such an example. Hudson runs on the build server as a service and is configured via a Web browser interface. Other tools such as AnthillPro have a similar approach that simplifies this configuration.

In fact, many current CI tools are also capable of handling the preparatory tasks that we included in the CIBuild.build file. They can establish the build workspace, check out the project files from version control, execute the build file, and run the test suite. You'll need to decide how to delegate these tasks between your build tool and your CI tool.

CI build tools enable you to easily specify either scheduled or triggered builds along with a variety of parameters to control when builds occur. The following snippet is an example from a CruiseControl configuration file (ccnet.config). This bit of code specifies that CruiseControl should check the source control repository every 30 seconds and, if a modification exists, should trigger a build.

```
<project name="CIBuild">
...
<triggers>
  <intervalTrigger name="CIbuild"
      seconds="30"
      buildCondition="IfModificationExists"
      initialSeconds="30" />
```

```
</triggers>
<sourcecontrol type="svn">
  <executable>c:\program files\subversion\bin\svn.exe</executable>
  <trunkUrl>http://repos.flixbuster.com/dw/trunk</trunkUrl>
  <workingDirectory>c:\builds\checkout\project</workingDirectory>
</sourcecontrol>
...
</project>
```

One of the most important responsibilities of the CI tool is to broadcast
the results of the build to the team. Team members should be able to easily check the status of the most recent build at any time, but they should be
bothered by the CI process only when the build fails. Most CI tools provide
a project dashboard that presents the project build status at a glance. Agile
Analytics teams typically have a dedicated monitor in their team room that
constantly displays the CI dashboard. Figure 9.1 shows an example of a
project dashboard as presented by Hudson. Notice that team members can
subscribe to RSS feeds from Hudson for all builds, failed builds, or just the
latest build. Hudson can also be configured to send e-mails to team members when the build fails.

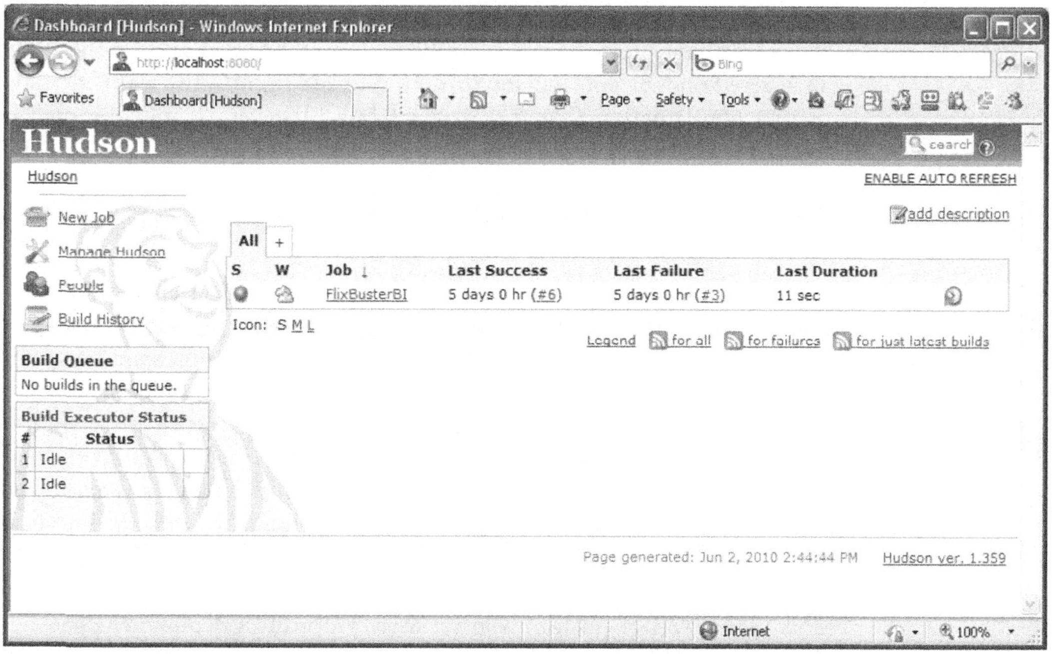

Figure 9.1 FlixBuster Analytics project dashboard using Hudson

Agile teams have invented many creative techniques to keep the team informed of the CI build status. One of the most famous examples is the use of red and green lava lamps in the team room. A bubbling green light indicates that the most recent build succeeded. A bubbling red lamp tells the team that there is a problem.

Agile Analytics Practice: A Broken Build Stops the Line

A broken build is the team's top priority. Everyone stops working to collaborate about the failure and how to fix it. Nobody checks in any new work until the build is fixed. If the build isn't fixed in 20 minutes, the team should undo changes and revert to the previous working version. When the build is fixed, the team reviews the results for acceptance before getting back to work.

Once you've set up a CI build for functional acceptance testing on your build server, it's a great idea to do the same thing for performance testing on your preproduction testing sandbox. As we discussed in Chapter 7, "Test-Driven Data Warehouse Development," your performance testing should simulate production data volumes, concurrent user loads, and other system stressors. Since running this suite of tests tends to be very time-intensive, the performance test is a good candidate for a scheduled build rather than a triggered one. By configuring this build to run nightly, the team will gain regular confirmation that the evolving DW/BI system is meeting performance goals.

PUSH-BUTTON RELEASES

Successful build automation and continuous integration enable teams to overcome the main impediments to the goal of delivering production-quality BI features every few weeks. This success means that the team has automated tests, the project is under version control, and the system is routinely built and tested to confirm its quality. The final goal in this project automation chain is production deployment of the DW/BI system quickly, easily, and reliably. Imagine if your DW/BI team could deploy newly accepted features into production frequently and without disrupting the user community.

This is the goal of push-button releases. We want a deployment package that resembles a software product that can be installed in any environment that meets the necessary prerequisites. Unlike the automated build and CI server, the production environment should not require any special tools or configurations other than those needed to run the DW/BI system. Moreover, it should be easy to determine the currently installed version of the system.

What Is a Release?

A release is a bundled collection of files from a specific point in the project repository (ideally a tagged point on a release branch). It includes the minimal set of files needed to deploy the complete working DW/BI system. Each release is marked by a distinct version number and includes a brief description of the newest features or enhancements. The release also includes essential documentation needed by end users and administrators.

At the heart of a good release package is single installation script or utility, hence the name *push-button release*. The installation script may require active involvement by an administrator to configure various aspects of the system during the install process. The release should be generated in the same way whether you are producing a release for a QA team, an internal deployment, or a productized DW/BI solution for a commercial market.

Design your release package so that it can be installed by someone outside the development team such as a systems admin, system tester, or support specialist. Think of the installers and ancillary support staff as extensions of the customer community. This customer community is much like your end-user customer community, and their user stories should be identified and prioritized just like the feature stories we discussed in Chapter 4, "User Stories for BI Systems." The release package is the primary product that you are developing for this customer community, and it deserves frequent review and acceptance just like BI features.

Preparing a Release

If you aren't careful, release packages can become elaborate, fancy affairs that are projects in their own right. It's best to start by building the smallest and simplest thing that is sufficient. (Is this a familiar theme?) Ideally, you've automated the build and your continuous integration is running regularly. As the end of the iteration nears, it's time to prepare for a release in the hope that customers will be demanding those great new features the team has just finished.

It's helpful to have a designated *release manager*, or even a separate *release team*, to coordinate this preparation. The role of the release manager is to oversee the release process and enable the development team to continue developing. The release manager helps the team properly follow and maintain the discipline of versioning, tagging, and branching strategies and manages the sandbox environment promotion. Additionally, the release manager is an important gatekeeper for production deployment. For large systems this can become a full-time job. The release manager guides the following release preparation processes:

1. **Team check-in.** All team members need to synchronize their workspaces with the version control system, making sure that all completed work is checked in.
2. **Sanity check.** Run the build one final time to be sure that everything is checked in, the system is working, and all tests are passing.
3. **Create the release branch.** Create a branch in the version control system specifically for this release (see Chapter 8, "Version Control for Data Warehousing," on creating release branches).
4. **Finalize the release branch.** Double-check to be sure that all documentation and ancillary files are updated for this release, including release notes, README files, installation instructions, and others.
5. **Configure CI for the release branch.** Just as we need continuous integration on the trunk, so we need to have CI running on the branch to validate the changes we make on the branch.
6. **Test the release branch.** Check out the release branch into a separate workspace and run the sanity check once more to be sure that the release branch is complete and correct.
7. **Tag the release branch.** Once everything on the branch is finalized and tested, tag the branch to mark the release point (see the discussion on release tagging in Chapter 8, "Version Control for Data Warehousing").
8. **Merge changes into the trunk.** Changes that are made along the release branch must be thoughtfully merged back into the trunk.

After these steps are complete, the release tag marks the version of the system that is ready to be bundled into a release. While the release manager is coordinating the release, the rest of the team is free to continue working on the project mainline.

Bundle the Release

Now that you have confirmed that the release is ready, it's time to bundle the release package. The release package will end up as a single distribution file that can be unpacked on the server(s) targeted for installation. When the admin doing the installation unpacks the distribution file, the result should be easy to navigate and execute. The instructions should be easy to find and follow, and the installation should be self-explanatory. Like project automation, a key benefit of creating an elegant and easy-to-use distribution package is that it frees developers to spend more time developing rather than supporting the deployment process.

What Goes in a Release Package?

The first order of business is to determine which files from your project repository belong in the release package, which files do not, and how to organize the files. Review your project repository and identify the files and directories that are not part of the production DW/BI system such as the following:

- **Test suites and testing frameworks.** You won't be running your tests in production, so be sure to leave out test suites and any testing frameworks and tools.
- **Development utilities.** Scripts, tools, or utilities used to make development easier are not part of production deployment. These should be left behind.
- **Build and CI scripts.** These were designed to build the system and run the tests and should be left behind. However, you may have specially developed deployment scripts that are variations of the build and CI scripts.
- **Compilable source code.** If your DW/BI system includes components that are compiled, such as homegrown BI applications, they should be precompiled. The compiled executable file is included in the distribution bundle, but the source files are not.

Evaluate your project files carefully and select only those files that are essential. In addition to these files, it may be necessary to develop some scripts to assist in the deployment. For example, the following deployment processes should be scripted:

- **Data archive.** If the DW/BI deployment is an upgrade from a previous version, all the data in the previous version should be archived before the upgrade. This will make it feasible to revert to the prior version if something goes wrong with the upgrade. Although this is a routine DBA procedure for DW/BI systems, your DW/BI team may want to consider developing scripts to automate this as part of the upgrade.

- **Data migration.** Iterative DW/BI development often results in changes to the data models. Migrating historical data from older data models to newer ones may require some conversion scripts.
- **Data loaders.** Upon deployment, DW/BI systems must be primed with initial data. On the first deployment all required source data must be "pumped" into the system. But iterative DW/BI development routinely calls for adding new source data alongside already existing data. Both cases call for scripts or utilities to perform these initial data loads and data alignments.
- **User authentication and security.** Depending on how user authorization and role-based access control are handled in your DW/BI system, it may be necessary to develop scripts to migrate user authorization data from prior versions to the latest version during deployment.
- **User-defined views/reports.** Nothing annoys BI system users more than having their custom reports disappear after a system upgrade. And there is little that is more tedious than having to manually re-create these views and reports for users. Create the necessary scripts to back up these user-defined features and restore them in the new system. Occasionally during iterative BI development, the data elements or metadata used in these reports changes, so it is important to automate the migration of old user-defined features to work with new data elements.

Carefully evaluate your deployment preparation and transition process and identify any other steps in the workflow that can and should be automated as part of push-button deployment. If you are concerned about the time required to automate these steps, consider that they already consume substantial time to execute manually. Part of the ability to deploy frequently is the freedom to move unimpeded by time-consuming manual preparatory and transition steps.

How to Organize the Release Package

Once you've determined what goes into the distribution bundle, you need to think carefully about how to organize its contents. The project directory structure is designed to support current and future developers, but will it also make sense to the installer? Ideally, the project directory structure will require minimal changes to be suitable as a distribution structure. For example, Figure 9.2 depicts how a release package might be organized after eliminating the unnecessary directories.

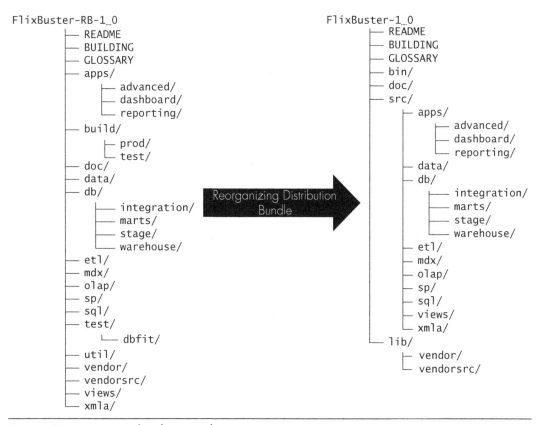

Figure 9.2 An example release package structure

Packing It All Up

Now that all the deployment scripts, files, directories, and structure have been determined, it's time to pack them into a single container like a .zip, .tar, or .rar file. In keeping with the spirit of this chapter, we should automate this process as well. The good news is that tools like Ant and NAnt can help with this step. For example, a NAnt script that packages the FlixBuster DW/BI system into a .zip file named FlixBuster-1_0.zip might include the following:

```
...
<zip zipfile="FlixBuster-1_0.zip">
  <zipfileset basedir=".">
    <include name="README" />
    <include name="BUILDING" />
    <include name="GLOSSARY" />
```

```
      </zipfileset >
      <zipfileset basedir="${bin.dir}" prefix="bin">
        <include name="**/*" />
      </zipfileset>
      <zipfileset basedir="${doc.dir}" prefix="doc">
        <include name="**/*" />
      </zipfileset>
      ...
  </zip>
  ...
```

It is relatively simple using tasks like this one to create an Ant or NAnt script to handle the bundling for you. Be sure to check this file into version control along with everything else.

Keeping Track of Versions

I was once on a non-Agile DW/BI team that was developing new features and enhancements for an existing DW/BI system. Even though we weren't Agile, we had multiple deployments scheduled to release new features at different points in the project schedule. After one deployment users began complaining about features missing that were previously available. Upon closer inspection we discovered that we had inadvertently installed an older version of the system rather than a newer one. We went backward! Not only did the deployment (a manual one) consume precious time, so did the root-cause analysis as well as the redeployment of the proper version.

Over time, and multiple deployments, it's easy to lose track of exactly which version of the DW/BI system is currently in production and what the delta is between versions. Like software, an installed DW/BI system should be able to tell us what version it is. Moreover, it's a really good idea to include database schema versions within each of the databases that make up your DW/BI system. I will defer to the many good articles available that describe how to instrument this versioning within your system. However, we need a similar capability for our release packaging. Notice that the preceding NAnt snippet has hard-coded version numbering in the distribution file name. We can take advantage of NAnt properties to make this more dynamic by defining the following properties in our bundling script:

```
...
<property name="name" value="FlixBuster" />
<property name="version" value="x_y" />
<property name="release" value="${name}-${version}" />
...
<zip zipfile="${release}">
...
```

Now, with these properties set, you can take advantage of the NAnt command parameter -D, which enables you to override the values of properties. So, assuming our NAnt file is named `releasePackage.build`, the NAnt execution command

```
> NAnt –buildfile: releasePackage.build –Dversion=1_0
```

will dynamically create the right file name for our release package. This technique can be used elsewhere in this and other NAnt scripts to physically tag a production deployment with a version number that can be easily located. Couple this approach with proper branching and tagging in the version control system, and you should be able to avoid experiences like the one I described.

WRAP-UP

Consider this chapter an introductory overview of project automation for business intelligence. Each project will be different because of the technology stack choices, the systems architecture, the development tools, and other factors. Because we aren't working with compiled source code like our software brethren, and we're working with a diverse set of technologies, project automation becomes somewhat more complicated. Nonetheless, it is worth the investment of effort to automate as much as possible on your DW/BI project. Not only will developers regain valuable time, but the DW/BI team can truly operate in Agile ways, frequently building and testing, frequently deploying, and always with the confidence of knowing that everything is still working.

If your head is as full after reading this chapter as mine is after writing it, I have a word of advice: Start automating early. If possible, start small during iteration zero by automating the simplest build, CI, and deployment processes. Then allocate some time in every iteration to gradually enhance and mature these processes so that your project automation progresses at the same rate as the project itself.

If your DW/BI project is already under way, then better late than never. But don't try to eat the elephant in one bite. Instead, allocate a little bit of time, starting in your next iteration, to begin automating the build. Once you have a commanded build working, focus on continuous integration followed by push-button releases. Don't stop delivering features to set this up if you can avoid it. Instead, reduce the size and number of features delivered for a few iterations. Although the team's velocity will suffer some in the interim, the payback will be evident once the project is automated.

As I have worked with Agile Analytics adopters, project automation is one of the technical practices that meets with significant resistance. Excuses include

- We don't know XML or Java or C# or . . .
- We don't have, or can't afford, a dedicated build server.
- We don't have time to automate the project; we have to get started developing.
- Project automation won't work for us because we are using XYZ technology.

Regarding not knowing the necessary language, I have this to say: DW/BI developers, like anyone in high tech, must constantly learn and grow their skills. Automation does not require object-oriented programming genius, nor does it require in-depth XML knowledge. Tools that support project automation are continuously advancing and making automation easier without any special skills. Meanwhile, the skills required are not difficult, and there are many good online resources and examples to help the neophyte.

Regarding the cost or availability of a dedicated build server: I recently finished a DW/BI project in which we configured a virtual server as a dedicated build server. The primary cost of this solution was in the allocation of disk storage for the server. Since build servers don't operate on large data volumes, this cost was nominal and the disk space was recovered at the end of the project. A dedicated build server need not be an expensive, high-powered computer. It is not uncommon for development teams to repurpose a mothballed computer as the build server. Regardless of the options available, the cost of developer time spent doing these things manually very quickly justifies an investment in a dedicated build server.

Regarding the lack of time to automate the project: A bit of time estimating and simple math should help put this excuse to rest. How much time will it take the team to do a manual build, a manual integration, and a manual deployment? Now, since Agile Analytics calls for frequent builds, system integration at regular intervals, and potential deployment every iteration, multiply the initial time estimates by the number of iterations in your project plan (at least). The time saved by project automation, coupled with the peace of mind it offers, far outstrips the time it takes to set everything up.

Alternatively, I would encourage the DW/BI team to ask itself, "How would our project benefit if we could build quickly, integrate continuously, and deploy frequently?" An honest assessment of those benefits will typically result in a strong argument in favor of this investment.

Regarding the argument about some DW/BI technologies being difficult to automate: There is no doubt that some technologies are more easily automated than others, and unfortunately I can't profess to having automated projects in every available DW/BI technology. However, I have yet to encounter a DW/BI technology that was impossible to incorporate into automated processes. Doing so may require creative thinking and a bit of exploration and experimentation.

As with all things Agile, if you move in small, incremental steps and in short iterations, before you know it your project will be fully automated and you'll wonder why you haven't always worked this way.

Chapter 10

FINAL WORDS

This book offers a point of departure to help launch you on a successful Agile Analytics trajectory. However, rather than covering all of the knotty problems you're bound to encounter on your journey, I've introduced a set of methods, techniques, and practices that support the core values and guiding principles of agility. Keeping your focus on these values and principles, rather than seeking a comprehensive methodology, will enable you to adapt your flavor of Agile Analytics to effectively handle the knotty problems in your environment.

It is my intention that this book be equally relevant to business leaders, stakeholders, project managers, and technical leaders and practitioners. One of the critical success factors of Agile adoption is the active participation of all of these groups. As you consider Agile Analytics adoption, I hope you will emphasize this community involvement within your organization.

The following sections are some of the topical areas that I believe either are important enough to reemphasize or deserve further attention even though they weren't addressed in this book. Some of these topics raise questions for which I don't have good answers but continue to explore. Other topics are so situational that there isn't one best approach. And still other topics in this chapter are cautionary messages to help you avoid many of the perils and pitfalls that can trap new Agile adopters.

FOCUS ON THE REAL PROBLEM

It pays to keep in mind the highest priority of Agile Analytics: to satisfy customers through the early and continuous delivery of working BI features. Whether you adopt the techniques presented in this book or another set of methods serving the same purpose matters less than keeping a focus on the real problem—that is, the DW/BI community's track record of not satisfying our customers.

In addition to the many IT industry reports presenting DW/BI project failure statistics, the proliferation of "spreadmarts" in most enterprises is another measure of our failure as a DW/BI community to respond to the needs of our customers. Wayne Eckerson coined the term *spreadmart* in 2002 to describe the proliferation of ad hoc spreadsheets within an organization for decision support (Eckerson 2002). Spreadmarts are created by various individuals, at various times, using different data sources and different business rules. They create a fractured view of the enterprise and are anathema to the goal of "one version of the truth." They typically bloom where standard BI reporting is too inflexible or too slow or fails to provide the needed features.

In discussions about different methods and techniques it is tempting to focus on how the new method will support our ability to do things the way we've done them in the past. We are drawn to what we know best. I recently had a conversation about Agile methods with a senior IT executive who has decades of experience in the industry. He said, "I know how to evaluate whether a waterfall project is on track by evaluating the initial project plan, the development artifacts, and whether or not the critical path tasks are being completed on time. But I can't see how to evaluate whether an Agile project is on track." I pointed out that effective Agile approaches result in the continuous delivery of production-quality, working features that customers have the opportunity to review and accept, suggesting that customer satisfaction is a better way of evaluating project status. We reflected on past projects that went according to plan but failed to delight customers versus projects that deviated from their plans and were ultimately considered big successes. He acknowledged that traditional project-tracking methods might be diverting his attention from the real problem, satisfying the actual needs of the customer community rather than rigidly following a plan.

Many Agile practices introduced in this book can be difficult, requiring investments of time, effort, and/or money. Test automation may require an entire shift in the way development teams work and may require developers to learn new tools and techniques. Keeping your project under version control may require an investment in procuring and configuring the right version control software. Build and deployment automation requires a different kind of discipline from what many DW/BI teams are experienced with. Focusing on value and quality may require managers and executives to view project results and status very differently. These and other Agile practices will initially be disruptive until they become team habits.

Agile adoptions tend to fail when the adopters "cherry-pick" the easy practices and ignore the hard ones. Efforts to justify ignoring hard practices include arguments like "We have a tight timeline and don't have time to learn *that* right now" or "Our situation is unique and *that practice* won't work for us." There is no mandate to adopt all of the recommended practices at once, or even to adopt all of them. However, as your team wrestles with whether or not to adopt a practice, consider the following questions:

- Will the goals of delivering customer value early and responding to change be better served if we adopt this practice?
- Will our team and our project be better off in the long run if we adopt this practice?
- Will the cost of adopting this practice be justified by its benefits? And how long will that return on investment take?

These questions will help your team keep its focus on the real problem rather than on reasons to ignore good practices. Also consider these questions as you roll out new practices over time. A particular practice may be valuable to implement, but others might need to be implemented first.

If you are adopting an Agile Analytics approach, you must be doing so because your previous methods were insufficient in some way. It pays to continuously reflect on those insufficiencies and evaluate your Agile adoption in light of how well it is helping you remedy the real problems.

BEING AGILE VERSUS DOING AGILE

I said it in the first chapter, but it bears repeating: Agile Analytics is not a methodology. Rather, it is a development style based on a set of core values (the Agile Manifesto) and supported by a set of guiding principles on which decisions are based. Agile's core values and guiding principles give rise to good process, not the other way around. In my experience helping to enable organizational agility I've seen success patterns and anti-patterns emerge. I've begun referring to success patterns as *Being Agile* and anti-patterns as *Doing Agile*. *Doing Agile* refers to teams that fail to move beyond the simpler trappings of agility: iterations, daily stand-up meetings, and the like. *Being Agile* refers to teams whose inherent values, behaviors, and mind-sets exhibit the essence and spirit of agility: adaptive, evolutionary, value-driven, and quality-driven development. Organizations that *are* Agile also *do* Agile, but the inverse is not necessarily true. Many organizations are decidedly non-Agile while still using many Agile practices. The following are some of the "smells" that suggest that a team or organization may be too fixated on Doing Agile:

- **Iron triangle planning.** Agile Analytics projects deserve sufficient planning, but Agile plans are projections, not promises. Leaders with lots of experience sometimes have difficulty breaking the habit of expecting a fixed-price, fixed-scope, and fixed-schedule project plan. An Agile plan reflects the teams' best projections based only on the information that is currently available. As requirements change and uncertainty is uncovered, those projections are likely to become obsolete. Agile leaders anticipate and adapt to this.

■ **Management styles don't change.** The best Agile Analytics teams are self-organizing, self-managing, and self-responsible. This doesn't mean that the role of management is subverted; instead, it changes. Managers are enablers, decision makers, and facilitators. They work with development teams to remove barriers and protect the team from unwanted outside pressures. Agile leaders are effective at replacing command-and-control leadership styles with more collaborative ones.

■ **Emphasis on productivity.** The promise of Agile Analytics is the delivery of a high-value, high-quality working system, not increased productivity. Leaders who emphasize productivity are surprised when quality suffers and end users are dissatisfied with results. Yet, when developers are pressured to be more productive, they take shortcuts such as reduced testing and hurried workmanship. Conversely, when the emphasis is on high-value and high-quality BI features, it is often the case that users' needs are met after only 60 to 70 percent of the planned features are done, effectively shortening the project cycle by shrinking the scope. Agile leaders emphasize quality and value and trust that productivity will take care of itself.

■ **Adapting to change is only lip service.** Agile or otherwise, anyone who has been in the DW/BI business for long knows that change is inevitable. This is perhaps more true in today's climate than ever before. Unfortunately, embracing and adapting to change are not normal parts of human nature. We go to great lengths to control and limit changes. We establish change control boards and change management processes. But instead of controlling changes, these processes only make them more disruptive. Embracing change means seeking it out, inviting it in, and encouraging more of it to ensure that we build the right solution for our customers. Agile leaders are eager to add new requirements, eliminate unnecessary requirements, overhaul project plans, rearrange priorities, and even discard working BI features in order to respond to and embrace change.

■ **Customer collaboration is short-circuited.** One of the four Agile core values is customer collaboration. Unfortunately, really effective customer collaboration is hard. Our customers are busy and hard to pin down. They sometimes tell us things that don't make sense or won't work. Customer collaboration cuts into development time. It is a mistake to defer to product owners or business analysts to be the complete "voice of the customer." It's easy to make this mistake, and it's almost never as effective as real customer collaboration. BI customers have really interesting stories to tell, and when developers get to hear these stories firsthand, they get a more holistic understanding of the BI system they are building—and they build it better. Agile leaders insist on frequent collaboration between BI development teams and end users, and they enable effective collaboration between these groups.

While Agile is not a prescriptive methodology, the Agile community has invented a number of technical and management practices that boost Agile performance, many of which have been adapted to analytics and are presented in this book. Although these practices are not mandatory, new Agile adopters tend to be more successful when they adhere to practices and follow them closely. Like people learning to play a musical instrument or sport, new Agile teams learn how to be effective by first learning and copying the habits and practices of seasoned teams. Once they've effectively copied these, they can benefit by selectively applying practices and tailoring how they are applied.

Agile skeptics sometimes focus on topics such as the value of comprehensive requirements and design up front; the importance of rigorous, formalized documentation; the need for detailed project plans; or other "sacred" aspects of their favorite methodology as arguments against Agile approaches. Conversely, Agile advocates can sometimes be overly evangelistic in their zeal, insisting that there is a single right method or a mandatory collection of practices required to be "truly Agile." It's often the excited new adopters who are the most zealous in their notion of Agile methods. As with most good ideas in our industry, one size never seems to fit all.

It's easy to get drawn into methodology debates, focusing on specific techniques while losing sight of the real problem. Methodology debates tend to cause us to focus on championing our favorite techniques rather than on their intended outcomes and results. Such debates can quickly become pedantic and lose focus on the real goal: doing what is right to deliver customer value early and often. If we've learned anything from various methodologies that have emerged over the years, it is that prescriptive methodologies are not a substitute for having motivated and talented people on the team. As Fred Brooks said, "There is no silver bullet" that will magically boost performance by orders of magnitude (Brooks 1975).

My hope is that you'll embrace the tenets of agility that have been presented throughout this book, if not the specific practices. By focusing on continuously *becoming* more Agile rather than on *doing* Agile methods, you will be more effective when faced with complex challenges for which there is no recommended practice. By blending and tailoring the good practices from a variety of Agile flavors, you will arrive at a customized Agile flavor that is most appropriate for the nuances of your environment.

For managers and leaders reading this book in the hope of urging your staff to adopt Agile approaches, I have a word of advice: Do your best to avoid imposing a single, standardized Agile method across all Agile teams. By focusing on the teams' outcomes and results to measure their performance, you can empower them to adopt and adapt the practices as they think best. Watch out for the temptation to monitor and measure performance using traditional performance-to-plan metrics. Keep in mind that we expect plans to change, and effective Agile teams embrace that change and adapt accordingly.

GNARLY PROBLEMS

Like all complex, technical domains we face problems in DW/BI that are just plain gnarly. These are problems that make our jobs both more interesting and frustrating at the same time. Issues such as extremely large data volumes, demand for near real-time analytics, and widely disparate or anomalous source data can all be gnarly problems. Furthermore, you may be facing some gnarly problems that are unique to your situation.

When I speak with experienced DW/BI practitioners about Agile Analytics, the conversation almost always involves a discussion of how to handle some particularly complex situation. I once spoke with a BI director who described a high-volume warehouse with over 20 fact tables of varying grain and a significant collection of conformed dimensions, all indexed on surrogate keys. The BI director was struggling with evolutionary data modeling because something as simple as adding a new column to a dimension table would adversely impact physical data storage, performance, the ability to backfill the new column with historical data, and other areas. The team would have to complete several database tasks to avoid incurring unwanted technical debt and performance hits.

Initially it did seem as if evolutionary database development would be impractical in this environment. However, as we talked further, I began to ask questions like "How easy will it be to get your data models correct and complete up front?" and "How long will comprehensive up-front modeling take?" We also talked about the fragile relationship between business and IT and the lack of confidence that business leaders had in IT. As we talked about the trade-offs between the cost of dealing with gnarly technical problems and the benefits of incrementally evolving toward the right solution, the BI director acknowledged that the benefits were probably worth the extra effort. The cost-benefit analysis doesn't always go like this for gnarly problems. Sometimes it makes sense to do a little more up-front work to avoid the high cost of change later. But the question should always include consideration of how much better off the project will be.

Another gnarly problem that I frequently encounter is that of data migration, including migrating data from one database or schema to another one or from one third-party technology to another. It is generally assumed that data migration cannot be iterative and incremental since that implies having one foot in the old schema and the other in the new one. The evolutionary modeling, database refactoring, and continuous delivery methods presented in Chapter 6, "Evolving Excellent Design," may address this problem in some situations. However, there are situations in which the data migration must occur all at once and must be correct on the first try. When very large data volumes are involved, these efforts are substantial and risky. Therefore, it makes sense to take an Agile approach leading up to the actual migration, using short iterations to build and test migration scripts. By working in small steps, and continuously integrating and testing those scripts in a preproduction "dry run" environment, you can be confident that the actual migration will succeed.

This book does not attempt to address all the various gnarly problems you may encounter in your DW/BI environment; nor does it try to answer the various forms of "How do I apply practice X given special circumstance Y?" My hope is that introducing the fundamentals of Agile Analytics will provide the jumping-off point needed to shape the techniques to work effectively for these difficult situations. I find that every new project I work on requires some new creative thinking about how to set up continuous integration, test automation, automated deployment, and other technical practices given the idiosyncrasies of the situation and technologies.

Finally, many Agile skeptics' arguments are based on avoiding rework and reducing technical effort. Agile Analytics does not ensure less technical effort or limited rework. In fact, it is through the continuous, incremental shaping of the solution, using good technical practices and refactoring, that the system evolves to become the right, well-designed solution.

WHAT ABOUT EMERGING TECHNOLOGIES?

Our discipline is continuously morphing and evolving. While not new, data mining and predictive analytics remain as advanced BI techniques. Complex event processing and real-time analytics have been increasing in popularity in recent years. On-demand and cloud-based DW/BI technologies are gaining momentum as alternatives for many enterprises. High-performance analytic databases based on massively parallel, shared-nothing architectures are boosting the performance of extremely high-volume data analysis. These are just a few of the current trends in our field, and it is reasonable to question how Agile Analytics applies to these and other emerging technologies.

Many of these technologies should be enhanced by Agile development. On-demand and cloud-based technologies offer a ready-to-go infrastructure and system architecture. These may provide a more advanced starting point, enabling Agile Analytics teams to get started sooner without the added burden of configuring technology stacks. Some analytic, cloud-based, and NoSQL[1] databases eliminate the need for traditional data modeling, instead using hidden/proprietary storage structures that are accessed via published interfaces. These technologies may enable Agile Analytics teams to be less bound to a particular data model, and therefore more easily able to adapt to change.

As organizations seek to explore new and emerging technologies, Agile techniques make perfect sense. By establishing timeboxed proof-of-concept projects, Agile Analytics teams can iteratively experiment with new technologies by building actual working BI features while uncovering the strengths and weaknesses of the technologies. This approach offers a much deeper exploration than traditional research and analysis techniques since developers actually work with the technologies and users actually experience the results, all the while using real operational data.

Conversely, many new and emerging technologies may change the nature of the development environment. The "sandbox infrastructure" presented in Chapter 7, "Test-Driven Data Warehouse Development," provides each developer with a private place to experiment, a separate sandbox for continuous integration, and a preproduction environment for final system readiness. This model may not be as easy to achieve when developing in on-demand and cloud-based platforms. However, the goals of these separate

---

1. A class of databases that do not adhere to a fixed relational model and do not expose a SQL interface (see http://en.wikipedia.org/wiki/NoSQL).

sandboxes remain relevant, and Agile Analytics teams may need to be creative in achieving these goals using new technologies.

The configuration of automated testing, continuous integration, and deployment automation may also be impacted by many of these emerging DW/BI technologies. As we saw in Chapter 8, "Version Control for Data Warehousing," and Chapter 9, "Project Automation," modern DW/BI tools using proprietary interfaces can be challenging to incorporate into project automation scripts. Doing so with on-demand and cloud-based technologies may be even more challenging. Ideally, popularizing these practices will encourage vendors to build better interfaces into their technologies to support them.

Agile approaches are very well suited to the development of complex event reporting and other near real-time BI requirements. By taking an incremental and iterative approach in this domain, Agile Analytics teams can converge on the right balance of functional and performance requirements needed to satisfy the customer community. Issues like the time-intensive nature of updating the warehouse and data marts can be counterbalanced with the time-sensitive needs of the business to receive data as soon as possible. Moreover, an Agile approach will enable the development team to keep the DW/BI system as lean as possible to better respond to the real-time demands of customers.

Adapting Agile methods to these new and emerging technologies is one of the next steps in Agile Analytics. As you encounter nontraditional technologies and analytical problems, consider the benefits of an adaptive, evolutionary approach that will enable the early and continuous delivery of business value. While the specific practices you employ may look different from the ones introduced in this book, you'll be able to align the constraints of your project with the values and principles of agility.

ADOPTION STRATEGIES

As you consider adopting an Agile Analytics approach in your organization, there are some things to consider and be prepared for. There may be a significant cultural impedance mismatch to overcome, and it's going to take time. In his keynote address at the Agile2010 conference in Orlando, Florida, Mike Cohn said, "Agile is not something you become, it is something you continue becoming more of." Organizations that successfully adopt Agile techniques do so by continuously reflecting and incrementally maturing and improving. Agile is simple in concept but is not easy to learn and practice well. You should expect some stumbles and challenges along the way. After helping many teams and organizations with their Agile adoptions, I have observed many such struggles and a few outright false starts.

The topic of Agile adoption could fill an entire book. In fact, it does, and you will benefit by adding Amr Elssamadisy's, *Agile Adoption Patterns* to your library (Elssamadisy 2008). However, I'll leave you with some suggestions and expectations to consider as you shape your Agile adoption strategy.

Expect Some Chaos

Whatever change you introduce, whether it is at the individual, team, or organizational level, will cause some initial disruption, discomfort, and chaos before the benefits are observed. If you play a musical instrument, a sport like golf, or any activity that requires proper technique, you've probably experienced this. Your technique may be working okay, but it includes some bad habits so you seek instruction from an expert. The expert shows you proper technique, but bad habits are hard to break. While you're trying to unlearn your old technique and relearn the better technique, your performance degrades below previous levels, you experience discomfort while learning new habits, and it may be frustrating until the change has become natural.

You can expect new Agile teams to experience initial frustration and discomfort as they integrate new principles, practices, and techniques. The Virginia Satir Change Model (see Figure 10.1) describes a pattern of events and stages a team or individual passes through when undergoing change. These stages affect team and individual feelings, thinking, performance, and psyche as a team shifts from the late performance status quo to the new one. These events and stages are summarized as follows:

1. **Late status quo.** The team is experiencing a consistent level of performance using familiar tools, processes, and techniques. Members know what to expect and how to behave and react.
2. **Foreign element.** The team is introduced to a new way of working that is expected to improve performance, for example, the Agile Analytics values, principles, and practices.
3. **Resistance.** The foreign element threatens the team's comfort with familiar structures and processes, and there is typically a period of resistance to the new and unfamiliar changes.
4. **Chaos.** As the team and individuals grapple with new techniques, their old expectations are no longer valid, and their old reactions

are no longer effective. There is often frustration and a sense that the new techniques aren't working. Performance during this stage is unpredictable.

5. **Transforming idea.** The group collectively discovers or embraces an idea that is transformational. For example, a Scrum team has a successful sprint and experiences the delight and excitement of the customer community during the feature showcase.

6. **Integration.** Team members begin to align with one another and embrace the changes with commitment. During this stage they may continue to revert to old habits and behaviors, but they are committed to breaking those habits.

7. **Practice.** The changes are becoming more routine and second nature. When team members encounter difficulty or frustration, they are able to identify problem areas and make effective adjustments.

8. **New status quo.** If the change is successfully assimilated, the team and the environment experience a consistent and predictable boost in performance. The team becomes healthier and better able to effectively react to uncertainty and difficulty.

Teams can get stuck in chaos and may need help moving out of this stage. By understanding the natural progression of a team undergoing change, leaders can provide the team with the necessary support and assistance to move efficiently toward the new status quo.

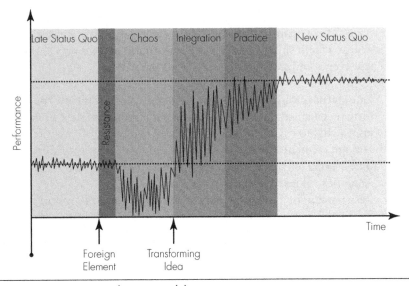

Figure 10.1 Satir Change Model

Leadership Responsibilities

Agile adoption is doomed without the sponsorship, support, and active involvement of management. Beware the temptation to treat Agile adoption as something limited to the development teams. Management styles may need to change as part of Agile adoption. Agile leaders provide Agile teams with focus and clarity of vision. They help the team strike the right balance among value delivery, focus on quality, and project constraints. Agile leaders guide the team by establishing core strategic vision and values. They facilitate team collaboration and work to foster team self-organization. Agile leaders provide the team with necessary constraints by making difficult decisions such as the allocation of people, money, priorities, and time. To do these things Agile leaders must have a solid understanding of Agile development and realistic expectations about its impact on products and projects.

Jim Highsmith, an expert on Agile leadership, outlines a few concrete things that Agile leaders should do in his blog, "What Do Agile Executives and Leaders Do" (Highsmith 2010d). These include aligning Agile transformation efforts to business strategy; helping teams understand and deliver on business, product, and project objectives; creating an Agile performance management system; facilitating a decentralized, empowered, collaborative workplace; fostering an adaptable product line and product architecture; creating an Agile proficiency framework; creating proactive and reactive organizational adaptation processes; understanding the Agile development process; and creating guidelines, training, and support for Agile processes, practices, and tools.

The Agile Project Leadership Network (www.apln.org) is an organization that is focused on developing Agile leadership qualities. The APLN helps leaders focus on value, customers, context, teams, individuals, and uncertainty and is founded on the values expressed in the Declaration of Interdependence (www.pmdoi.org).

Goals and Business Alignment

Understanding and clarifying your goals for adopting Agile Analytics are critical to success. Are you adopting Agile methods to address quality problems, improve customer responsiveness, rebuild the relationship with your customer community, better handle the risk and uncertainty inherent in your projects, address on-time delivery problems, or some other goal? Carefully evaluate your reasons for Agile adoption and establish a set of realistic indicators of success.

It is equally important to understand how these goals align with the strategic goals of the business. Doing so will ensure that you have executive support and buy-in and will enable you to show how improvements in your DW/BI processes directly tie to strategic organizational objectives.

Agile Adoption Road-Mapping

As a consultant helping organizations with Agile adoption (including software, product, and DW/BI agility), I have discovered tremendous benefit in the power of strategic road-mapping techniques. Road-mapping is commonly used for establishing long-range strategic objectives and analyzing the factors and prerequisites necessary for achieving those goals. Road-mapping is used by senior executives to clarifying strategic enterprise objectives, product managers to clarify strategic product objectives, and IT department leaders to align IT direction with enterprise goals.

A strategic road map is typically a two-dimensional chart showing a two- to five-year timeline along the horizontal axis. The vertical axis generally is divided into a series of swim lanes (see Figure 10.2). The topmost lane typically conveys strategic goals, and each of the others reflects a different business or functional perspective (technology, training, resources, etc.). Cambridge University professor Robert Phaal and colleagues have developed highly collaborative road-mapping workshop techniques that enable organizational leaders to fill in these swim lanes with key activities, precursors, and success factors (Phaal, Farrukh, and Probert 2010).

A collaborative road-mapping workshop focused on your Agile adoption is a powerful technique for achieving organizational alignment. The road map will enable you to visualize how the strategic goals behind the initiative will be achieved. My Agile enablement road maps typically include swim lanes such as training, projects, resources, technology, organizational capabilities, and internal coaching. You may uncover other valuable perspectives that make good swim lanes on your road map.

Training and Coaching

Training refers to the formalized classroom style of transferring knowledge. It is an effective method for helping newly formed Agile communities gain a shared and common understanding of Agile values, principles, and practices. An Agile coach is a key member of the Agile project community (sometimes the scrum master is the coach). The coach has deep knowledge of Agile techniques and is a team facilitator, teacher, mentor, problem solver, conflict navigator, collaboration conductor, and more (Adkins 2010).

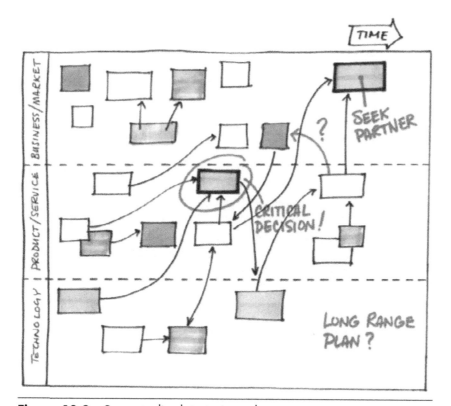

Figure 10.2   Conceptualized strategic road map
Image from Roadmapping for Strategy and Innovation *(Phaal, Farrukh, and Probert 2010), used with permission from Robert Phaal.*

Your Agile adoption strategy should include a substantial focus on both training and coaching. My friend and colleague Masa K. Maeda uses the analog of teaching someone to ride a bicycle. Training is like explaining bike-riding technique, including balance, braking, steering, and pedaling; coaching is like running alongside to keep the new rider from crashing until he or she learns to stay upright and steady. Training without coaching is likely to result in a conceptual understanding of bicycling followed by a series of painful crashes that may put the new rider off of bicycling forever.

Like learning to ride a bicycle, Agile adoption requires an effective blending of training and coaching to help new teams avoid painful crashes that may put the team off of Agile forever. Be sure that your trainers have good teaching skills combined with sufficient depth of experience to answer the hard questions that inevitably arise during training. Trainers whose knowledge is limited to textbook examples may fail to garner the confidence of those receiving training. Be sure that your Agile coaches are knowledgeable in Agile methods as well as the problem domain of the Agile project. The best coaches are those who are well respected by the team and who demonstrate agility through their behaviors and attitudes. Effective coaches are embedded with the project team and provide gentle guidance through behavioral modeling and silent influence rather than overbearing dominance.

Just as new Agile development teams need coaching, so do new Agile managers and leaders. As discussed, effective Agile leadership is essential to successful Agile adoption. While Agile development practices are tangible and well defined, Agile management practices are often less crisp. Agile managers are often faced with leadership challenges that rely on "Agile thinking" rather than well-defined practices. Agile management coaches can help leaders learn to think in an Agile fashion.

Measuring Success

Every Agile adoption strategy should include a well-defined and shared understanding of success. Moreover, this definition of success should be objectively measurable. Revisit the adoption goals and Agile enablement road map to align your success metrics with those goals and timelines. There must be very good reasons to adopt Agile Analytics since it will be disruptive to your current processes. If your aim is to improve responsiveness to your BI users, then establish metrics that reflect that. If the goal is to deliver high-priority BI value early, then establish value delivery metrics. Similarly, on-time delivery goals require timeliness metrics and quality goals require defect density metrics.

As you craft your success metrics, be realistic. As discussed previously, the stages of change will take time. Things will initially get worse before they improve. Build these expectations into your monitoring and metrics collection processes. Additionally, take the time to baseline your organization's pre-Agile performance so that you can evaluate performance improvements in relative terms. Be realistic and conservative in setting expectations for improvement. Metrics expert Michael Mah has observed that it takes high-performing Agile teams at least two years to achieve the expected performance increases (Mah 2008). During that time teams continuously improve but have more room for growth.

CLOSING THOUGHTS . . .

At the time of this writing there are a few of us in the data warehousing and business intelligence community who have been successfully applying agility to DW/BI projects. Until recently our sub-community seemed to be relatively small, but 2010 has seen a marked increase in the attention being given to Agile in data warehousing, business intelligence, and analytics.

There is an increasing body of written knowledge on this topic. Ralph Hughes's book *Agile Data Warehousing* offers a great introduction to applying Scrum practices on DW projects (Hughes 2008). Scott Ambler is a prolific writer who has written extensively about Agile data techniques as well as providing thought leadership on many other important Agile topics. Chris Sorensen is an Agile data warehouse practitioner at WestJet who has taken the time to maintain a blog on his experiences and ideas (www. theagiledatawarehouse.com). The Data Warehousing Institute (TDWI) instructor and DW/BI author Larissa Moss has been teaching and writing about Agile approaches to scoping and development for the past several years. BI thought leaders Claudia Imhoff and Len Silverston have been including Agile topics in their DW/BI presentations recently. Ralph Kimball and Joy Mundy of the Kimball Group have periodically addressed Agile techniques in their publications. Jill Dyche's 2010 blogs on Agile BI were both thought-provoking and highly ranked by *Information Management* magazine.[2] Steve Hitchman and Phil Consadine, of the Australian consultancy MIP, have authored a number of Agile BI articles and are active in the Agile DW/BI movement. In addition to these notable authors there are many others who are active contributors to Agile DW/BI forums, blogs, and discussion threads, many of whom are practitioners willing to share their firsthand experiences and lessons learned.

In addition to the growing body of knowledge in this field, an increasing number of DW/BI technology vendors are offering Agile enabling technologies. Open-source business intelligence vendor Pentaho has established an Agile BI initiative as part of its strategic direction and actively markets agility as being integral to its products and services. New Zealand technology vendor WhereScape has long supported rapid data warehouse development and deployment with its RED product and in 2010 launched WhereScape RED—The Agile Edition, which is further tuned to support many of the technical practices introduced in this book. In-memory BI technology

---

2. www.information-management.com/blogs/business_intelligence_TDWI_
   analytics-10018597-1.html

vendors like QlikView offer Agile-enabling technologies as do many providers of SaaS data warehouse and business intelligence products.

I expect that in the next few years we will see continued growth and refinement of Agile DW/BI concepts, techniques, and approaches. Through experience these ideas will continue to evolve and take shape. Regardless of the specific techniques, an adaptive and evolutionary approach to large, complex projects is simply the right thing to do; and before long I expect that we will no longer distinguish development as being Agile or not.

I leave you with my best wishes on your Agile journey. I hope it is as rewarding as mine has been so far. I can be found online at www.theagilist.com. Please contact me with your experiences, questions, discoveries, and other Agile thoughts. I'm interested in knowing about the lessons you learn along the way.

This page intentionally left blank

References and
Recommended Reading

Abdel-Hamid, T., and S. Madnick. 1991. *Software Project Dynamics: An Integrated Approach.* Upper Saddle River, NJ: Prentice Hall.

Adkins, L. 2010. *Coaching Agile Teams: A Companion for ScrumMasters, Agile Coaches, and Project Managers in Transition.* Boston: Addison-Wesley.

Ambler, S. W. 2002. *Agile Modeling: Effective Practices for eXtreme Programming and the Unified Process.* New York: John Wiley & Sons, Inc.

———. 2003. *Agile Database Techniques: Effective Strategies for the Agile Software Developer.* Danvers: John Wiley & Sons.

———. 2004. *The Object Primer: Agile Model-Driven Development with UML 2.0.* Cambridge: Cambridge University Press.

———. 2005a. "Agile Best Practice: Prioritized Requirements." Retrieved November 2, 2010, from Agile Modeling, www.agilemodeling.com/essays/prioritizedRequirements.htm.

———. 2005b. "Requirements Envisioning: An Agile Best Practice." Retrieved November 1, 2010, from Agile Modeling, www.agilemodeling.com/essays/initialRequirementsModeling.htm.

———. 2006. "Iteration Modeling: An Agile Best Practice." Retrieved November 1, 2010, from Agile Modeling, www.agilemodeling.com/essays/iterationModeling.htm.

———. 2007. "Test-Driven Development of Relational Databases," *IEEE Software* 24, no. 3 (May): 37–43.

———. 2008a. "Active Stakeholder Participation: An Agile Best Practice." Retrieved October 19, 2010, from Agile Modeling, www.agilemodeling.com/essays/activeStakeholderParticipation.htm#Stakeholders.

———. 2008b. "Surveys Exploring the Current State of Information Technology Practices," December 5. Retrieved October 18, 2010, from 2008 IT Project Success Rates Survey Results, www.ambysoft.com/surveys/success2008.html.

————. 2009a. "Communication on Agile Software Projects." Retrieved October 18, 2010, from Agile Modeling, www.agilemodeling.com/essays/communication.htm.

————. 2009b. "Examining the 'Big Requirements Up Front (BRUF) Approach.'" Retrieved October 14, 2010, from www.agilemodeling.com/essays/examiningBRUF.htm.

————. 2010. "How Agile Are You? 2010 Survey Results." Retrieved November 18, 2010, from Ambysoft, www.ambysoft.com/surveys/howAgileAreYou2010.html.

Ambler, S. W., and P. J. Sadalage. 2006. *Refactoring Databases: Evolutionary Database Design.* Boston: Addison-Wesley.

Beck, K. 2003. *Test-Driven Development: By Example.* Boston: Addison-Wesley.

————. 2008. *Implementation Patterns.* Boston: Addison-Wesley.

Beck, K., and C. Andres. 2004. *Extreme Programming Explained: Embrace Change, 2nd Edition.* Boston: Addison-Wesley.

Blaha, M. 2010. *Patterns of Data Modeling.* Boca Raton, FL: CRC Press.

Brand, S. 1995. *How Buildings Learn: What Happens After They're Built.* New York: Penguin.

Brooks, F. J. 1975. *The Mythical Man-Month: Essays on Software Engineering.* Reading, MA: Addison-Wesley.

Calero, C., M. Piattini, C. Pascual, and M. Serrano. 2001. "Towards Data Warehouse Quality Metrics," pp. 2.1–2.8. In *Design and Management of Data Warehouses.* Interlaken, Switzerland: CEUR Workshop Proceedings.

Clark, M. 2004. *Pragmatic Project Automation: How to Build, Deploy, and Monitor Java Applications.* Raleigh: Pragmatic Bookshelf.

Cockburn, A. 2000. *Writing Effective Use Cases.* Boston: Addison-Wesley.

————. 2001. *Agile Software Development.* Boston: Addison-Wesley.

————. 2004. *Crystal Clear: A Human-Powered Methodology for Small Teams.* Boston: Addison-Wesley.

Cohn, M. 2004. *User Stories Applied: For Agile Software Development.* Boston: Addison-Wesley.

————. 2006. *Agile Estimating and Planning.* Upper Saddle River, NJ: Prentice Hall.

Collier, K. 2005. "Agile Database Testing." *Cutter IT Journal* (December): 14–22.

Collier, K., and D. O'Leary. 2009. *The Message Driven Warehouse*. Cambridge, MA: Cutter Consortium.

Constantine, L. L., and E. Yourdon. 1979. *Structured Design: Fundamentals of a Discipline of Computer Program and Systems Design*. Upper Saddle River, NJ: Prentice Hall.

Cox, S. 2006. "Observations and Measurements," September 21. Retrieved April 2009 from OpenGIS Standards and Specifications, http://portal. opengeospatial.org/files/?artifact_id=17038.

Cunningham, W. 1992. "The WyCash Portfolio Management System." *ACM OOPSLA Conference Proceedings*. Reading, MA: Addison-Wesley.

de Bono, E. 1999. *Six Thinking Hats*. Boston: Back Bay Books.

DeGrace, P., and L. H. Stahl. 1990. *Wicked Problems, Righteous Solutions: A Catalog of Modern Engineering Paradigms*. Upper Saddle River, NJ: Prentice Hall.

DSDM Consortium. 2002. "Timeboxing." Retrieved October 14, 2010, from DSDM Consortium, www.dsdm.org/version4/2/public/Timeboxing. asp#Timebox_Schedule.

Eckerson, W. 2002. "Taming Spreadsheet Jockeys." *Application Development Trends (ADTmag.com)* September 1, http://adtmag.com/articles/2002/ 09/01/taming-spreadsheet-jockeys.aspx.

Elssamadisy, A. 2008. *Agile Adoption Patterns: A Roadmap to Organizational Success*. Boston: Addison-Wesley.

Farley, D., and J. Humble. 2010. *Continuous Delivery: Reliable Software Releases through Build, Test, and Deployment Automation*. Boston: Addison-Wesley.

Feathers, M. 2004. *Working Effectively with Legacy Code*. Upper Saddle River, NJ: Prentice Hall.

Fowler, M. 1997. *Analysis Patterns: Reusable Object Models*. Menlo Park, CA: Addison Wesley Longman.

———. 1999. *Refactoring: Improving the Design of Existing Code*. Boston: Addison Wesley Longman.

———. 2002. "The XP 2002 Conference," June. Retrieved July 14, 2010, from Martin Fowler.com, http://martinfowler.com/articles/xp2002.html.

Gamma, E., R. Helm, R. Johnson, and J. Vlissides. 1994. *Design Patterns: Elements of Reusable Object-Oriented Software.* Reading, MA: Addison Wesley Longman.

Gat, I. 2009. "Technical Debt on Your Balance Sheet," September 29. Retrieved November 19, 2010, from The Agile Executive, http://theagileexecutive.com/2009/09/29/technical-debt-on-your-balance-sheet/.

———. 2010. "The Nine Transformative Aspects of the Technical Debt Metric," October 28. Retrieved November 19, 2010, from The Agile Executive, http://theagileexecutive.com/2010/10/28/the-nine-transformative-aspects-of-the-technical-debt-metric/.

Hay, D. C. 1996. *Data Model Patterns: Conventions of Thought.* New York: Dorset House Publishing.

———. 2006. *Data Model Patterns: A Metadata Map.* San Francisco: Morgan Kaufman.

Highsmith, J. A. 2000. *Adaptive Software Development: A Collaborative Approach to Managing Complex Systems.* New York: Dorset House Publishing.

———. 2002. *Agile Software Development Ecosystems.* Boston: Addison-Wesley.

———. 2010a. *Agile Project Management: Creating Innovative Products, 2nd Edition.* Boston: Addison-Wesley.

———. 2010b. "The Financial Implications of Technical Debt," October 19. Retrieved November 19, 2010, from Adaptive Imagineering: Changing the Way IT Does Business, www.jimhighsmith.com/2010/10/19/the-financial-implications-of-technical-debt/.

———. 2010c. "Tracing a Continuum of Trust: Compliance, Cooperation, Collaboration," June 17. Retrieved November 16, 2010, from Cutter Consortium: Agile Product & Project Management, www.cutter.com/content/project/fulltext/advisor/2010/apm100617.html.

———. 2010d. "What Do Agile Executives and Leaders Do," November 4. Retrieved December 27, 2010, from Agile Project Leadership Network, www.apln.org/profiles/blogs/what-do-agile-executives-amp.

Hughes, R. 2008. *Agile Data Warehousing: Delivering World-Class Business Intelligence Systems Using Scrum and XP.* Bloomington: iUniverse.

Inmon, W. 2005. *Building the Data Warehouse, 4th Edition.* New York: John Wiley & Sons.

————. 2007. "Corporate Information Factory (CIF) Overview," January 1. Retrieved November 11, 2008, from Corporate Information Factory, www.inmoncif.com/library/cif/.

————. 2008. "The Virtual Data Warehouse (Again)," December 4. Retrieved December 4, 2008, from BeyeNetwork, www.b-eye-network.com/newsletters/inmon/9018.

Jankovsky, B. 2008. "ETL Patterns," August 28. Retrieved November 23, 2010, from http://bobjankovsky.org/showx.php?class=ETL%20PATTERNS.

Jones, M. E., and I.-Y. Song. 2005. "Dimensional Modeling: Identifying, Classifying & Applying," pp. 29–38. In *Proceedings of the 8th ACM International Workshop on Data Warehousing and OLAP*. Bremen: ACM.

Katzenbach, J. R., and D. K. Smith. 2006. *The Wisdom of Teams: Creating the High-Performance Organization*. New York: Collins.

Kerievsky, J. 2004. *Refactoring to Patterns*. Boston: Addison-Wesley.

Kernighan, B. W. 1974. *The Elements of Programming Style*. New York: McGraw-Hill Education.

Kimball, R., and M. Ross. 2002. *The Data Warehouse Toolkit: The Complete Guide to Dimensional Modeling, 2nd Edition*. New York: John Wiley & Sons.

Leishman, T. R., and D. A. Cook. 2002. "Requirements Risks Can Drown Software Projects." *CrossTalk: The Journal of Defense Software Engineering* (April): 4–8.

Longman, C. 2005. "Data Warehousing Meeting—December 7, 2005," December 7. Retrieved November 16, 2008, from DAMA UK—Data Management Association, www.damauk.org/Building%20the%20adaptive%20data%20warehouse%20-%20Cliff%20Longman.pdf.

Mah, M. 2008. *How Agile Projects Measure Up, and What This Means to You*. Cambridge, MA: Cutter Consortium.

Marick, B. 1994. *The Craft of Software Testing: Subsystems Testing Including Object-Based and Object-Oriented Testing*. Upper Saddle River, NJ: Prentice Hall.

Mason, M. 2006. *Pragmatic Version Control: Using Subversion, 2nd Edition*. Raleigh, NC: Pragmatic Bookshelf.

Moss, L., and S. Adelman. 2000. "Data Warehouse Failures," October 1. Retrieved October 1, 2007, from *The Data Administration Newsletter*, www.tdan.com/i014fe01.htm.

Palmer, S. R., and M. J. Felsing. 2002. *A Practical Guide to Feature-Driven Development.* Upper Saddle River, NJ: Prentice Hall.

Phaal, R., C. Farrukh, and D. Probert. 2010. *Roadmapping for Strategy and Innovation: Aligning Technology and Markets in a Dynamic World.* Cambridge: University of Cambridge, Institute for Manufacturing.

Pink, D. H. 2009. *Drive: The Surprising Truth about What Motivates Us.* New York: Riverhead.

Pixton, P., N. Nickolaisen, T. Little, and K. McDonald. 2009. *Stand Back and Deliver: Accelerating Business Agility.* Boston: Addison-Wesley.

Sadalage, P. J. 2007. *Recipes for Continuous Database Integration.* Boston: Addison-Wesley.

Schwaber, K., and M. Beedle. 2001. *Agile Software Development with Scrum.* Upper Saddle River, NJ: Prentice Hall.

Thomas, D., and A. Hunt. 2004. *Pragmatic Version Control Using CVS.* Raleigh: Pragmatic Bookshelf.

Tuckman, B. 1965. "Developmental Sequence in Small Groups." *Psychological Bulletin* 63: 384–99.

Viesturs, E., and D. Roberts. 2006. *No Shortcuts to the Top: Climbing the World's 14 Highest Peaks.* New York: Broadway Books.

Yoder, J. W., and R. E. Johnson. 2002. "The Adaptive Object-Model Architectural Style." *IFIP Conference Proceedings* 224: 3–27. Deventer: Kluwer, B.V.

INDEX

Numbers

90-day (six-iteration) planning cycle, dividing project plan into iterations, 88–89

A

Acceptance testing. *See also* Functional testing
  in Agile testing framework, 199
  for failed DW/BI project, xxi
  key perspectives in testing software and systems, 197–198
  process under test, 204
  in traditional development, 193
  WatiN utility for, 195
  in waterfall development, 31
Accountability, of teams, 128
Accuracy, traits of Agile modeling, 150
Adaptive Object Modeling (AOM), 153–154
Adaptive Object Modeling (Yoder and Johnson), 190
Adaptive Software Development (Highsmith), 5
Adkins, Lyssa, 67, 69, 303
ADM (adaptive data model), 179
  in architecture of message-driven warehouse, 188–189
  creating adaptive warehouses, 190
  SOR (System of Record) database built on, 177, 179
  use of design patterns in, 153–154
Administrative skills, for implementing DW/BI systems, 16
Adoption strategies
  expecting some chaos while making change, 300–301
  goals and business alignment and, 302–303
  leadership responsibilities regarding, 302
  measuring success of, 305
  overview of, 299–300
  road map for, 303
  training and coaching in, 303–305
Adzic, Gojko, 206

Agile Adoption Patterns (Elssamadisy), 300
Agile Alliance
  guiding principles of, 9–10
  overview of, 6
Agile Analytics, introduction to
  Agile approach to developing DW/BI systems, 4–7
  challenges of applying Agile methods to DW/BI, 20–22
  data warehousing architectures and, 13–16
  difficulty of building DW/BI systems, 16–17
  fail fast and adapt approach, 18–19
  FlixBuster example, 22–23
  frequent failure of DW/BI development projects, 17–18
  guiding principles, 9–10
  myths and misconceptions, 10–13
  overview of, 3
  relating Agile approach to success rate, 19–20
  summary (wrap up) of, 23–24
  what it is, 7–9
  what the term means, xxvi–xxvii
  why it is needed, 16
Agile Best Practice (Ambler), 108
Agile Data Warehousing (Hughes), 306, xxv
Agile Database Techniques (Ambler), 226
Agile, defined, 3
Agile Manifesto, 6
Agile Model Driven Development (AMDD), 33
Agile Modeling (Ambler), 151
Agile Project Leadership Network (APLN), 302
Agile Project Management. *See* APM (Agile Project management)
Agile Project Management (Highsmith), 39
Agreements, working agreements required by self-organizing teams, 130–131
Aguirre, Ricardo, xxxiii
Ambler, Scott, 19–20, 31, 33, 40, 44, 72–73, 91–92, 108, 146, 151, 158, 162–163, 165–166, 168, 194, 212, 226, xxv, xxxiv

Made in the USA
Monee, IL
07 October 2020